W9-BMY-710

RESTful Web Services Cookbook

RESTful Web Services Cookbook

Subbu Allamaraju

O'REILLY®

Beijing · Cambridge · Farnham · Köln · Sebastopol · Tokyo

RESTful Web Services Cookbook

by Subbu Allamaraju

Copyright © 2010 Yahoo!, Inc. All rights reserved.
Printed in the United States of America.

Published by O'Reilly Media, Inc., 1005 Gravenstein Highway North, Sebastopol, CA 95472.

O'Reilly books may be purchased for educational, business, or sales promotional use. Online editions are also available for most titles (*http://my.safaribooksonline.com*). For more information, contact our corporate/institutional sales department: (800) 998-9938 or *corporate@oreilly.com*.

Editor: Mary E. Treseler		**Cover Designer:** Karen Montgomery	
Production Editor: Sumita Mukherji		**Interior Designer:** David Futato	
Production Services: Molly Sharp		**Illustrator:** Robert Romano	

Printing History:

March 2010: First Edition.

Nutshell Handbook, the Nutshell Handbook logo, and the O'Reilly logo are registered trademarks of O'Reilly Media, Inc. *RESTful Web Services Cookbook*, the image of a great fringed lizard, and related trade dress are trademarks of O'Reilly Media, Inc.

Many of the designations used by manufacturers and sellers to distinguish their products are claimed as trademarks. Where those designations appear in this book, and O'Reilly Media, Inc., was aware of a trademark claim, the designations have been printed in caps or initial caps.

While every precaution has been taken in the preparation of this book, the publisher and author assume no responsibility for errors or omissions, or for damages resulting from the use of the information contained herein.

ISBN: 978-0-596-80168-7

[LSI]   [2011-08-12]

1313125201

Table of Contents

Preface

In 2000, Roy Fielding, one of the key contributors to HTTP and URI, codified the architecture of the Web in his doctoral thesis titled "Architectural Styles and the Design of Network-Based Software Architectures." In this thesis, he introduced an architecture style known as Representational State Transfer (REST). This style, in abstract terms, describes the foundation of the World Wide Web. The technologies that make up this foundation include the Hypertext Transfer Protocol (HTTP), Uniform Resource Identifier (URI), markup languages such as HTML and XML, and web-friendly formats such as JSON.

REST is an architectural style for networked applications. It consists of several constraints to address separation of concerns, visibility, reliability, scalability, performance, etc. See Appendix B for a brief overview of these constraints. What makes REST attractive to build distributed and decentralized client/server applications is the infrastructure of the Web. Deploying web services on this infrastructure lets you take advantage of a wide range of existing infrastructure that includes web servers, client libraries, proxy servers, caches, firewalls, and so on. Although, in theory, it is possible to build RESTful applications without relying on HTTP, attempting to do so can be an expensive proposition. In this book, *RESTful web services* means web services built using HTTP, URIs, XML, JSON, Atom, etc.

Scope of the Book

This book is not a discourse on REST or its merits over other styles of architecture. This is a cookbook for designers and developers of RESTful web services.

Plenty of material exists that describes the REST architectural style. Wikipedia's entry on Representational State Transfer (*http://en.wikipedia.org/wiki/Representational_State _Transfer*) provides a concise description of REST's underlying concepts, its constraints, and the guiding principles to design applications. Leonard Richardson and Sam Ruby's *RESTful Web Services* (O'Reilly) provides a more in-depth coverage on the basics of this topic detailing how to use *resources* as the core building blocks. But how do you find help with day-to-day design and implementation questions? This is the book to fill that gap.

This book consists of recipes to help design and implement RESTful client/server applications. It presents these recipes in a manner that lets you take advantage of the web infrastructure and REST without having to ponder whether your web service is RESTful. Each recipe includes one or more problem statements and a solution, followed by a detailed discussion with examples, commentary on implementation, and any trade-offs involved.

Much of the material for the recipes is based on common design problems found while developing RESTful web services. The problems include usage of HTTP, resource and representation design, URIs, caching, concurrency control, partial updates, batch processing, transactions, security, versioning, compatibility, etc.

This book is not programming language specific. It uses HTTP request and response messages to illustrate implementation. You can use languages such as C#, C++, Java, Ruby, Python, PHP, and Perl to implement these recipes. See Appendix A for a list of programming language–specific books, or search your favorite bookstore.

This book does not also deal with installing, administering, or securing web servers, caches, and proxies. See books such as *Apache Cookbook* by Ken Coar and Rich Bowen, *Apache Security* by Ivan Ristic, and *Squid: The Definitive Guide* by Duane Wessels (all from O'Reilly), or product manuals to learn such topics.

Companion Material

See *http://www.restful-webservices-cookbook.org* for additional material, errata, comments, and questions about this book.

You may find the following additional resources helpful:

REST-Discuss Yahoo! Group (http://tech.groups.yahoo.com/group/rest-discuss)
> If you have questions on the REST architectural style, search the archives of this group. Better yet, join this group to post your questions and engage in conversations about the merits and demerits of REST, commonly encountered problems, and usage of HTTP for RESTful web services.

Leonard Richardson and Sam Ruby's RESTful Web Services *(O'Reilly)*
> See this book to learn more about REST and how to use the Web as a platform for building RESTful web services.

RESTwiki (http://rest.blueoxen.net/cgi-bin/wiki.pl)
> This wiki contains a collection of articles written over years that describe various aspects of REST and its application.

Chris Shiflett's HTTP Developer's Handbook *(Sams)*
> See this book if you have questions about using HTTP in client or server applications.

Undoubtedly, there will be additional design and implementation problems that are not addressed by this book or the previously discussed resources. Visit *http://www.restful-webservices-cookbook.org* to post your questions, suggestions, or alternative solutions you have had success with in your experience. In due course, this site will include additional recipes, and they will be included in the next revision of this book.

How This Book Is Organized

This book is organized into 14 chapters followed by 5 appendixes as follows:

Chapter 1, Using the Uniform Interface
> This chapter describes the details of using HTTP's uniform interface and deals with issues such as statelessness, visibility, safety and idempotency, extensibility, new resource creation, GET versus POST, etc. The recipes in this chapter primarily deal with using HTTP's uniform interface.

Chapter 2, Identifying Resources
> This chapter describes how to identify resources to cover some commonly encountered application scenarios.

Chapter 3, Designing Representations
> This chapter describes how to design representations, how to use HTTP headers on requests and responses, how to choose media types and formats, and how to do error handling.

Chapter 4, Designing URIs
> This chapter describes common patterns for designing URIs, using URIs as identifiers, and keeping URIs cool.

Chapter 5, Web Linking
> This chapter shows when and how to use links in representations and covers details of links in the body of representations, link headers, URI templates, and applications of links.

Chapter 6, Atom and AtomPub
> This chapter presents how to use Atom feeds, entries, media resources, and service documents as resources; how to use the AtomPub protocol; and when to use Atom to design resource representations.

Chapter 7, Content Negotiation
> This chapter shows how to negotiate for representations based on media type, character encoding, content encoding, or content language; how to use the Vary header; and when to use content negotiation.

Chapter 8, Queries
> This chapter shows some approaches for designing URIs for queries, handling large queries, and storing queries.

Chapter 9, Web Caching
> This chapter describes how to support expiration caching in servers and deal with caching in clients.

Chapter 10, Conditional Requests
> This chapter describes how to implement conditional requests in servers and clients for various HTTP methods and shows how conditional requests can help caching, optimistic concurrency control, and idempotency.

Chapter 11, Miscellaneous Writes
> This chapter shows how to solve a variety of design problems that at first glance may seem outside the scope of REST and HTTP. Topics include copying, merging, partial updates, batch processing, and transactions.

Chapter 12, Security
> This chapter shows how to address common security needs such as authentication, authorization, delegation, etc.

Chapter 13, Extensibility and Versioning
> This chapter shows how to write extensible servers, how to keep clients resilient to change, and how to implement versioning.

Chapter 14, Enabling Discovery
> This chapter describes how to document RESTful web services.

Appendix A, Additional Reading
> This appendix lists places where you can find more information about REST and the underlying technologies.

Appendix B, Overview of REST
> This appendix provides a brief introduction to REST with an example.

Appendix C, HTTP Methods
> This appendix shows how to use standard HTTP methods.

Appendix D, Atom Syndication Format
> This appendix provides a reference to Atom feed and entry documents.

Appendix E, Link Relation Registry
> This appendix lists link relation types that you can use in links.

Conventions Used in This Book

The following typographical conventions are used in this book:

Italic
> Indicates new terms, URLs, email addresses, filenames, and file extensions.

`Constant width`
> Used for program listings, as well as within paragraphs to refer to program elements such as variable or function names, databases, datatypes, environment variables, statements, and keywords.

`Constant width starting with "#"`

Used for comments in HTTP requests and response messages. For instance:

```
# This is a request
GET /toc
Host: www.restful-webservices-cookbook.org

# This is a response
HTTP/1.1 200 OK
Date: Sat, 07 Nov 2009 03:14:05 GMT
Last-Modified: Sat, 07 Nov 2009 03:14:05 GMT
Content-Type: text/html; charset=UTF-8

<html>...</html>
```

 This icon signifies a tip, suggestion, or general note.

 This icon indicates a warning or caution.

Using Code Examples

This book is here to help you get your job done. In general, you may use the code in this book in your programs and documentation. You do not need to contact us for permission unless you're reproducing a significant portion of the code. For example, writing a program that uses several chunks of code from this book does not require permission. Selling or distributing a CD-ROM of examples from O'Reilly books does require permission. Answering a question by citing this book and quoting example code does not require permission. Incorporating a significant amount of example code from this book into your product's documentation does require permission.

We appreciate, but do not require, attribution. An attribution usually includes the title, author, publisher, and ISBN. For example: "*RESTful Web Services Cookbook* by Subbu Allamaraju. Copyright 2010 Yahoo!, Inc., 978-0-596-80168-7."

If you feel your use of code examples falls outside fair use or the permission given here, feel free to contact us at *permissions@oreilly.com*.

Safari® Books Online

 Safari Books Online is an on-demand digital library that lets you easily search over 7,500 technology and creative reference books and videos to find the answers you need quickly.

With a subscription, you can read any page and watch any video from our library online. Read books on your cell phone and mobile devices. Access new titles before they are available for print, and get exclusive access to manuscripts in development and post feedback for the authors. Copy and paste code samples, organize your favorites, download chapters, bookmark key sections, create notes, print out pages, and benefit from tons of other time-saving features.

O'Reilly Media has uploaded this book to the Safari Books Online service. To have full digital access to this book and others on similar topics from O'Reilly and other publishers, sign up for free at *http://my.safaribooksonline.com*.

How to Contact Us

Please address comments and questions concerning this book to the publisher:

O'Reilly Media, Inc.
1005 Gravenstein Highway North
Sebastopol, CA 95472
800-998-9938 (in the United States or Canada)
707-829-0515 (international or local)
707-829-0104 (fax)

We have a web page for this book, where we list errata, examples, and any additional information. You can access this page at:

http://www.oreilly.com/catalog/9780596801687

To comment or ask technical questions about this book, send email to:

bookquestions@oreilly.com

For more information about our books, conferences, Resource Centers, and the O'Reilly Network, see our website at:

http://www.oreilly.com

Acknowledgments

Many people have helped this book happen. Mary Treseler, the editor for this book at O'Reilly, helped shape the outline for this book by asking the right questions. She provided much needed support, encouragement, and polite nudging to transform ideas into a reality.

Many thanks to Mark Nottingham and Hugo Haas for helping me draft an initial outline for this book.

Mike Amundsen, who contributed to parts of this book, spent countless hours and red pens to review and comment on the book line by line. His suggestions on improving the tone of this book were invaluable. Despite his limited availability, Mike was always on call to discuss the merits and demerits of solutions and the real-world trade-offs.

Thanks to Havi Hoffman, who manages Yahoo! Press, for patiently guiding me through the process of writing a proposal and for pulling the right strings to shield me from the elaborate process. My thanks to Neal Sample, James Lok, Jay Rossiter, and Tony Ng (all from Yahoo! Inc.) for their support during the course of writing this book. I would also like to thank Korby Parnell for planting the seeds to write this book.

I am profoundly grateful to Mark Nottingham, Eben Hewitt, Colin Jack, Stefan Tilkov, Norbert Lindenberg, Chris Westin, Dan Theurer, Shaunak Kashyap, Larry Cable, Alan Dean, Surya Suravarapu, Jim D'Ambrosia, Randolph Kahle, Dhananjay Nene, and Brian Sletten for their valuable and critical feedback on the clarity, approach, quality, and accuracy of the material in this book.

Thanks to the members of the REST-Discuss Yahoo! Group (*http://tech.groups.yahoo .com/group/rest-discuss*) for all the passionate, tough, and insightful discussions on all things related to REST.

Thanks also to all the readers who provided feedback on the rough cuts drafts of this book.

Mike Amundsen's Contribution

Mike Amundsen contributed to Recipes 4.1, 4.3, 6.1, 6.4, 9.1, 9.4, 9.5, 11.8, 11.9, 11.12, and Appendix D.

## CHAPTER 1

Using the Uniform Interface

HTTP is an application-level protocol that defines operations for transferring representations between clients and servers. In this protocol, methods such as GET, POST, PUT, and DELETE are operations on resources. This protocol eliminates the need for you to invent application-specific operations such as createOrder, getStatus, updateStatus, etc. How much you can benefit from the HTTP infrastructure largely depends on how well you can use HTTP as an application-level protocol. However, a number of techniques including SOAP and some Ajax web frameworks use HTTP as a protocol to transport messages. Such usage makes poor use of HTTP-level infrastructure. This chapter presents the following recipes to highlight various aspects of using HTTP as an application protocol:

Recipe 1.1, "How to Keep Interactions Visible"
   Visibility is one of the key characteristics of HTTP. Use this recipe to learn how to maintain visibility.

Recipe 1.2, "When to Trade Visibility"
   There are cases when you may need to forgo visibility to meet application needs. Use this recipe to find some scenarios.

Recipe 1.3, "How to Maintain Application State"
   Use this recipe to learn the best way to manage state.

Recipe 1.4, "How to Implement Safe and Idempotent Methods on the Server"
   Maintaining safety and idempotency helps servers guarantee repeatability for requests. Use this recipe when implementing servers.

Recipe 1.5, "How to Treat Safe and Idempotent Methods in Clients"
   Follow this recipe to implement clients for safety and idempotency principles.

Recipe 1.6, "When to Use GET"
   Use this recipe to learn when to use GET.

Recipe 1.7, "When to Use POST"
   Use this recipe to learn when to use POST.

1.1 How to Keep Interactions Visible

As an application protocol, HTTP is designed to keep interactions between clients and servers visible to libraries, servers, proxies, caches, and other tools. Visibility is a key characteristic of HTTP. Per Roy Fielding (see Appendix A for references), visibility is "the ability of a component to monitor or mediate the interaction between two other components." When a protocol is visible, caches, proxies, firewalls, etc., can monitor and even participate in the protocol.

Problem

You want to know what visibility means and what you can do to keep HTTP requests and responses visible.

Solution

Once you identify and design resources, use GET to get a representation of a resource, PUT to update a resource, DELETE to delete a resource, and POST to perform a variety of potentially nonidempotent and unsafe operations. Add appropriate HTTP headers to describe requests and responses.

Discussion

Features like the following depend entirely on keeping requests and responses visible:

Caching
    Caching responses and automatically invalidating cached responses when resources are modified

Optimistic concurrency control
> Detecting concurrent writes and preventing resource changes when such operations are based on stale representations

Content negotiation
> Selecting a representation among alternatives available for a given resource

Safety and idempotency
> Ensuring that clients can repeat or retry certain HTTP requests

When a web service does not maintain visibility, such features will not work correctly. For instance, when the server's usage of HTTP breaks optimistic concurrency, you may be forced to invent application-specific concurrency control mechanisms on your own.

 Maintaining visibility lets you use existing HTTP software and infrastructure for features that you would otherwise have to build yourself.

HTTP achieves visibility by virtue of the following:

- HTTP interactions are stateless. Any HTTP intermediary can infer the meaning of any given request and response without correlating them with past or future requests and responses.

- HTTP uses a uniform interface consisting of OPTIONS, GET, HEAD, POST, PUT, DELETE, and TRACE methods. Each method in this interface operates on one and only one resource. The syntax and the meaning of each method do not change from application to application or from resource to resource. That is why HTTP is known as a *uniform interface.*

- HTTP uses a MIME-like envelope format to encode representations. This format maintains a clear separation between headers and the body. Headers are visible, and except for the software that is creating the message and the software that is processing the message, every piece of software in between can treat the body as completely opaque.

Consider an HTTP request to update a resource:

```
# Request
PUT /movie/gone_with_the_wind HTTP/1.1 ❶
Host: www.example.org ❷
Content-Type: application/x-www-form-urlencoded

summary=...&rating=5&... ❸

# Response
HTTP/1.1 200 OK ❹
Content-Type: text/html;charset=UTF-8 ❺
Content-Length: ...
```

```
<html>❻
    ...
</html>
```

❶ Request line containing HTTP method, path to the resource, and HTTP version

❷ Representation headers for the request

❸ Representation body for the request

❹ Response status line containing HTTP version, status code, and status message

❺ Representation headers for the response

❻ Representation body for the response

In this example, the request is an HTTP message. The first line in this message describes the protocol and the method used by the client. The next two lines are request headers. By simply looking at these three lines, any piece of software that understands HTTP can decipher not only the intent of the request but also how to parse the body of the message. The same is the case with the response. The first line in the response indicates the version of HTTP, the status code, and a message. The next two lines tell HTTP-aware software how to interpret the message.

For RESTful web services, your key goal must be to maintain visibility to the extent possible. Keeping visibility is simple. Use each HTTP method such that it has the same semantics as specified by HTTP, and add appropriate headers to describe requests and responses.

Another part of maintaining visibility is using appropriate status codes and messages so that proxies, caches, and clients can determine the outcome of a request. A status code is an integer, and the status message is text.

As we will discuss in Recipe 1.2, there are cases where you may need to trade off visibility for other characteristics such as network efficiency, client convenience, and separation of concerns. When you make such trade-offs, carefully analyze the effect on features such as caching, idempotency, and safety.

1.2 When to Trade Visibility

This recipe describes some common situations where trading off visibility may be necessary.

Problem

You want to know common situations that may require you to keep requests and responses less visible to the protocol.

Solution

Whenever you have multiple resources that share data or whenever an operation modifies more than one resource, be prepared to trade visibility for better abstraction of information, loose coupling, network efficiency, resource granularity, or pure client convenience.

Discussion

Visibility often competes with other architectural demands such as abstraction, loose coupling, efficiency, message granularity, etc. For example, think of a person resource and a related address resource. Any client can submit GET requests to obtain representations of these two resources. For the sake of client convenience, the server may include data from the address resource within the representation of the person resource as follows:

```
# Request to get the person
GET /person/1 HTTP/1.1
Host: www.example.org
Content-Type: application/xml;charset=UTF-8

<person>
  <name>John Doe</name>
  <address type="home">
    <street>1 Main Street</street>
    <city>Bellevue</city>
    <state>WA</state>
  </address>
</person>

# Request to get the address
GET /person/1/address HTTP/1.1
Host: www.example.org
Content-Type: application/xml;charset=UTF-8

<address type="home">
  <street>1 Main Street</street>
  <city>Bellevue</city>
  <state>WA</state>
</address>
```

Let's assume that the server allows clients to submit PUT requests to update these resources. When a client modifies one of these resources, the state of the related resource also changes. However, at the HTTP level, these are independent resources. Only the server knows that they are dependent. Such overlapping data is a common cause of reduced visibility.

One of the important consequences of reduced visibility is caching (see Chapter 9). Since these are two independent resources at the HTTP level, caches will have two copies of the address: one as an independent address representation and the other as part of the person representation. This can be inefficient. Also, invalidating one representation from the cache will not invalidate the other representation. This can leave stale representations in the cache.

In this particular example, you can eliminate the overlap between these resources by including a reference to the address from the person resource and avoid including address details. You can use links (see Chapter 5) to provide references to other resources.

Although providing a link may minimize overlaps, it will force clients to make additional requests.

In this example, the trade-off is between visibility and client convenience and, potentially, network efficiency. A client that always deals with person resources can make a single request to get information about the person as well as the address.

Here are some more situations where you may need to give up visibility for other benefits:

Client convenience

Servers may need to design special-purpose coarse-grained composite resources for the sake of client convenience (e.g., Recipe 2.4).

Abstraction

In order to abstract complex business operations (including transactions), servers may need to employ controller resources to make changes to other resources (e.g., Recipe 2.6). Such resources can hide the details used to implement business operations.

Network efficiency

In cases where a client is performing several operations in quick succession, you may need to combine such operations into batches to reduce network latency (e.g., Recipes 11.10 and 11.13).

In each of these cases, if you focus only on visibility, you may be forced to design your web service to expose all data as independent resources with no overlaps. A web service designed in that manner may lead to fine-grained resources and poor separation of concerns between clients and servers. For an example, see Recipe 2.6. Other scenarios such as copying or merging resources and making partial updates (see Chapter 11) may also require visibility trade-offs.

Provided you are aware of the consequences early during the design process, trading off visibility for other benefits is not necessarily bad.

1.3 How to Maintain Application State

Often when you read about REST, you come across the recommendation to "keep the application state on the client." But what is "application state" and how can you keep that state on the client? This recipe describes how best to maintain state.

Problem

You want to know how to manage state in RESTful web services such that you do not need to rely on in-memory sessions on servers.

Solution

Encode application state into URIs, and include those URIs into representations via links (see Chapter 5). Let clients use these URIs to interact with resources. If the state is large or cannot be transported to clients for security or privacy reasons, store the application state in a durable storage (such as a database or a filesystem), and encode a reference to that state in URIs.

Discussion

Consider a simplified auto insurance application involving two steps. In the first step, the client submits a request with driver and vehicle details, and the server returns a quote valid for a week. In the second step, the client submits a request to purchase insurance. In this example, the application state is the quote. The server needs to know the quote from the first step so that it can issue a policy based on that quote in the second request.

 Application state is the state that the server needs to maintain between each request for each client. Keeping this state in clients does not mean serializing some session state into URIs or HTML forms, as web frameworks like ASP.NET and JavaServer Faces do.

Since HTTP is a stateless protocol, each request is independent of any previous request. However, interactive applications often require clients to follow a sequence of steps in a particular order. This forces servers to temporarily store each client's current position in those sequences outside the protocol. The trick is to manage state such that you strike a balance between reliability, network performance, and scalability.

The best place to maintain application state is within links in representations of resources, as in the following example:

```
# Request
POST /quotegen HTTP/1.1
Host: www.example.org
Content-Type: application/x-www-form-urlencoded
```

```
fname=...&lname=...&..

# Response
HTTP/1.1 200 OK
Content-Type: application/xml;charset=UTF-8

<quote xmlns:atom="http://www.w3.org/2005/Atom">
  <driver>
    ...
  </driver>
  <vehicle>
    ...
  </vehicle>
  <offer>
    ...
    <valid-until>2009-10-02</valid-until>
    <atom:link href="http://www.example.org/quotes/buy?quote=abc1234"
         rel="http://www.example.org/rels/quotes/buy"/> ❶
  </offer>
</quote>
```

❶ A link containing application state

In this example, the server stores the quote data in a data store and encodes its primary key in the URI. When the client makes a request to purchase insurance using this URI, the server can reinstate the application state using this key.

Choose a durable storage such as a database or a filesystem to store application state. Using a nondurable storage such as a cache or an in-memory session reduces the reliability of the web service as such state may not survive server restart. Such solutions may also reduce scalability of the server.

Alternatively, if the amount of data for the quote is small, the server can encode the state within the URI itself, as shown in the code below.

When you store application state in databases, use database replication so that all server instances have access to that state. If the application state is not permanent, you may also need to clean up the state at some point.

```
# Request
GET /quotegen?fname=...&lname=...&... HTTP/1.1
Host: www.example.org

# Response
HTTP/1.1 200 OK
Content-Type: application/xml;charset=UTF-8

<quote xmlns:atom="http://www.w3.org/2005/Atom">
  <driver>
```

```
   ...
  </driver>
  <vehicle>
    ...
  </vehicle>
  <offer>
    ...
    <valid-until>2009-08-02</valid-until>
    <atom:link href="http://www.example.org/quotes/buy?fname=...&lname=...&..."
          rel="http://www.example.org/quotes/buy"/>
  </offer>
</html>
```

Since the client will need to send all that data back in every request, encoding the application state in links may reduce network performance. Yet it can improve scalability since the server does not need to store any data, and it may improve reliability since the server does not need to use replication. Depending on your specific use case and the amount of state, use a combination of these two approaches for managing application state, and strike a balance between network performance, scalability, and reliability.

 When you store application state in links, make sure to add checks (such as signatures) to detect/prevent the tampering of state. See Recipe 12.5 for an example.

1.4 How to Implement Safe and Idempotent Methods on the Server

Safety and idempotency are guarantees that a server must provide to clients in its implementation for certain methods. This recipe discusses why these matter and how to implement safety and idempotency on the server.

Problem

You want to know what idempotency and safety mean, and what you can do to ensure that the server's implementation of various HTTP methods maintain these two characteristics.

Solution

While implementing GET, OPTIONS, and HEAD methods, do not cause any side effects. When a client resubmits a GET, HEAD, OPTIONS, PUT, or DELETE request, ensure that the server provides the same response except under concurrent conditions (see Chapter 10).

Discussion

Safety and idempotency are characteristics of HTTP methods for servers to implement. Table 1-1 shows which methods are safe and which are idempotent.

Table 1-1. Safety and idempotency of HTTP methods

Method	Safe?	Idempotent?
GET	Yes	Yes
HEAD	Yes	Yes
OPTIONS	Yes	Yes
PUT	No	Yes
DELETE	No	Yes
POST	No	No

Implementing safe methods

In HTTP, safe methods are not expected to cause side effects. Clients can send requests with safe methods without worrying about causing unintended side effects. To provide this guarantee, implement safe methods as read-only operations.

Safety does not mean that the server must return the same response every time. It just means that the client can make a request knowing that it is not going to change the state of the resource. For instance, both the following requests *may be* safe:

```
# First request
GET /quote?symb=YHOO HTTP/1.1
Host: www.example.org

HTTP/1.1 200 OK
Content-Type: text/plain;charset=UTF-8

15.96

# Second request 10 minutes later
GET /quote?symb=YHOO HTTP/1.1
Host: www.example.org

HTTP/1.1 200 OK
Content-Type: text/plain;charset=UTF-8

16.10
```

In this example, the change in response between these two requests may have been triggered by some other client or some backend operation.

Implementing idempotent methods

Idempotency guarantees clients that repeating a request has the same effect as making a request just once. Idempotency matters most in the case of network or software failures. Clients can repeat such requests and expect the same outcome. For example, consider the case of a client updating the price of a product.

```
# Request
PUT /book/gone-with-the-wind/price/us HTTP/1.1
Host: www.example.org
Content-Type: application/x-www-form-urlencoded

val=14.95
```

Now assume that because of a network failure, the client is unable to read the response. Since HTTP says that PUT is idempotent, the client can repeat the request.

```
# Request
PUT /book/gone-with-the-wind/price/us HTTP/1.1
Host: www.example.org
Content-Type: application/x-www-form-urlencoded

val=14.95

# Response
HTTP/1.1 200 OK
Content-Type: application/xml;charset=UTF-8

<value>14.95</value>
```

For this approach to work, you must implement all methods except POST to be idempotent. In programming language terms, idempotent methods are similar to "setters." For instance, calling the setPrice method in the following code more than once has the same effect as calling it just once:

```
class Book {
    private Price price;
    public void setPrice(Price price) {
        this.price = price;
    }
}
```

Idempotency of DELETE

The DELETE method is idempotent. This implies that the server must return response code 200 (OK) even if the server deleted the resource in a previous request. But in practice, implementing DELETE as an idempotent operation requires the server to keep track of all deleted resources. Otherwise, it can return a 404 (Not Found).

```
# First request
DELETE /book/gone-with-the-wind HTTP/1.1
Host: www.example.org

# Response
HTTP/1.1 200 OK

# Second request
DELETE /book/gone-with-the-wind HTTP/1.1
Host: www.example.org
```

```
# Response
HTTP/1.1 404 Not Found
Content-Type: text/html;charset=UTF-8

<html>
  ...
</html>
```

Even when the server has a record of all the deleted resources, security policies may require the server to return a 404 (Not Found) response code for any resource that does not currently exist.

1.5 How to Treat Safe and Idempotent Methods in Clients

Problem

You want to know how to implement HTTP requests that are idempotent and/or safe.

Solution

Treat GET, OPTIONS, and HEAD as read-only operations, and send those requests whenever required.

In the case of network or software failures, resubmit GET, PUT, and DELETE requests to confirm, supplying If-Unmodified-Since and/or If-Match conditional headers (see Chapter 10).

Do not repeat POST requests, unless the client knows ahead of time (e.g., via server's documentation) that its implementation of POST for any particular resource is idempotent.

Discussion

Safe methods

Any client should be able to make GET, OPTIONS and HEAD requests as many times as necessary. If a server's implementation causes unexpected side effects when processing these requests, it is fair to conclude that the server's implementation of HTTP is incorrect.

Idempotent methods

As discussed in Recipe 1.4, idempotency guarantees that the client can repeat a request when it is not certain the server successfully processed that request. In HTTP, all methods except POST are idempotent. In client implementations, whenever you encounter a software or a network failure for an idempotent method, you can implement logic to retry the request. Here is a pseudocode snippet:

```
try {
    // Submit a PUT request
    response = httpRequest.send("PUT", ...);
    if(response.code == 200) {
        // Success
        ...
    }
    else if(response.code >= 500) {
        // Failure due to server error
        ...
    }
    else if(response.code >= 400) {
        // Failure due to client error
        ...
    }
    ...
}
catch(NetworkFailure failure) {
    // Retry the request now or later
    ...
}
```

In this example, the client implements logic to repeat the request only in the case of network failures, not when the server returned a **4xx** or **5xx** error. The client must continue to treat various HTTP-level errors as usual (see Recipe 3.14).

Since POST is not idempotent, do not apply the previous pattern for POST requests unless told by the server. Recipe 10.8 describes a way for servers to provide idempotency for POST requests.

1.6 When to Use GET

The infrastructure of the Web strongly relies on the idempotent and safe nature of GET. Clients count on being able to repeat GET requests without causing side effects. Caches depend on the ability to serve cached representations without contacting the origin server.

Problem

You want to know when and when not to use GET and the potential consequences of using GET inappropriately.

Solution

Use GET for safe and idempotent information retrieval.

Discussion

Each method in HTTP has certain semantics. As discussed in Recipe 1.1, the purpose of GET is to get a representation of a resource, PUT is to create or update a resource,

DELETE is to delete a resource, and POST is either to create new resources or to make various other changes to resources.

Of all these methods, GET can take the least amount of misuse. This is because GET is both safe and idempotent.

 Do not use GET for unsafe or nonidempotent operations. Doing so could cause permanent, unexpected, and undesirable changes to resources.

Most abuse of GET happens in the form of using this method for unsafe operations. Here are some examples:

```
# Bookmark a page
GET /bookmarks/add_bookmark?href=http%3A%2F%2F
    www.example.org%2F2009%2F10%2F10%2Fnotes.html HTTP/1.1
Host: www.example.org

# Add an item to a shopping cart
GET /add_cart?pid=1234 HTTP/1.1
Host: www.example.org

# Send a message
GET /messages/send?message=I%20am%20reading HTTP/1.1
Host: www.example.org

# Delete a note
GET /notes/delete?id=1234 HTTP/1.1
Host: www.example.org
```

For the server, all these operations are unsafe and nonidempotent. But for any HTTP-aware software, these operations are safe and idempotent. The consequences of this difference can be severe depending on the application. For example, a tool routinely performing health checks on a server by periodically submitting a GET request using the fourth URI shown previously will delete a note.

If you must use GET for such operations, take the following precautions:

- Make the response noncacheable by adding a Cache-Control: no-cache header.
- Ensure that any side effects are benign and do not alter business-critical data.
- Implement the server such that those operations are repeatable (i.e., idempotent).

These steps may help reduce the impact of errors for certain but not all operations. The best course of action is to avoid abusing GET.

1.7 When to Use POST

This recipe summarizes various applications of POST.

Problem

You want to know the potential applications of the POST method.

Solution

Use POST for the following:

- To create a new resource, using the resource as a factory as described in Recipe 1.8
- To modify one or more resources via a controller resource as described in Recipe 2.6
- To run queries with large inputs as described in Recipe 8.3
- To perform any unsafe or nonidempotent operation when no other HTTP method seems appropriate

Discussion

In HTTP, the semantics of method POST are the most generic. HTTP specifies that this method is applicable for the following.[*]

- Annotation of existing resources;
- Posting a message to a bulletin board, newsgroup, mailing list, or similar group of articles;
- Providing a block of data, such as the result of submitting a form, to a data-handling process;
- Extending a database through an append operation.

All such operations are unsafe and nonidempotent, and all HTTP-aware tools treat POST as such:

- Caches do not cache responses of this method.
- Crawlers and such tools do not automatically activate POST requests.
- Most generic HTTP tools do not resubmit POST requests automatically.

Such a treatment gives great latitude for servers to use POST as a general-purpose method for a variety of operations, including tunneling. Consider the following:

```
# An XML-RPC message tunneled over HTTP POST
POST /RPC2 HTTP/1.1
Host: www.example.org
Content-Type: text/xml;charset=UTF-8

<methodCall>
  <methodName>messages.delete</methodName>
  <params>
    <param>
      <value><int>1234</int></value>
```

---

[*] From Sec 9.5 of RFC 2616 (*http://tools.ietf.org/html/rfc2616#section-9.5*).

```
      </param>
    </params>
</methodCall>
```

This is an example of XML-RPC (*http://www.xmlrpc.com/*) tunneling an operation via the POST method. Another popular example is SOAP with HTTP:

```
# A SOAP message tunneled over HTTP POST
POST /Messages HTTP/1.1
Host: www.example.org
Content-Type: application/soap+xml; charset=UTF-8

<soap:Envelope xmlns:soap="http://www.w3.org/2001/12/soap-envelope"
    soap:encodingStyle="http://www.w3.org/2001/12/soap-encoding">

  <soap:Body xmlns:ns="http://www.example.org/messages">
    <ns:DeleteMessage>
      <ns:MessageId>1234</ns:MessageId>
    </ns:DeleteMessage>
  </soap:Body>
</soap:Envelope>
```

Both these approaches misuse the method POST. For this example, the DELETE method is more appropriate:

```
# Using DELETE
DELETE /message/1234 HTTP/1.1
Host: www.example.org
```

When there is no such direct mapping between the application's operations and HTTP, using POST has less severe consequences than overloading other HTTP methods.

In addition, the following situations force you to use POST even when GET is the right method to use:

- HTML clients like browsers use the URI of the page as the Referer header while making requests to fetch any linked resources. This may leak any sensitive information contained in the URI to external servers.

  In such cases, if using Transport Layer Security (TLS, a successor to SSL) or if the encryption of any sensitive information in the URI is not possible, consider using POST to serve HTML documents.

- As discussed in Recipe 8.3, POST may be the only option when queries from clients contain too many parameters.

Even in these conditions, use POST only as the last resort.

1.8 How to Create Resources Using POST

One of the applications of POST is to create new resources. The protocol is similar to using the "factory method pattern" for creating new objects.

Problem

You want to know how to create a new resource, what to include in the request, and what to include in the response.

Solution

Identify an existing resource as a factory for creating new resources. It is common practice to use a collection resource (see Recipe 2.3) as a factory, although you may use any resource.

Let the client submit a POST request with a representation of the resource to be created to the factory resource. Optionally support the Slug header to let clients suggest a name for the server to use as part of the URI of the resource to be created.

After creating the resource, return response code 201 (Created) and a Location header containing the URI of the newly created resource.

If the response body includes a complete representation of the newly created resource, include a Content-Location header containing the URI of the newly created resource.

Discussion

Consider the case of creating an address resource for a user. You can take the user resource as a factory to create a new address:

```
# Request
POST /user/smith HTTP/1.1 ❶
Host: www.example.org
Content-Type: application/xml;charset=UTF-8
Slug: Home Address ❷

<address>
  <street>1, Main Street</street>
  <city>Some City</city>
</address>

# Response
HTTP/1.1 201 Created
Location: http://www.example.org/user/smith/address/home_address ❸
Content-Location: http://www.example.org/user/smith/address/home_address ❹
Content-Type: application/xml;charset=UTF-8

<address>
  <id>urn:example:user:smith:address:1</id>
  <atom:link rel="self" href="http://www.example.org/user/smith/address/home_address"/>
  <street>1, Main Street</stret>
  <city>Some City</city>
</address>
```

❶ User resource acting as a factory to create a home address resource

❷ A suggestion for naming the URI of the new resource

❸ URI of the newly created resource

❹ URI of representation in the response

In this example, the request contains data to create a new resource, and a `Slug` header with a suggestion for the URI of the new resource. Note that the `Slug` header is specified by AtomPub (RFC 5023). This header is just a suggestion from the client. The server need not honor it. See Chapter 6 to learn about AtomPub.

The status code of the response `201` indicates that the server created a new resource and assigned the URI `http://www.example.org/user/smith/address/home_address` to it, as indicated by the `Location` response header. The `Content-Location` header informs the client that the body of the representation can also be accessed via the URI value of this header.

 Along with the `Content-Location` header, you can also include the `Last-Modified` and `ETag` headers of the newly created resource. See Chapter 10 to learn more about these headers.

1.9 When to Use PUT to Create New Resources

You can use either HTTP `POST` or HTTP `PUT` to create new resources. This recipe discusses when to use `PUT` to create new resources.

Problem

You want to know when to use `PUT` to create new resources.

Solution

Use `PUT` to create new resources only when clients can decide URIs of resources. Otherwise, use `POST`.

Discussion

Here is an example of a client using `PUT` to create a new resource:

```
# Request
PUT /user/smith/address/home_address HTTP/1.1  ❶
Host: www.example.org
Content-Type: application/xml;charset=UTF-8

<address>
  <street>1, Main Street</street>
  <city>Some City</city>
</address>

# Response
HTTP/1.1 201 Created
```

```
Location: http://www.example.org/user/smith/address/home_address
Content-Location: http://www.example.org/user/smith/address/home_address
Content-Type: application/xml;charset=UTF-8

<address>
  <id>urn:example:user:smith:address:1</id>
  <atom:link rel="self" href="http://www.example.org/user/smith/address/home_address"/>
  <street>1, Main Street</street>
  <city>Some City</city>
</address>
```

❶ Client using PUT to create a new resource

Use PUT to create new resources only when the client can control part of the URI. For instance, a storage server may allocate a root URI for each client and let clients create new resources using that root URI as a root directory on a filesystem. Otherwise, use POST.

When using POST to create new resources, the server decides the URI for the newly created resource. It can control its URI naming policies along with any network security-level configurations. You can still let servers use information in the representation (such as the Slug header) while generating URIs for new resources.

When you support PUT to create new resources, clients must be able to assign URIs for resources. When using this method to create new resources, take the following into consideration:

- To let clients assign URIs, the server needs to explain to clients how URIs on the server are organized, what kind of URIs are valid, and what kind are not.
- You also need to consider any security and filtering rules set up on servers based on URI patterns and may want to restrict clients to use a narrow range of URIs while creating new URIs.

In general, any resource that can be created via PUT can equivalently be created by using POST with a factory resource. Using a factory resource gives the server more control without explaining its URI naming rules. An exception is the case of servers providing a filesystem-like interface for clients to manage documents. WebDAV (see Recipe 11.4) is an example.

1.10 How to Use POST for Asynchronous Tasks

HTTP is a synchronous and stateless protocol. When a client submits a request to a server, the client expects an answer, whether the answer is a success or a failure. But this does not mean that the server must finish processing the request before returning a response. For example, in a banking application, when you initiate an account transfer, the transfer may not happen until the next business day, and the client may be required to check for the status later. This recipe discusses how to use this method to process requests asynchronously.

Problem

You want to know how to implement POST requests that take too long to complete.

Solution

On receiving a POST request, create a new resource, and return status code 202 (Accepted) with a representation of the new resource. The purpose of this resource is to let a client track the status of the asynchronous task. Design this resource such that its representation includes the current status of the request and related information such as a time estimate.

When the client submits a GET request to the task resource, do one of the following depending on the current status of the request:

Still processing
> Return response code 200 (OK) and a representation of the task resource with the current status.

On successful completion
> Return response code 303 (See Other) and a Location header containing a URI of a resource that shows the outcome of the task.

On task failure
> Return response code 200 (OK) with a representation of the task resource informing that the resource creation has failed. Clients will need to read the body of the representation to find the reason for failure.

Discussion

Consider an image-processing web service offering services such as file conversions, optical character recognition, image cleanup, etc. To use this service, clients upload raw images. Depending on the nature and size of images uploaded and the current server load, the server may take from a few seconds up to several hours to process each image. Upon completion, client applications can view/download processed images.

Let's start with the client submitting a POST request to initiate a new image-processing task:

```
# Request
POST /images/tasks HTTP/1.1
Host: www.example.org
Content-Type: multipart/related; boundary=xyz

--xyz
Content-Type: application/xml;charset=UTF-8

...
```

```
--xyz
Content-Type: image/png

...

--xyz--
```

In this example, the client uses a multipart message, with the first part containing an XML document describing the kind of image-processing operations the server needs to perform and the second part containing the image to be processed.

Upon ensuring that the contents are valid and that the given image-processing request can be honored, let the server create a new task resource:

```
# Response
HTTP/1.1 202 Accepted  ❶
Content-Type: application/xml;charset=UTF-8
Content-Location: http://www.example.org/images/task/1
Date: Sun, 13 Sep 2009 01:49:27 GMT

<status xmlns:atom="http://www.w3.org/2005/Atom">
  <state>pending</state>
  <atom:link href="http://www.example.org/images/task/1" rel="self"/>
  <message xml:lang="en">Your request has been accepted for processing.</message>
  <ping-after>2009-09-13T01:59:27Z</ping-after>  ❷
</status>
```

❶ Response code indicating that the server accepted the request for processing

❷ A hint to check for the status at a later time

The client can subsequently send a GET request to this task resource. If the server is still processing the task, it can return the following response:

```
# Request
GET /images/task/1 HTTP/1.1
Host: www.example.org

# Response
HTTP/1.1 200 OK
Content-Type: application/xml;charset=UTF-8

<status xmlns:atom="http://www.w3.org/2005/Atom">
  <state>pending</state>
  <atom:link href="http://www.example.org/images/task/1" rel="self"/>
  <message xml:lang="en">Your request is currently being processed.</message>
  <ping-after>2009-09-13T02:09:27Z</ping-after>
</status>
```

 See Recipe 3.9 to learn the rationale behind the choice of the date-time value for the ping-after element.

After the server successfully completes image processing, it can redirect the client to the result. In this example, the result is a new image resource:

```
# Request
GET /images/task/1 HTTP/1.1
Host: www.example.org

# Response
HTTP/1.1 303 See Other   ❶
Location: http://www.example.org/images/1
Content-Location: http://www.example.org/images/task/1

<status xmlns:atom="http://www.w3.org/2005/Atom">
  <state>done</state>
  <atom:link href="http://www.example.org/images/task/1" rel="self"/>
  <message xml:lang="en">Your request has been processed.</message>
</status>
```

❶ See the target resource for the result.

> The response code 303 merely states that the result exists at the URI indicated in the Location header. It does not mean that the resource at the request URI (e.g., http://www.example.org/images/task/1) has moved to a new location.

This representation informs the client that it needs to refer to http://www.example.org/images/1 for the result. If, on the other hand, the server fails to complete the task, it can return the following:

```
# Request
GET /images/task/1 HTTP/1.1
Host: www.example.org

# Response
HTTP/1.1 200 OK
Content-Type: application/xml;charset=UTF-8

<status xmlns:atom="http://www.w3.org/2005/Atom">
  <state>failed</state>
  <atom:link href="http://www.example.org/images/task/1" rel="self"/>
  <message xml:lang="en">Failed to complete the request.</message>
  <detail xml:lang="en">Invalid image format.</detail>
  <completed>2009-09-13T02:10:00Z</completed>
</status>
```

1.11 How to Use DELETE for Asynchronous Deletion

This recipe outlines an approach for using DELETE for asynchronous tasks. This recipe is appropriate when resource deletion takes a significant amount of time for cleanup and archival tasks in the backend.

Problem

You want to know how to implement DELETE requests that take too long to complete.

Solution

On receiving a DELETE request, create a new resource, and return 202 (Accepted) with the response containing a representation of this resource. Let the client use this resource to track the status. When the client submits a GET request to the task resource, return response code 200 (OK) with a representation showing the current status of the task.

Discussion

Supporting asynchronous resource deletion is even simpler than creating or updating resources. The following sequence of steps illustrates an implementation of this recipe:

1. To begin, a client submits a request to delete a resource.

   ```
   DELETE /users/john HTTP/1.1
   Host: www.example.org
   ```

2. The server creates a new resource and returns a representation indicating the status of the task.

   ```
   HTTP/1.1 202 Accepted
   Content-Type: application/xml;charset=UTF-8

   <status xmlns:atom="http://www.w3.org/2005/Atom">
     <state>pending</state>
     <atom:link href="http://www.example.org/task/1" rel="self"/>
     <message xml:lang="en">Your request has been accepted for processing.</message>
     <created>2009-07-05T03:10:00Z</ping>
     <ping-after>2009-07-05T03:15:00Z</ping-after>
   </status>
   ```

3. The client can query the URI http://www.example.org/task/1 to learn the status of the request.

You can use the same approach for asynchronously updating a resource via the PUT method.

1.12 When to Use Custom HTTP Methods

There were several attempts to extend HTTP with new methods. The most prominent attempt was WebDAV (*http://www.webdav.org*). WebDAV defines several HTTP methods, such as PROPFIND, PROPPATCH, MOVE, LOCK, UNLOCK, etc., for distributed authoring and versioning of documents (see Recipe 11.4). Other examples include PATCH (Recipe 11.9) for partial updates and MERGE (*http://msdn.microsoft.com/en-us/library/cc668771.aspx*) for merging resources.

Problem

You want to know the consequences of using custom HTTP methods.

Solution

Avoid using nonstandard custom HTTP methods. When you introduce new methods, you cannot rely on off-the-shelf software that only knows about the standard HTTP methods.

Instead, design a controller (see Recipe 2.6) resource that can abstract such operations, and use HTTP method POST.

Discussion

The most important benefit of extending methods is that they let servers define clear semantics for those methods and keep the interface uniform. But unless widely supported, extension methods reduce interoperability.

For example, WebDAV defines the semantics of MOVE as a "logical equivalent of a copy (COPY), followed by consistency maintenance processing, followed by a delete of the source, where all three actions are performed atomically." Any client can submit an OPTIONS request to determine whether a WebDAV resource implements MOVE. When necessary, if a resource supports this method, the client can submit a MOVE request to move a resource from one location to another.

```
# Request to discover supported methods
OPTIONS /docs/annual_report HTTP/1.1
Host: www.example.org

# Response
HTTP/1.1. 204 No Content
Allow: GET, PUT, DELETE, MOVE

# Move
MOVE /docs/annual_report HTTP/1.1
Host: www.example.org
Destination: http://www.example.org/docs/annual_report_2009

# Response
HTTP/1.1 201 Created
Location: http://www.example.org/docs/annual_report_2009
```

It is certainly possible to follow WebDAV's approach and design a new method, say, CLONE, to create a clone of an existing resource:

```
# Request to clone
CLONE /po/1234 HTTP/1.1
Host: www.example.org

# Clone created
HTTP/1.1 201 Created
Location: www.example.org/po/5678
```

Clients will then be able to discover support for this method and submit a CLONE request.

In reality, proxies, caches, and HTTP libraries will treat such methods as nonidempotent, unsafe, and noncacheable. In other words, they apply the same rules to such extension methods as POST, which is nonidempotent, unsafe, and most often noncacheable. This is because idempotency and safety are guarantees that the server must explicitly provide. For unknown custom methods, proxies, caches, and HTTP libraries cannot assume that the server provides such guarantees. Therefore, for most HTTP-aware software and tools, custom HTTP methods are synonymous with POST.

```
# Request to clone
POST /clone-orders HTTP/1.1
Host: www.example.org
Content-Type: application/x-www-form-urlencoded

id=urn:example:po:1234

# Clone created
HTTP/1.1 201 Created
Location: www.example.org/po/5678
```

Moreover, not all HTTP software (including firewalls) may support arbitrary extension methods. Therefore, use custom methods only when wide interoperability is not a concern.

 Prefer POST over custom HTTP methods. Not every HTTP software lets you use custom HTTP methods. Using POST is a safer option.

1.13 When and How to Use Custom HTTP Headers

It is not uncommon to find HTTP servers using custom headers. Some well-known custom headers include X-Powered-By, X-Cache, X-Pingback, X-Forwarded-For, and X-HTTP-Method-Override. HTTP does not prohibit such extension headers, but depending on what clients and servers use custom headers for, custom headers may impede interoperability. This recipe discusses when and how to use custom HTTP headers.

Problem

You want to know the common conventions and best practices for using custom HTTP headers.

Solution

Use custom headers for informational purposes. Implement clients and servers such that they do not fail when they do not find expected custom headers.

Avoid using custom HTTP headers to change the behavior of HTTP methods. Limit any behavior-changing headers to the method POST.

If the information you are conveying through a custom HTTP header is important for the correct interpretation of the request or response, include that information in the body of the request or response or the URI used for the request. Avoid custom headers for such usages.

Discussion

Most websites using the WordPress blogging platform (*http://wordpress.org*) include the following HTTP headers in responses:

```
X-Powered-By: PHP/5.2.6-2ubuntu4.2
X-Pingback: http://www.example.org/xmlrpc.php
```

Such headers are not part of HTTP. The first header is generated by the PHP runtime that WordPress is built on. It indicates that the server is using a particular version of PHP on Ubuntu. The X-Pingback header contains a URI that clients can use to notify WordPress when a reference is made on some other server to the resource. Similarly, HTTP caching proxy Squid uses X-Cache headers to inform clients whether the representation in the response is being served from the cache.

Such usages are informational. Clients receiving those headers are free to ignore them without loss of functionality. Another commonly used informational header is X-Forwarded-By.

```
X-Forwarded-For: 192.168.123.10, 192.168.123.14
```

The purpose of this header is to convey the source of the request to the server. Some proxies and caches add this header to report the source of the request to the server. In this example, the server received a request from 192.168.123.10 via 192.168.123.14. If all proxies and caches that the request is served through augment this header, then the server can determine the IP address of the client.

 Although names of some custom headers start with X-, there is no established convention for naming these headers. When you introduce custom headers, use a convention such as X-{company-name}-{header-name}.

The following custom HTTP headers are not informational and may be required for the correct processing of requests or responses:

```
# A version number of the resource
X-Example-Version: 1.2

# An identifier for the client
X-Example-Client-Id: 12345

# An operation
X-Example-Update-Type: Overwrite
```

Avoid such usages. They weaken the use of URIs as resource identifiers and HTTP methods as operations.

Another commonly used custom header is X-HTTP-Method-Override. This header was initially used by Google as part of the Google Data Protocol (*http://code.google.com/apis/gdata/docs/2.0/basics.html*). Here is an example:

```
# Request
POST /user/john/address HTTP/1.1
X-HTTP-Method-Override: PUT
Content-Type: application/xml;charset=UTF-8

<address>
  <street>...</street>
  <city>...</city>
  <postal-code>...</postal-code>
</address>
```

In this case, the client uses X-HTTP-Method-Override with a value of PUT to override the behavior of the method used for the request, which is POST. The rationale for this extension was to tunnel the method PUT over POST so that any firewalls configured to block PUT will permit the request.

> Instead of using X-HTTP-Method-Override to override POST, use a distinct resource to process the same request using POST without that header. Any HTTP intermediary between the client and the server may omit custom headers.

## CHAPTER 2

Identifying Resources

One of the first steps in developing a RESTful web service is designing the resource model. The resource model identifies and classifies all the resources the client uses to interact with the server. Of all the aspects of designing a RESTful web service, such as identification of resources, choice of media types and formats, and application of the uniform interface, resource identification is the most flexible part.

Because of the visible nature of HTTP (see Recipe 1.1), you can use tools like Firebug (*http://getfirebug.com*), Yahoo! YSlow (*http://developer.yahoo.com/yslow/*), or Resource Expert Droid (*http://redbot.org/*) to make reasonable assertions about whether the server is implementing HTTP correctly. But you cannot do the same with resources. *There is no right or wrong resource model.* All that matters is whether you can use HTTP's uniform interface reasonably correctly to implement your web service. This chapter goes through the following recipes to help identify resources for a number of common situations:

Recipe 2.1, "How to Identify Resources from Domain Nouns"
   Use this recipe to identify an initial set of resources from domain entities.

Recipe 2.2, "How to Choose Resource Granularity"
   Use this recipe to guide resource granularity.

Recipe 2.3, "How to Organize Resources into Collections"
   When you have several resources of the same kind, use this recipe to group those into collection resources.

Recipe 2.4, "When to Combine Resources into Composites"
   Use this recipe to combine resources into composites, based on client usage patterns.

Recipe 2.5, "How to Support Computing/Processing Functions"
   Apply this recipe to identify resources that implement processing functions.

Recipe 2.6, "When and How to Use Controllers to Operate on Resources"
   Use this recipe to design controller resources to make changes across several resources.

Designing a resource model is usually an iterative process. While developing a web service, look at backend design constraints and client needs along with other use cases, and revisit these recipes to improve resources iteratively.

2.1 How to Identify Resources from Domain Nouns

Both object-oriented design and database modeling techniques use domain entities as a basis for design. You can use the same technique to identify resources. But be warned. As you shall see later in this chapter, this recipe is simplistic and can, in some cases, provide a misleading outcome.

Problem

You want to start identifying resources from the use cases and a description of the web service.

Solution

Analyze your use cases to find domain nouns that can be operated using "create," "read," "update," or "delete" operations. Designate each noun as a resource. Use POST, GET, PUT, and DELETE methods to implement "create," "read," "update," and "delete" operations, respectively, on each resource.

Discussion

Consider a web service for managing photos. Clients can upload a new photo, replace an existing photo, view a photo, or delete a photo. In this example, "photo" is an entity in the application domain. The actions a client can perform on this entity include "create a new photo," "replace an existing photo," "view a photo," and "delete a photo."

You can apply this recipe to identify each "photo" as a resource such that clients can use HTTP's uniform interface to operate on these photos as follows:

- Method GET to get a representation of each photo
- Method PUT to update a photo
- Method DELETE to delete a photo
- Method POST to create a new photo

This recipe is what gives REST the perception that REST is suitable for CRUD-style (Create, Read, Update, Delete) applications only. If you limit yourself to identifying resources based on domain nouns alone, you are likely to find that the fixed set of methods in HTTP is quite a limitation. In most applications, CRUD operations make only part of the interface. Consider some examples:

- Find traffic directions from Seattle to San Francisco.
- Generate random numbers, or convert a given distance from miles to kilometers.

- Provide a way for a client to get a user's profile with a minimal set of properties, list of the 10 latest photos uploaded by the user, and 10 news stories that match the user's interest all in one single request.
- Approve a requisition to buy software.
- Transfer money from one bank account to another bank account.
- Merge two address books.

In all these use cases, it is easy to spot the nouns. But in each case, if you designate those nouns as resources, you will find that the corresponding actions do not map to HTTP methods such as GET, POST, PUT, and DELETE. You will need additional resources to tackle such use cases. See the rest of the recipes in this chapter to identify those additional resources.

2.2 How to Choose Resource Granularity

Bluntly mapping domain entities into resources may lead to resources that are inefficient and inconvenient to use. This recipe discusses criteria that you can use to determine appropriate granularity for resources.

Problem

You want to know the criteria for determining an appropriate granularity of resources.

Solution

Use network efficiency, size of representations, and client convenience to guide resource granularity.

Discussion

Looking at the scenarios of your application, you may find several nouns of different granularity. Take, for example, a social network where the interactions happen in the context of a "user." Each user's data may include an activity stream, list of friends, list of followers, links to share, etc. In such an application, should you model each user as a coarse-grained resource to encapsulate all this data? Or should you make the resources less coarse-grained and offer activity streams, friends, followers, etc., as resources as well? The answer depends on what a typical client for your web service does. With the former approach, user representations may be too big for clients to handle, and the latter may be more flexible. If most of the clients download the user's data onto the user's computers, store it, and then present it using some rich user interface, then offering the user resource containing all its data makes sense.

Take a much simpler case such as a user with an address. You may want to maintain a proxy HTTP cache to keep representations of all users in its memory so that clients can quickly access these representations. In this example, the representation of the user resource that also includes the address may be too big to fit into the cache. Offering the address of each user as a separate resource makes more sense, although it can make client/server interactions chatty because of the reduced granularity.

Similarly, mapping database tables or object models in your application to resources may not produce the best results. A number of factors, such as domain modeling and allowing for efficient data access and processing, influence the design of database tables and object models. HTTP clients, on the other hand, access resources over the network using HTTP's uniform interface. Therefore, you need to design resources to suit clients' usage patterns and not design them based on what exists in a database or the object model.

So, how can you determine nouns that are candidate resources? How granular should you design them? The best way to answer these questions is to think from the client's perspective. In the first example shown previously, coarse granularity is more convenient for rich-client applications, whereas in the second example, the resources are more fine-grained to meet caching requirements. Therefore, look from the client and network point of view to determine resource granularity. The following factors may further influence resource granularity:

- Cacheablility
- Frequency of change
- Mutability

Refining resource granularity to ensure that more cacheable, less frequently changing, or immutable data is separated from less cacheable, more frequently changing, or mutable data can improve the efficiency of both clients and servers.

2.3 How to Organize Resources into Collections

Organizing resources into collections gives clients and servers an ability to refer to a group of a resources as one, to perform queries on the collection, or even to use the collection as a factory to create new resources.

Problem

You want to know how best to group together resources that share some commonality.

Solution

Identify similar resources based on any application-specific criteria. Common examples are resources that share the same database schema or the same set of attributes or properties or look similar to clients. Group similar resources into a collection resource for each similarity.

Design a representation for each collection such that it contains information about all or some of its member resources (see Recipe 3.7).

Discussion

Once you group several similar resources under a collection resource, you can refer to the group as a whole, as in the following example. You can, for instance, submit a GET request to fetch an entire collection instead of fetching individual resources one after the other.

Consider a social network, where all user records share the same database schema. Each user in this network has a list of friends and a list of followers. Friends and followers are other users in the same database. Users are categorized based on personal interests, such as running, cycling, swimming, hiking, etc. In this example, you can identify the following collections whose members are user resources:

- Collection of user resources
- Collection of friends of any given user
- Collection of followers of a given user
- Collections of users by the same interest

Here is an example of a users collection resource returned in response to a GET request to that collection:

```
# Request
GET /users HTTP/1.1
Host: www.example.org

# Response
IITTP/1.1 200 OK
Content-Type: application/xml;charset=UTF-8

<users xmlns:atom="http://www.w3.org/2005/Atom"> ❶
  <atom:link rel="self" href="http://www.example.org/users"/>
  <user> ❷
    <id>urn:example:user:001</id>
    <atom:link rel="self" href="http://www.example.org/user/user001"/>
    <name>John Doe</name>
    <email>john.doe@example.org</email>
  </user>
  <user>
    <id>urn:example:user:002</id>
    <atom:link rel="self" href="http://www.example.org/user/user002"/>
    <name>Jane Doe</name>
    <email>jane.doe@example.org</email>
  </user>
  ...
</users>
```

❶ A collection resource

❷ A member of the collection

Note that a collection does not necessarily imply hierarchical containment. A given resource may be part of more than one collection resource. For example, a user resource may be part of several collections such as "users," "friends," "followers," and "hikers." Here is a friends collection for a user:

```
# Request
GET /user/user001/friends HTTP/1.1
Host: www.example.org

# Response
HTTP/1.1 200 OK
Content-Type: application/xml;charset=UTF-8

<users xmlns:atom="http://www.w3.org/2005/Atom">
  <atom:link rel="self" href="http://www.example.org/user/user001/friends"/>
  <user>
    <id>urn:example:user:002</id>
    <atom:link rel="self" href="http://www.example.org/user/user002"/>
    <name>Jane Doe</name>
    <email>jane.doe@example.org</email>
  </user>
  ...
</users>
```

You can use collection resources for the following:

- To retrieve paginated views of a collection, such as browsing through the friends collection of a user, obtained 10 at a time (see Recipe 3.7).

- To search the collection for its members or to obtain a filtered view of the collection. For instance, you could search for friends who are swimmers (see Recipe 8.2).

- To create new member resources using the collection as a factory, by submitting HTTP POST requests to the collection resource.

- To perform the same operation on a number of resources at once (see Recipe 11.10).

2.4 When to Combine Resources into Composites

When you look at the home pages of sites like *http://www.yahoo.com* or *http://www .msn.com*, you will notice that these pages aggregate information from a number of sources, such as news, email, weather, entertainment, finance, etc. If you think of each of these sources as resources, serving each of these home pages is a result of combining those disparate resources into a single resource whose representation is an HTML page. Such web pages are composite resources; i.e., they combine information from other resources. This recipe uses the same technique to identify composite resources.

Problem

You want to know how to provide a resource whose state is made up of states from two or more resources.

Solution

Based on client usage patterns and performance and latency requirements, identify new resources that aggregate other resources to reduce the number of client/server round-trips.

Discussion

A composite resource combines information from other resources. Consider a snapshot page for each customer in an enterprise application. This page shows the customer information, such as the name, the contact information, a summary of the latest purchase orders from the customer, and any pending requests for quotes. Using the recipes discussed in this chapter so far, you can identify the following resources:

- Customer, with name, contact information, and other details
- Collection of purchase orders for each customer
- Collection of pending quotes for each customer

Given these resources, you can make the following GET requests and, using the responses, build a customer snapshot page:

```
# Get the customer data
GET /customer/1234 HTTP/1.1
Host: www.example.org

# Get the 10 latest purchase orders
GET /orders?customerid=1234&sortby=date_desc&limit=10 HTTP/1.1
Host: www.example.org

# Get the 10 latest pending quotes
GET /quotes?customerid=1234&sortby=date_desc&status=pending&limit=10 HTTP/1.1
Host: www.example.org
```

Although this sequence of GET requests may be acceptable for the server, these requests are very chatty. It may be more efficient for the client to send a single network request for all the data needed to render the page.

For the customer snapshot page, you can design a "customer snapshot" composite resource that combines all the information needed for the client to render the page. Assign a URI of the form http://www.example.org/customer/1234/snapshot where 1234 is an identifier that identifies a customer. Here is an example of this resource in use:

```
# Request
GET /customer/1234/snapshot HTTP/1.1
Host: www.example.org
```

```
# Response
HTTP/1.1 200 OK
Content-Type: application/xml;charset=UTF-8

<snapshot xmlns:atom="http://www.w3.org/2005/Atom">
  <!-- Customer info -->
  <customer>
    <id>1234</id>
    <atom:link rel="self" href="http://www.example.org/customer/1234">
    <name>...</name>
    <address>...</address>
  </customer>
  <!-- Most 10 recent orders placed by the customer -->
  <orders>
    <atom:link rel="http://www.example.org/rels/orders/recent"
          href="http://www.example.org/orders?customerid=1234&sortby=date_desc&"/>
    <order>
      <id>...</id>
      ...
    </order>
    ...
  </orders>
  <!-- Most 10 pending quotes for the customer -->
  <quotes>
    <atom:link rel="http://www.example.org/rels/quotes/recent"
          href="http://www.example.org/quotes?customerid=1234&sortby=date_desc&"/>
    ...
  </quotes>
</snapshot>
```

This response is an aggregate of representations that the client would get by submitting three GET requests.

Composite resources reduce the visibility of the uniform interface since their representations contain overlapping data with other resources. Therefore, before offering composite resources, consider the following:

- If requests for composites are rare in your application, composites may be a poor choice. The client may benefit from relying on a caching proxy to fetch those resources from a cache instead.

- Another factor is the network cost between the client and the server and between the server and any backend services or data stores it relies upon. If the cost of the latter is significant, then retrieving large amounts of data and combing them on the server into a composite may increase the latency for the client and reduce throughput for the server.

  In this case, you may be able to improve latency by adding a caching layer between clients and servers and avoiding composites. Conduct load tests to verify whether a composite would help.

- Finally, creating special-purpose composites for the sake of every client is not a pragmatic task. Pick the clients that are most important for your web service, and design composites to suit the needs of those clients.

2.5 How to Support Computing/Processing Functions

Processing functions are not uncommon. Websites like Babel Fish (*http://babelfish.ya hoo.com/*), XE.com (*http://www.xe.com/*), and Google Maps (*http://maps.google.com*) take some inputs, process them with the help of data stored in their backend servers and some algorithms, and return results. These are all processing functions.

Problem

You want to know how to provide resource abstractions for tasks such as performing computations or validating data.

Solution

Treat the processing function as a resource, and use HTTP GET to fetch a representation containing the output of the processing function. Use query parameters to supply inputs to the processing function.

Discussion

One of the most common perceptions of REST's architectural constraints is that they only apply to resources that are "things" or "entities" in the application domain. Although this may be true in a number of cases, scenarios that involve processing functions challenge that perception. Here are some examples:

Distance between two places
> A client submits latitude and longitude values of both the locations to the server. The server then computes and returns the distance to the client.

Driving directions
> A client submits two locations in free form, say, "Seattle, WA" and "San Francisco, CA," and the server returns the directions as a list of driving segments and turn directions.

Validate a credit card
> The client submits credit card data such as the name of the cardholder, card number, and expiry date to the server, and the server returns data to the client indicating whether the card is valid.

All these examples share the same peculiarity. In each case, if you apply Recipe 2.1, you will find nouns on which you cannot easily apply the uniform interface. For example, if you identify each "place" as a resource, you will find that there is no HTTP equivalent of the operation "compute distance."

One way to address such use cases is to treat the processing function itself as a resource. In the first example, you can treat the distance calculator as a resource and the distance as its representation. The following request and response illustrate this resource:

```
# Request
GET /distance_calc?lats=47.610&lngs=-122.333&late=37.788&lnge=-122.406 HTTP/1.1
Host: www.example.org

# Response
HTTP/1.1 200 OK
Content-Type: application/xml;charset=UTF-8

<result xmlns:atom="http://www.w3.org/2005/Atom">
  <atom:link rel="self"
     href="http://www.example.org/distance_calc?lats=47.610&
           lngs=-122.333&late=37.788&lnge=-122.406"/>
  <distance unit="miles">808.0</distance>
</result>
```

Similarly, "direction finder," "points of interest finder," and "credit card validator" can all be resources with "directions," "points of interest," and "validation result" as representations of those resources:

```
# Request to find directions
GET /directions?from=Seattle,WA&to=San%20Francisco HTTP/1.1
Host: www.example.org

# Response
HTTP/1.1 200 OK
Content-Type: application/xml;charset=UTF-8

<directions>
  <step>
    ...
  </step>
  <step>
    ...
  </step>
</directions>

# Request to find points of interest
GET /poi?lat=47.610&lng=-122.333 HTTP/1.1
Host: www.example.org

# Response
HTTP/1.1 200 OK
Content-Type: application/atom+xml;charset=UTF-8

<atom:feed xmlns:atom="http://www.w3.org/2005/Atom">
  <atom:title>Points of Interest</atom:title>
  <atom:link href="http://www.example.org/poi?lat=47.610&lng=-122.333/" rel="self"/>
  <atom:updated>2009-10-01T18:30:02Z</atom:updated>
  <atom:author>
    <atom:name>All Names Made Up Inc.</atom:name>
  </atom:author>
```

```
  <atom:id>urn:uuid:60a76c80-d399-11d9-b93C-0003939e0af6</atom:id>
  <atom:entry>
    <atom:id>urn:example:poi:0012</atom:id>
    <atom:title>...</atom:title>
    <atom:updated>2009-09-13T18:30:02Z</atom:updated>
    <atom:link rel="alternate" href="http://www.example.org/poi/0012.html"/>
    <atom:content type="text">...</atom:content>
  </atom:entry>
  ...
</atom:feed>

# Request to validate a credit card (sent via HTTPS)
GET /validate?ccnum=1234567890123456 HTTP/1.1
Host: www.example.org

# Response
HTTP/1.1 200 OK
Content-Type: text/plain;charset=UTF-8

invalid
```

Because all these methods are safe and idempotent, GET is the most appropriate HTTP method for implementing processing functions.

> URIs such as https://www.example.org/validate appear to denote "operations," thus undermining the uniform interface. However, URIs merely identify resources, and the syntax of URIs does not matter as far as HTTP is concerned.

2.6 When and How to Use Controllers to Operate on Resources

In the case of RESTful web services, controllers can help increase the separation of concerns between servers and clients, improve network efficiency, and let servers implement complex operations atomically.

Problem

You want to know how to tackle write operations that involve modifying more than one resource atomically, or whose mapping to PUT or DELETE is not obvious.

Solution

Designate a controller resource for each distinct operation. Let clients use the HTTP method POST to submit a request to trigger the operation. If the outcome of the operation is the creation of a new resource, return response code 201 (Created) with a Location header referring to the URI of the newly created resource. If the outcome is the modification of one or more existing resources, return response code 303 (See Other) with a Location with a URI that clients can use to fetch a representation of those modifications. If the server cannot provide a single URI to all the modified resources, return response code 200 (OK) with a representation in the body that clients can use to learn about the outcome. Handle errors as described in Recipe 3.13.

Discussion

A *controller* is a resource that can atomically make changes to resources. The need for such a resource may not be apparent from your domain model, but it can help the server abstract complex business operations and provide a way for clients to trigger those operations. This in turn reduces coupling between clients and servers.

Consider merging two address books for a user. A client on the mobile phone needs a way to synchronize all the contacts with the current address book on the server. One option is to use PUT as follows:

1. Submit a GET request to the address book resource to download the complete address book from the server.
2. Load the local list of contacts, and merge them with the address book downloaded from the server.
3. Submit a PUT request to the address book resource to replace the entire address book with the merged one.

This will do the job but with some limitations. For the client's environment, downloading the entire address book and then merging it with the local list of contacts makes the client's use of the network inefficient. Moreover, some users may have very large address books on the server, and not all fields in the address book may be relevant for the client. The client may not have enough computing power for handling the merge operation. More importantly, the application logic to merge entries in the address book belongs to the server, not the client. Expecting clients to deal with this task results in the duplication of code and poor separation of concerns.

Here is another option:

1. Get each address in the address book from the server.
2. If that address matches with an entry in the local storage, merge it, and update it by submitting a PUT request.
3. If there is a new contact in the local storage that does not exist on the server, submit a POST request to the address book to add it.

This approach has the additional drawback of network chattiness, which again is not suitable for the client's constrained environment such as a mobile phone.

A more effective solution is to employ a controller resource to solve this problem. For this example, design a controller resource, and allow the client to submit the address book to the server for a merge.

```
# Request to merge an address book
POST /user/smith/address_merge HTTP/1.1
Host: www.example.org
```

```
Content-Type: text/csv;charset=UTF-8

John Doe, 1 Main Street, Seattle, WA
Jane Doe, 100 North Street, Los Angeles, CA
...

# Response
HTTP/1.1 303 See Other
Location: http://www.example.org/user/smith/address_book
Content-Type: text/html;charset=UTF-8

<html>
  <body>
    <p>See <a href="http://www.example.org/user/smith/address_book">address
    book</a> for the merged address book.</p>
  </body>
</html>
```

After merging the address books, the server redirects the client to the user's updated address book. The client can fetch a copy of the merged address book, if necessary.

Here is another example. Consider a bookstore where a store operator wants to reduce the pretax price of a book by 15 percent, and update the posttax price to reflect this discount. The server can offer the discount percentage as a resource, and clients can submit a PUT request to modify the current discount. The server can update the total price of the book as part of the same request.

```
# Request to update the discount value
PUT /book/1234/discount HTTP/1.1
Host: www.example.org
Content-Type: application/x-www-urlencoded

value=15

# Response
HTTP/1.1 204 No Content
```

Now consider that the client wants to offer a 30-day free access to an online version of the same book along with this 15 percent discount. The server can maintain a collection of all books that are currently being offered in the 30-day free plan, and the client can submit a POST request to add this particular book to that collection.

```
# Request to add the book to the list of offers
POST /30dayebookoffers HTTP/1.1
Host: www.example.org
Content-Type: application/x-www-urlencoded

id=1234&from=2009-10-10&to=2000-11-10

# Response
HTTP/1.1 201 Created
Location: http://www.example.org/30dayebookoffer/1234
Content-Length: 0
```

If your business case requires that these two changes be done atomically, you can employ a controller resource for this purpose.

```
# Request to add a discount offer and 30-day free access
POST /book/1234/discountebookoffer HTTP/1.1
Host: www.example.org
Content-Type: application/x-www-urlencoded

id=1234&discount=15&ebook_from=2009-10-10&ebook_to=2000-11-10

# Response
HTTP/1.1 303 See Other
Location: http://www.example.org/book/1234
Content-Length: 0

# Request to get the updated book
GET /book/1234 HTTP/1.1
Host: www.example.org

# Response
HTTP/1.1 200 OK
Content-Type: application/xml;charset=UTF-8

<book xmlns:atom="http://www.w3.org/2005/Atom">
  <id>urn:example:book:1234</id>
  <atom:link rel="self" href="http://www.example.org/book/1234"/>
  ...
  <discount>15</discount>
  ...
  <atom:link rel="http://www.example.org/rels/offer"
        href="http://www.example.org/30dayebookoffer/1234"/>
  ...
</book>
```

In the response, the server includes a link to let clients discover the 30-day offer. If the client is presenting a user interface to end users, it can provide a link to this offer for users to navigate to.

The key point to notice from these examples is the difficulty you might find in mapping operations in your application to the methods in the uniform interface. For example, in the discount example, the server identifies the current discount value as a resource so that clients can use PUT to update it. Similarly, the server identifies 30-day free electronic book offers as a collection and lets clients use POST to add a new book to this collection. But when it comes to combining these two tasks into a single request, a direct mapping to any HTTP method is not obvious. Controllers are most appropriate in such cases.

For use cases like the previous one, do not use the method POST directly on the book resource because it could lead to tunneling. Tunneling occurs whenever the client is using the same method on a single URI for different actions. Here is an example of tunneling:

```
# Request to add a discount offer
POST /book/1234 HTTP/1.1
Host: www.example.org
Content-Type: application/x-www-urlencoded

op=updateDiscount&discount=15

# Response
HTTP/1.1 200 OK
Content-Type: application/xml;charset=UTF-8

<book xmlns:atom="http://www.w3.org/2005/Atom">
  <id>urn:example:book:1234</id>
  <atom:link rel="self" href="http://www.example.org/book/1234"/>
  ...
  <discount>15</discount>
  ...
</book>

# Request to add the book for 30-day offers
POST /book/1234 HTTP/1.1
Host: www.example.org
Content-Type: application/x-www-urlencoded

op=30dayOffer&ebook_from=2009-10-10&ebook_to=2000-11-10

# Response
HTTP/1.1 200 OK
Content-Type: application/xml;charset=UTF-8

<book xmlns:atom="http://www.w3.org/2005/Atom">
  <id>urn:example:book:1234</id>
  <atom:link rel="self" href="http://www.example.org/book/1234"/>
  ...
  <atom:link rel="http://www.example.org/rels/offer"
        href="http://www.example.org/30dayebookoffer/1234"/>
</book>
```

In the requests, the parameters op=updateDiscount and op=30dayOffer signify the operation. This leads to tunneling.

Tunneling reduces protocol-level visibility (see Recipe 1.1) because the visible parts of requests such as the request URI, the HTTP method used, headers, and media types do not unambiguously describe the operation.

 Avoid tunneling at all costs. Instead, use a distinct resource (such as a controller) for each operation.

## CHAPTER 3

Designing Representations

As far as clients are concerned, a *resource* is an abstract entity that is identified by a URI. A *representation*, on the other hand, is concrete and real since that is what you program to and operate upon in clients and servers.

Recall from Recipe 1.1 that HTTP provides an envelope format for representations in requests and responses. Designing a representation involves (a) using that envelope format to include the right headers, and (b) when there is a body for the representation, choosing a media type and designing a format for the body. This chapter presents the following recipes covering various aspects of representation design:

Recipe 3.1, "How to Use Entity Headers to Annotate Representations"
Use this to decide what entity headers to include when sending a representation.

Recipe 3.2, "How to Interpret Entity Headers"
Use this to decide how to interpret entity headers from a representation received.

Recipe 3.3, "How to Avoid Character Encoding Mismatch"
Use this recipe to learn about some precautions about character encoding mismatch.

Recipe 3.4, "How to Choose a Representation Format and a Media Type"
Use this recipe to find the criteria to choose a representation format and a media type.

Recipe 3.5, "How to Design XML Representations"
Use this recipe to decide the essential ingredients for XML-formatted representations.

Recipe 3.6, "How to Design JSON Representations"
Use this recipe to learn how to design JSON-formatted representations.

Recipe 3.7, "How to Design Representations of Collections"
Refer to this recipe to learn about the conventions used to design representations of collections.

Recipe 3.8, "How to Keep Collections Homogeneous"
Use this recipe to check for guidelines on how to keep collections easy to iterate.

3.1 How to Use Entity Headers to Annotate Representations

A representation is much more than just data serialized in a format. It is a sequence of bytes and metadata that describes those bytes. In HTTP, representation metadata is implemented as name-value pairs using entity headers. These headers are as important as the application data itself. They ensure visibility, discoverability, routing by proxies, caching, optimistic concurrency, and correct operation of HTTP as an application protocol.

Problem

You want to know what HTTP headers to send in a request to a server or in a response to a client.

Solution

Use the following headers to annotate representations that contain message bodies:

- `Content-Type`, to describe the type of the representation, including a `charset` parameter or other parameters defined for that media type.
- `Content-Length`, to specify the size in bytes of the body of the representation.
- `Content-Language`, to specify the language if you localized the representation in a language.
- `Content-MD5`, to include an MD5 digest of the body of the representation when the tools/software processing or storing representations may be buggy and need to

provide consistency checks. Note that TCP uses checksums at the transport level for consistency checking.

- Content-Encoding, when you encode the body of the representation using gzip, compress, or deflate encoding.
- Last-Modified, to specify the last time the server modified the representation or the resource.

Discussion

HTTP is designed such that the sender can describe the body (also called the *entity body* or *message body*) of the representation using a family of headers known as *entity headers*. With the help of these headers, recipients can make decisions on how to process the body without looking inside the body. These headers also minimize the amount of out-of-band knowledge and guesswork needed to parse the body.

Here is an example of a representation annotated:

```
Content-Type: application/xml;charset=UTF-8
Content-Language: en-US
Content-MD5: bbdc7bbb8ea5a689666e33ac922c0f83
Last-Modified: Sun, 29 Mar 2009 04:51:38 GMT

<user xmlns:atom="http://www.w3.org/2005/Atom">
  <id>user001</id>
  <atom:link rel="self" href="http://example.org/user/user001"/>
  <name>John Doe</name>
  <email>john@example.org</email>
</user>
```

Let's now look at each of the headers.

Content-Type

This header describes the "type" of a representation and is more generally known as the *media-type* or *MIME type*. Examples include text/html, image/png, application/xml, and text/plain. These are all identifiers of the format used to encode the body of the representation. Roughly speaking, a format is the way you encode information into some medium, such as a file, a disk, or the network. XML, JSON, text, CSV, PDF, etc. are formats. A media type identifies the format used and describes the semantics of how to interpret the body of a representation. application/xml, application/json, text/plain, text/csv, application/pdf, etc., are all media types.

This header informs the receiver of how to parse the data. For instance, if the value of the header is application/xml or any value that ends with +xml, you can use an XML parser to parse the message. If the value is application/json, you can use a JSON parser. When this header is absent, all you are left with is guesswork about the nature of the body.

Content-Length

Originally introduced in HTTP 1.0, the purpose of this header is to let the recipient of a message know whether it has read the correct number of bytes from the connection. To send this header, the sender needs to compute the size of the representation before writing the body. HTTP 1.1 supports a more efficient mechanism known as *chunked transfer encoding*. This makes the `Content-Length` header redundant. Here is a representation using chunked encoding:

```
HTTP/1.1 200 OK
Last-Modified: Thu, 02 Apr 2009 02:32:28 GMT
Content-Type: application/xml;charset=UTF-8
Transfer-Encoding: chunked

FF
[some bytes here]

58
[some bytes here]
0
```

Include the `Content-Length` if the client does not support HTTP 1.1.

 For `POST` and `PUT` requests, even if you are using `Transfer-Encoding: chunked`, include the `Content-Length` header in requests from client applications. Some proxies reject `POST` and `PUT` requests that contain neither of these headers.

Content-Language

Use this header when the representation is localized for a specific language. The value of this header is a two-letter RFC 5646 language tag, optionally followed by a hyphen (-) and any two-letter country code. Here is an example:

```
# Response
HTTP/1.1 200 OK
Content-Language: kr

<address type="work">
  <street-address>강남구 삼성동 144-19,20 번지 JS 타워</street-address>
  <locality>서울특별시</locality>
  <postal-code>135-090</postal-code>
  <country-name>대한민국</country-name>
  <country-code>KR</country-code>
</address>
```

Content-MD5

Recipients can use this header to validate the integrity of entity body. The value of this header is an MD5 digest of the body of the representation computed after applying the content encoding (`gzip`, `compress`, etc.) but before applying the transfer encoding (e.g., chunked encoding).

Since this header does not guarantee that the message has not been tampered with, do not use this header as a measure of security. Whoever altered the body can also update the value of this header.

This header can be useful when sending or receiving large representations over potentially unreliable networks. When the sender of a representation includes the Content-MD5 header, the recipient can verify the integrity of the message before attempting to parse it.

Content-Encoding

The presence of this header indicates the type of compression applied to the body of the representation. The value of this header is a string like `gzip`, `compress`, or `deflate`. Here is a gzip-encoded representation:

```
Content-Type: application/xml;charset=UTF-8
Content-Language: en-US
Content-MD5: b7c50feb215b112d3335ad0bd3dd88c1
Content-Encoding: gzip
Last-Modified: Sun, 29 Mar 2009 04:51:38 GMT

... gzip encoded bytes ...
```

The recipient of this message needs to decompress this message before parsing the body.

Clients can indicate their preference for Content-Encoding using the Accept-Encoding header (see Chapter 7 for more details). However, there is no standard way for the client to learn whether a server can process representations compressed in a given encoding.

Unless you know out of band that the target server supports a particular encoding method, avoid using this header in HTTP requests.

Last-Modified

This header applies for responses only. This value of this header is the timestamp of the last time the server modified the representation of the resource. We will discuss this header in Chapter 9.

3.2 How to Interpret Entity Headers

When a server or client receives a representation, correctly interpreting entity headers before processing a request is vital. This recipe discusses how to interpret a representation from the headers included.

Problem

You want to know how to interpret the entity headers included in a representation, and how to process the representation using those headers.

Solution

Content-Type

> When you receive a representation with no `Content-Type`, avoid guessing the type of the representation. When a client sends a request without this header, return error code 400 (`Bad Request`). When you receive a response without this header from a server, treat it as a bad response.

Content-Length

> Do not check for the presence of the `Content-Length` header in a representation you receive without first confirming the absence of `Transfer-Encoding: chunked`.

Content-Encoding

> Let your network library deal with uncompressing compressed representations.

Content-Language

> Read and store the value of this header, if present, to record the language used.

Discussion

In most cases, client applications need only deal with checking the `Content-Type` header and character encoding to determine how to parse the body of a representation. Client-side HTTP libraries must be able to deal with `Content-Encoding` transparently.

Some software applications assume that the `Content-Length` header must always be present and reject representations that do not contain this header. This is an incorrect assumption. If you must determine the message length before processing a request or a response in your code, follow the procedure outlined in Section 4.4 of RFC 2616.

Make sure to process representations in responses based on the values of the `Content-Type`, `Content-Language`, and `Content-Encoding` headers. For instance, just because the client sent an `Accept: application/json` header or because the URI for the resource ends with `.json`, don't assume the response will be JSON formatted. See Recipe 7.1 for how to inform the server of what types of representations the client can process.

3.3 How to Avoid Character Encoding Mismatch

Character encoding mismatch between the sender and receiver of a representation usually results in data corruption and often in parse errors.

Problem

You want to know how to ensure that the characters in your representations are interpreted correctly by the recipients.

Solution

When sending a representation, if the media type allows a `charset` parameter, include that parameter with a value of the character encoding used to convert characters into bytes.

When you receive a representation with a media type that supports the `charset` parameter, use the specified encoding when constructing a character stream from bytes in the body of the representation. If you ignore the sender-supplied `charset` value and use some other value, your applications may misinterpret the characters.

If you receive an XML, JSON, or HTML representation with a missing `charset` parameter, let your XML, JSON, or HTML parsers interpret the character set by inspecting the first several bytes as per algorithms outlined in specifications of those formats.

Discussion

Text and XML media types such as `application/xml`, `text/html`, `application/atom+xml`, and `text/csv` let you specify the character encoding used to convert characters into bytes in the entity body via a `charset` parameter of the `Content-Type` header. Here is an example:

```
Content-Type: application/xml;charset=UTF-8
```

The JSON media type `application/json` does not specify a `charset` parameter but uses UTF-8 as the default encoding. RFC 4627 specifies ways to determine the character encoding of JSON-formatted data.

Errors due to character encoding mismatch can be hard to detect. For instance, when a sender uses UTF-8 encoding to encode some text into bytes and the recipient uses `Windows-1252` encoding to decode those bytes into text, you will not detect any issues as long as the characters the sender used have the same code values in both the encodings. For instance, a phrase such as "`Hello World`" will appear the same on both sides, but a phrase such as "`2 €s for an espresso?`" will appear as "`2 ?Ǩs for an espresso?`" because of differences between these encodings.

 Such mismatch is described by the term *Mojibake*. See *http://en.wikipedia.org/wiki/Mojibake* for more examples.

Another common way to introduce a character encoding mismatch in XML representations is to report one encoding in the Content-Type header and report another in the body as in the following example:

```
Content-Type: application/xml; charset=UTF-8 ❶

<?xml version="1.0" encoding="ISO-8859-1"?> ❷
<user> ... </user>
```

❶ UTF-8 declared in the Content-Type header

❷ ISO-8859-1 declared in the prolog of the XML document

In this case, if you ignore supplying the encoding from the charset parameter (UTF-8) to the XML parser, the parser will attempt to determine the character encoding from the prolog and will find it as ISO-8859-1. This will cause the recipient to misinterpret the characters in the body.

Also avoid using the text/xml media type for XML-formatted representations. The default charset for text/xml is us-ascii, whereas application/xml uses UTF-8.

3.4 How to Choose a Representation Format and a Media Type

This may be one of the first questions to come to mind when designing a RESTful web service. However, no single format may be right for all kinds of resources and representations. Picking up a format like JSON or XML for all representations may reduce the flexibility that HTTP has to offer.

Problem

You want to know how to choose a format and a media type for representations.

Solution

Keep the choice of media types and formats flexible to allow for varying application use cases and client needs for each resource.

Determine whether there is a standard format and media type that matches your use cases. The best place to start your search is the Internet Assigned Numbers Authority (IANA, *http://www.iana.org/assignments/media-types/*) media type registry.

If there is no standard media type and format, use extensible formats such as XML (application/xml), Atom Syndication Format (application/atom+xml), or JSON (application/json).

Use image formats like image/png or rich document formats like application/vnd.ms-excel or application/pdf to provide alternative representations of data. When using such formats, consider adding a Content-Disposition header, as in

`Content-Disposition: attachment; filename=<status.xls>` to give a hint of the file-name that the client could use to save the representation to the filesystem.

Prefer to use well-known media types for representations. If you are designing a new media type, register the format and media type with IANA by following the procedure outlined in RFC 4288.

Discussion

HTTP's message format is designed to allow different media types and formats for requests and responses. Some resources may require XML-formatted representations, others may require HTML representations, while still others may require PDF-format-ted representations. Similarly, some resources can process `application/x-www-form-urlencoded` but return XML-formatted representations in response. Leaving room for such flexibility is a vital part of designing representations. For instance, a system man-aging customer accounts may need to provide a variety of media types and formats.

- An XML-formatted representation for each customer account
- An Atom feed of all new customers
- Customer trends presented as a spreadsheet
- HTML pages for summary of each customer

When it comes to format and media type selection, the rule of thumb is to let the use cases and the types of clients dictate the choice. For this reason, it is important not to pick up a development framework that rigidly enforces one or two formats for all re-sources with no flexibility to use other formats.

Using standard or well-known media types

When selecting a format and a media type for representations, first check whether there is a standard or well-known format and media type that matches your use cases. The IANA media type registry lists media types by primary types such as `text` and `application` and subtypes such as `plain`, `html`, and `xml` and provides additional refer-ences to the media type and the underlying format. For example, at *http://www.iana .org/assignments/media-types/application/*, you will find that RFC 4627 defines the me-dia type `application/json`. If you decide to use JSON as a format for your representa-tions, that is the document to consult to learn the semantics of this format. Table 3-1 lists some commonly used standard or well-known media types.

Table 3-1. Well-known/standard media types

Media types	Format	Reference
application/xml	Generic XML format	RFC 3023
application/*+xml	Special-purpose media types using the XML format	RFC 3023
application/atom+xml	An XML format for Atom documents	RFC 4287 and RFC 5023

Media types	Format	Reference
application/json	Generic JSON format	RFC 4627
application/javascript	JavaScript, for processing by JavaScript-capable clients	RFC 4329
application/x-www-form-urlencoded	Query string format	HTML 4.01
application/pdf	PDF	RFC 3778
text/html	Various versions of HTML	RFC 2854
text/csv	Comma-separated values, a generic format	RFC 4180

In this table, the first column specifies the media type, whereas the second one specifies the format used by the media type. *The generic formats in this table have no application-specific semantics.* For example, an XML-formatted representation for a customer account resource will have widely different semantics than, say, an XML-formatted representation for a purchase order resource. In this example, it is up to the server to define the semantics of various XML elements in these representations.

```
# A customer representation
Content-Type: application/xml;charset=UTF-8

<customer>
  <id>urn:example:customer:cust001</id>
  ...
</customer>

# A purchase customer representation
Content-Type: application/xml;charset=UTF-8

<po>
  <id>urn:example:po:po001</id>
  ...
</po>
```

On the other hand, specialized formats such as Atom, PNG, HTML, and PDF have concrete semantics specified by the respective RFCs or other documents listed in Table 3-1. Take, for example, the following HTML representation of a customer:

```
# A customer representation
Content-Type: text/html;charset=UTF-8

<html>
  <head>
    <title>Customer Xyz</title>
  </head>
  <body>
    ...
  </body>
</html>
```

The HTML specifications describe the semantics of this representation. If you decide to use a generic format such as XML or JSON, you should document the semantics of the representations in as much detail as possible.

Introducing new formats and media types

You can design completely new textual or binary formats with application-specific rules for encoding and decoding data, and you can assign new media types for those formats. For instance, you can assign the media type `application/vnd.example.customer+xml` for the XML format used for customer account resource. Here `vnd` stands for "vendor," implying that this is a vendor/implementation-specific media type:

```
# A customer representation
Content-Type: application/vnd.example.customer+xml;charset=UTF-8

<customer>
  <id>urn:example:customer:cust001</id>
  ...
</customer>
```

In this case, by looking at the `Content-Type` header and without parsing the XML, any software that is aware of this media type can recognize that this is a customer account representation. The following two things may motivate the introduction of such new media types:

New formats
> In some cases, your application data may be specialized and significantly differs from any existing related media types. Examples include new audio, video, or document formats or binary formats for encoding data.

Visibility
> As shown in the previous example, application-specific media types promote visibility as long as such media types are widely supported.

If you choose to create new media types of your own, consider the following guidelines:

- If the media type is XML based, use a subtype that ends with `+xml`.
- If the media type is for private use, use the subtype starting with `vnd.`. For example, you can use a media type such as `application/vnd.example.org.user+xml`. This is another convention used by some application-specific media types.
- If the media type is for public use, register your media type with IANA as per RFC 4288.

Note that new media types that are not widely recognized may reduce interoperability with clients as well as tools such as proxies, log file analyzers, monitoring software, etc.

Avoid introducing new application-specific media types unless they are expected to be broadly used. Proliferation of new application-specific media types may impede interoperability.

Although custom media types improve protocol-level visibility, existing protocol-level tools for monitoring, filtering, or routing HTTP traffic pay little or no attention to media types. Hence, using custom media types only for the sake of protocol-level visibility is not necessary.

3.5 How to Design XML Representations

For representations that are application specific, such as a customer profile or a purchase order, it is natural to include application data in representations. In addition, in order to make representations in your web service consistent with each other and to improve the usability of those representations, it is essential that you include certain additional details in each representation.

Problem

You want to know what data to include in XML-formatted representations.

Solution

In each representation, include a self link (i.e., a link with the link relation type `self`) to the resource (see Chapter 5), and include identifiers for each of the application domain entities that makes up a resource (Recipe 3.10).

If part of the representation contains natural-language text, add `xml:lang` attributes indicating the language that the contents of that element are localized in.

Discussion

Including common elements such as identifiers and links in all representations makes it easier for clients and servers to process requests and generate responses. For instance, the self link can help clients know the URI for the representation, and clients can use that as an identifier for the resource.

The self link serves the same purpose as the request URI when the response contains the representation of the resource at that URI, or as the `Content-Location` header when the representation in the response does not correspond to the resource at the request URI. For instance, in the first request shown here, the request URI corresponds to the location of the resource for the response in the representation. In the second request, the `Content-Location` provides the URI of the resource:

```
# Request
GET /user/smith/address/0 HTTP/1.1
Host: www.example.org

# Response
HTTP/1.1 200 OK
Content-Type: application/xml;charset=UTF-8
```

```
<address>
  <id>urn:example:user:smith:address:0</id>
  <atom:link rel="self" href="http://www.example.org/user/smith/address/0"/>
  <street>1, Olympia Dr</street>
  <city>Some City</city>
</address>


# Second request to create a resource
POST /user/smith HTTP/1.1
Host: www.example.org
Content-Type: application/xml;charset=UTF-8

<address>
  <street>1, Main Street</stret>
  <city>Some City</city>
</address>

# Response
HTTP/1.1 201 Created
Location: http://www.example.org/user/smith/address/1
Content-Location: http://www.example.org/user/smith/address/1
Content-Type: application/xml;charset=UTF-8

<address>
  <id>urn:example:user:smith:address:1</id>
  <atom:link rel="self" href="http://www.example.org/user/smith/address/1"/>
  <street>1, Main Street</street>
  <city>Some City</city>
</address>
```

 Including self links in the body of the representation may be useful when the code used for processing the body does not have access to the request URI or the response headers.

For representations that contain data localized in more than one language, the Content-Language header is not sufficient. In such cases, include language tags directly to the body of the representation. Here is an example, adapted from the XML 1.0 specification:

```
# Response
HTTP/1.1 200 OK
Content-Type: application/xml;charset=UTF-8
Content-Language: en

<content>
  <text>The quick brown fox jumps over the lazy dog.</text> ❶
  <text xml:lang="en-GB">What colour is it?</text> ❷
  <text xml:lang="en-US">What color is it?</text> ❸
  <text xml:lang="de"> ❹
    <p>Habe nun, ach! Philosophie,</p>
    <p>Juristerei, und Medizin</p>
```

```
      <p>und leider auch Theologie</p>
      <p>durchaus studiert mit heißem Bemüh'n.</p>
    </text>
  </content>
```

❶ Text in the default language for the representation, as specified by the Content-Language header

❷ Text in the en-GB language

❸ Text in the en-US language

❹ Text in all the child elements in the de language

3.6 How to Design JSON Representations

JSON is a JavaScript-based data format. Like XML, it is a general-purpose, human-readable, and extensible format. In languages like JavaScript and PHP, parsing JSON structures is easier than parsing XML. Most web services that are consumed by browser-based clients often prefer JSON over representation formats.

Problem

You want to know what data to include in JSON-formatted representations.

Solution

In each representation, include a self link to the resource (see Recipe 5.2), and include identifiers for each of the application domain entities that make up resource (Recipe 3.10).

If an object in the representation is localized, add a property to indicate the language its contents are localized in.

Discussion

The approach presented in this recipe is similar to that of XML (Recipe 3.5). Here is an example of a representation of a person resource:

```
{
  "name" : "John",
  "id" : "urn:example:user:1234",
  "link" : {
    "rel : "self",
    "href" : "http://www.example.org/person/john"
  },
  "address" : {
    "id" : "urn:example:address:4567",
    "link" : {
      "rel : "self",
      "href" : "http://www.example.org/person/john/address"
    }
```

```
    ...
  }
}
```

When the Content-Language header does not sufficiently describe the locale of the representation, add a property to express the language, as in the following example:

```
{
  "content" : {
    "text" : [{
        "value" : "The quick brown fox jumps over the lazy dog."
      },
      {
        "lang" : "en-GB",
        "value" : "What colour is it"
      },
      {
        "lang" : "en-US",
        "value" : "What color is it"
      }
    ]
  }
}
```

3.7 How to Design Representations of Collections

Clients use collections to iterate through its members. Since some collections contain a large number of member resources, clients need a way to paginate/scroll through the collection.

Problem

You want to know what to include in representations of collection resources.

Solution

Include the following in each collection representation:

- A self link to the collection resource
- If the collection is paginated and has a next page, a link to the next page
- If the collection is paginated and has a previous page, a link to the previous page
- An indicator of the size of the collection

Discussion

A collection resource is like any other resource except that, in some case, it contains a large number of members. When a server returns only a subset of members in the representation of a collection, the server should also provide links to allow the client to paginate through all the members. Here is a collection resource containing several articles:

```
# Request
GET /articles?contains=cycling&start=10 HTTP/1.1
Host: www.example.org

# Response
HTTP/1.1 200 OK
Content-Type: application/xml;charset=UTF-8
Content-Language: en

<articles total="1921" xmlns:atom="http://www.w3.org/2005/Atom">
  <atom:link rel="self"
    href="http://www.example.org/articles?contains=cycling&start=10"/> ❶
  <atom:link rel="prev"
    href="http://www.example.org/articles?contains=cycling"/> ❷
  <atom:link rel="next"
    href="http://www.example.org/articles?contains=cycling&start=20"/> ❸
  <article>
    <atom:link rel="self"
      href="http://www.nytimes.com/2009/07/15/sports/cycling/15tour.html"/>
    <title>For Italian, Yellow Jersey Is Fun While It Lasts</title>
    <body>...</body>
  </article>
  <article>
    <atom:link rel="alternate"
      href="http://www.nytimes.com/2009/07/27/sports/cycling/27tour.html"/>
    <title>Contador Wins, but Armstrong Has Other Victory</title>
    <body>...</body>
  </article>
  ...
</articles>
```

❶ A link to the collection itself

❷ A link to the previous page

❸ A link to the next page

This representation is the result of searching a large collection of news articles. This representation has three links—a link with the self relation type to get the representation itself, a link with the prev relation type to get the previous 10 articles, and another link with the next relation type to get the next 10 articles. Clients can use these links to navigate through the entire collection.

The total attribute gives the client an indication of the number of members in the collection.

Although the size of the collection is useful for building user interfaces, avoid computing the exact size of the collection. It may be expensive to compute, volatile, or even confidential for your web service. Providing a hint is usually good enough.

At the HTTP level, each page is a different resource. This is because each page of results in this example has a different URI such as http://www.example.org/books?contains= cycling and http://www.example.org/books?contains=cycling&start=10.

3.8 How to Keep Collections Homogeneous

Depending on use cases, you can group resources into collections by using similarities. However, no matter what criteria you choose for any collection, it is important to keep the representation homogeneous so that it is easy to use by clients.

Problem

You want to know how to design a representation format for a collection whose members don't completely look alike.

Solution

Design the representation of the collection such that members in a collection are structurally and syntactically similar.

Discussion

When designing a representation format for the collection, include only the homogeneous aspects of its member resources. For instance, if your collection of products can contain cars, boats, and motorcycles, include just the common aspects of those resources in the product collection. Note that collections are meant for grouping resources that are similar in some sense, and when you include resource-specific information that is not common across other resources within the same collection, it usually is a result of poor abstraction. Here is an example of such a poor abstraction:

```
<!-- Avoid this -->
<products xmlns:atom="http://www.w3.org/2005/Atom">
  <atom:link rel="self" href="http://www.example.org/catalog/products"/>
  <!-- The first member is an automobile. -->
  <automobile>
    <id>9001</id>
    <atom:link rel="self" href="http://www.example.org/catalog/product/9001"/>
    <make>Smart</make>
    <model>Fortwo Convertible</model>
    <year>2009</year>
    <class classid="small">Small Car</class>
    <mpg>
      <city>33</city>
      <highway>41</highway>
    </mpg>
    <drivetrain>2WD</drivetrain>
    <list-price currency="USD">19495</list-price>
  </automobile>
  <!-- The second member is a boat! -->
  <sailboat>
```

```
    <id>10101</id>
    <atom:link rel="self" href="http://www.example.org/catalog/product/10101"/>
    <make>Jeanneau</make>
    <model>Sunfast 3200</model>
    <year>2008</year>
    <length unit="ft">32</length>
    <hull-type>fiberglass</hull-type>
    <number-of-engines>1</number-of-engines>
    <list-price currency="USD">95995</list-price>
  </sailboat>
</products>
```

In this example, although the automobile and sailboat share common properties, they have properties that are specific to each product. For a client application iterating over such a collection, those specific properties may not make sense, and clients may not be able to cope with such a representation. Consider avoiding such representations, and keep the representation of collections homogeneous, as in the following:

```
<products xmlns:atom="http://www.w3.org/2005/Atom">
  <atom:link rel="self" href="http://www.example.org/catalog/products"/>
  <product type="automobile">
    <id>9001</id>
    <atom:link rel="self" href="http://www.example.org/catalog/product/9001"/>
    <make>Smart</make>
    <model>Fortwo Convertible</model>
    <year>2009</year>
    <list-price currency="USD">19495</list-price>
  </product>
  <product type="sailboat">
    <id>10101</id>
    <atom:link rel="self" href="http://www.example.org/catalog/product/10101"/>
    <make>Jeanneau</make>
    <model>Sunfast 3200</model>
    <year>2008</year>
    <list-price currency="USD">95995</list-price>
  </product>
</products>
```

This homogeneous form is more convenient for the client than the previous example.

3.9 How to Use Portable Data Formats in Representations

There are a number of ways to encode dates, times, countries, numbers, and time zones in representations. For instance, you can format date-time values as using the Unix date format, Unix epoch time, or plain MM-DD-YYYY and DD-MM-YYYY formats. Most date-time formats require clock synchronization between clients and servers or depend on local time. These formats cause interoperability problems because of differences in clocks, time zones, or even daylight saving time. Similarly, currency and number formats vary from country to country, and representations designed for audiences in one country may not interoperate with clients or servers in another country unless you use portable data formats.

Problem

You want to know the appropriate formats to choose for dates, times, numbers, currencies, etc.

Solution

Except when the text is meant for presentation to end users, avoid using language-, region-, or country-specific formats or format identifiers. Instead, use the following portable formats:

- Use decimal, float, and double datatypes defined in the W3C XML Schema for formatting numbers including currency.
- Use ISO 3166 codes for countries and dependent territories.
- Use ISO 4217 alphabetic or numeric codes for denoting currency.
- Use RFC 3339 for dates, times, and date-time values used in representations.
- Use BCP 47 language tags for representing the language of text.
- Use time zone identifiers from the Olson Time Zone Database to convey time zones.

Discussion

Choosing portable formats for data eliminates interoperability errors. See examples below for some commonly used formats. Note that your application domain may involve additional types of data not included here. Look for industry- or domain-specific standards before inventing your own.

Numbers

The formats specified by the XML Schema for numbers are language and country independent and hence are portable:

```
123.456    +1234.456    -1234.456    -.456, 123.
```

However, formats like the following are not portable:

```
1,234,567    12,34,567    1,234
```

Countries and territories

ISO 3166-1, the first part of ISO 3166, specifies two-letter country codes such as US for the United States, Dk for Denmark, IN for India, etc.

ISO 3166-2, the second part of ISO 3166, specifies codes for subdivisions of countries such as states and provinces. Examples include US-WA, US-CO, CA-BC, IN-AP, etc.

Currencies

ISO 4217 specifies three-letter currency codes for names of currencies. The first two letters of these codes represent ISO 3166-1 two-letter country codes, and the third letter is usually the initial for the currency. Examples include USD for the U.S. dollar, CAD for the Canadian dollar, and DKK for the Danish krone. These codes represent revaluation and changes in currencies. Using these codes with currency values removes ambiguity with currency names such as "dollar" or symbols such as $.

Dates and times

RFC 3339 is a profile of ISO 8601, which is a standard for representing dates and times using the Gregorian calendar. RFC 3339–formatted dates, times, and date-time values have the following characteristics:

- You can compare two values by sorting them as strings.
- This format is human readable.
- Dates can use either Coordinated Universal Time (UTC) or an offset from the UTC, thus avoiding issues related to time zones and daylight saving time.

Here are some examples of properly formatted date, time, and date-time values:

```
2009-09-18Z
23:05:08Z
2009-09-18T23:05:08Z
2009-09-18T23:05:08-08:00
```

The date, time, and dateTime datatypes in the W3C XML Schema follow RFC 3339, and you can use libraries that support these datatypes to read and parse these values.

Language tags

BCP stands for "best current practice." BCP 47 currently refers to RFC 5646 and RFC 5645 that define values of language tags such as the HTML lang attribute and XML xml:lang attribute. Examples include en for English, en-CA for Canadian English, and ja-JP for Japanese as used in Japan.

Time zone identifiers

The Olso Time Zone Database provides a uniform convention for time zone names and contains data about time zones. This database accounts for time zones, seasonal changes such as daylight saving time, and even historical time zone changes. Most programming languages support time zone classes/utilities that support this database. Examples include Java's java.util.Timezone, Ruby's TZInfo, Python's tzinfo, and C#'s System.TimeZoneInfo.

3.10 When to Use Entity Identifiers

For RESTful web services, URIs are the unique identifiers for resources. However, application code usually has to deal with identifiers of domain entities. When a client or a server is part of a larger heterogeneous set of applications, information from resources may cross several system boundaries, and entity identifiers can be used to cross-reference or transform data.

Problem

You want to know when to include entity identifiers in representations along with resource URIs.

Solution

For each of the application domain entities included in the representation of a resource, include identifiers formatted as URNs.

Discussion

Although URIs uniquely identify resources, entity identifiers come in handy for the following:

- When your clients and servers are part of a larger environment containing applications using RPC, SOAP, asynchronous messaging, stored procedures, and even third-party applications, entity identifiers may be the only common denominator across all those systems to provide the identity of data uniformly.

- Clients and servers can maintain their own stored copies of entities included in a resource without having to decode from resource URIs or having to use URIs as database keys. Although not ideal, URIs may change. Clients can use these identifiers to cross-reference various entities referred to from different representations.

- When not all entities in your application domain are mapped to resources, entity identifiers can help provide uniqueness for data contained in representations.

Even if you mapped all the entities in your application to resources with unique URIs, including entity identifiers in representations will future-proof your application when it needs to integrate with non-HTTP web services. To maintain the uniqueness of identifiers, consider formatting identifiers as URNs.

Here is an example, where the database identifier of the user resource is 1234 and that of the user's address is 4567:

```
<person xmlns:atom="http://www.w3.org/2005/Atom">
  <atom:link rel="self" href="http://example.org/person/john"/>
  <id>urn:example:user:1234</id>
  <name>John Doe</name>
  <address>
    <id>urn:example:address:4567</id>
```

```
    <street>1 Main Street</street>
    <city>Seattle</city>
    <state>WA</state>
  </address>
</person>
```

3.11 How to Encode Binary Data in Representations

Not every representation can completely rely on textual formats such as XML and JSON. Some representations may need to contain binary data within textual representations. Examples include a video preview of a movie in a movie catalog or some image cover art of a representation of an audio sample in a music store.

Problem

You want to know how to encode binary data in representations that also contain textual data.

Solution

Use multipart media types such as `multipart/mixed`, `multipart/related`, or `multipart/alternative`. Avoid encoding binary data within textual formats using Base64 encoding.

Discussion

Multipart messages give you the ability to combine dissimilarly formatted data into one single HTTP message. A multipart message is a message containing several message parts each separated by a boundary. Each part can contain a message of a different media type. Here is an example:

```
Content-type: multipart/mixed; boundary="abcd"

--abcd
Content-Type: application/xml;charset=UTF-8

<movie> ... </movie>
--abcd
Content-type: video/mpeg

... image here ...

--abcd--
```

This multipart message has two parts, one containing an XML document and the other containing a video. Consider one of the multipart media types listed in Table 3-2 for such use cases.

Table 3-2. Using multipart media types

Media type	Usage
multipart/ form-data	To encode name-value pairs of data mixed with parts containing data of arbitrary media types. The usage is the same as you would use to upload files using HTML forms.
multipart/ mixed	To bundle several parts of arbitrary media types. In the previous example, the multipart message combined the metadata of a movie represented as application/xml and the video as video/mpeg into a single HTTP message.
multipart/ alternative	Use this when sending alternative representations of the same resource using different media types. The best example for this media type is sending email as plain text (media type text/plain) and HTML (media type text/html).
multipart/ related	Use this when the parts are interrelated and you need to process the parts together. The first part is the root part and can refer to various other parts via a Content-ID header.

 Creating and parsing multipart messages in some programming languages may be cumbersome and complex. As an alternative, instead of including binary data in representations, provide a link to fetch the binary data as a separate resource. For instance, in the previous example, you can provide a link to the video.

3.12 When and How to Serve HTML Representations

HTML is a popular hypermedia format, and with browsers as universal clients, users can interact with HTML representations without any application-specific logic implemented in browsers. Moreover, you can use JavaScript and HTML parsers to extract or infer data from HTML. This recipe discusses the pros and cons and when HTML may be appropriate.

Problem

You want to know if you must design HTML representations along with XML or JSON-formatted representations, and if so, how.

Solution

For resources that are expected to be consumed by end users, provide HTML representations. Avoid designing HTML representations for machine clients. To enable web crawlers and such software, use microformats or RDFa to annotate data within the markup.

Discussion

HTML is widely understood and supported by client software such as browsers, HTML parsers, authoring tools, and generating tools. It is also self-describing, enabling users to use any HTML-compliant client to interact with servers. This makes it a suitable format for human consumption. For instance, consider the following XML-formatted representation of a resource:

```
<person xmlns:atom="http://www.w3.org/2005/Atom">
  <atom:link rel="self" href="http://example.org/person/john"/>
  <id>urn:example:user:1234</id>
  <name>John</name>
  <address>
     <atom:link rel="self" href="http://example.org/person/john"/>
     <id>usr:example:address:4567</id>
     <street>1 Main Street</street>
     <city>Seattle</city>
     <state>WA</state>
  </address>
</person>
```

You can design the following equivalent HTML representation (without any CSS styles, for the sake of simplicity) for the same resource:

```
<html>
  <head>
    <title>John</title>
    <link rel="self" href="http://example.org/person/john"/>
  </head>
  <body>
    <h1>John</h1>
    <div>
       <div>1 Main Street</div>
       <div>Seattle</div>
       <div>WA</div>
    </div>
  </body>
</html>
```

When offering some or all of your representations as HTML documents, consider annotating HTML with microformats or RDFa. Doing so allows web crawlers and such software to extract information from your HTML documents without depending on the structure of your HTML documents. Here is an example of the previous HTML representation annotated with the hcard microformat (*http://microformats.org/wiki/ hcard*):

```
<html>
  <head>
    <title>John</title>
  </head>
  <body>
    <h1 class="fn">John</h1>
    <div class="vcard">
      <div class="adr">
        <div class="street-address">1 Main Street</div>
        <div class="locality">Seattle</div>
        <div><abbr class="region" title="Washington">WA</abbr></div>
      </div>
    </div>
```

```
      </body>
    </html>
```

Microformats use HTML `class` attributes to annotate various HTML elements so that HTML-aware clients can interpret the semantics of those elements. The `hcard` microformat is a mapping of the `vcard` format (RFC 2426) to HTML. The `vcard` format is an interoperable standard for representing addresses. The `hcard` microformat specifies several CSS class names. The previous example uses the class name `fn` for the name, `adr` for the address, `street-address` for street names, `locality` for location names, and `region` for regions such as states.

Any microformat-capable HTML parser can interpret the address from this HTML document. Adding this format need not affect the rendering of the document in browsers since microformats use the `class` attribute to extend HTML.

You can similarly use RDFa:

```
<html>
  <head>
    <title>John</title>
  </head>
  <body>
    <div xmlns:v="http://www.w3.org/2001/vcard-rdf/3.0#"
        about="http://example.org/person/john">
      <h1 property="v:FN" href="http://example.org/person/john">John</h1>
      <div role="v:ADR">
        <div property="v:Street">1 Main Street</div>
        <div property="v:Locality">Seattle</div>
        <div><abbr property="v:Region" title="Washington">WA</abbr></div>
      </div>
    </div>
  </body>
</html>
```

The only difference is that it uses RDFa and the `vcard` format to annotate HTML elements. Some search engines use these annotations to decipher the semantics of information from HTML documents.

 Note that RDFa is specified only for XHTML 1.1. However, all currently deployed browsers do support RDFa for HTML documents.

3.13 How to Return Errors

HTTP is based on the exchange of representations, and that applies to errors as well. When a server encounters an error, either because of problems with the request that a client submitted or because of problems within the server, always return a representation that reflects the state of the error condition. This includes the response status code, response headers, and a body containing the description of the error.

Problem

You want to know how to return errors to clients.

Solution

For errors due to client inputs, return a representation with a 4xx status code. For errors due to server implementation or its current state, return a representation with a 5xx status code. In both cases, include a Date header with a value indicating the date-time at which the error occurred.

Unless the request method is HEAD, include a body in the representation formatted and localized using content negotiation (see Chapter 7) or in human-readable HTML or plain text.

If information to correct or debug the error is available as a separate human-readable document, include a link to that document via a Link header (see Recipe 5.3) or a link in the body.

If you are logging errors on the server side for later tracking or analysis, provide an identifier or a link that can be used to refer to that error. For instance, clients can report the error code to the server's team while reporting problems.

Keep the response body descriptive, but exclude details such as stack traces, errors from database connection failures, etc. If appropriate, describe any actions that the client can take to correct the error or to help the server debug and fix the errors.

Discussion

HTTP 1.1 defines two classes of error codes, one in the range of 400 to 417 and the other in the range of 500 to 505. One common mistake that some web services make is to return a status code that reflects success (status codes from 200 to 206 and from 300 to 307) but include a message body that describes an error condition.

```
# Avoid returning success code with an error in the body.
HTTP/1.1 200 OK
Content-Type: application/xml;charset=UTF-8

<error>
  <message>Account limit exceeded.</message>
</error>
```

Doing this prevents HTTP-aware software from detecting errors. For example, a cache will store it as a successful response and serve it to subsequent clients even when clients may be able to make a successful request.

Errors due to client inputs: 4xx

The following list shows error codes you are likely to generate in your server-side application code and not codes that will be automatically by generated by your web/application server:

400 (Bad Request)

> You can return this error when your server cannot decipher client requests becasue of syntactical errors.
>
> HTTP 1.1 defines only one condition under which you can return this error. That is when the request does not include a Host header.

401 (Unauthorized)

> Return this when the client is not authorized to access the resource but may be able to gain access after authentication. If your server will not let the client access the resource even after authentication, then return 403 (Forbidden) instead.
>
> When returning this error code, include a WWW-Authenticate header field with the authentication method to use. Commonly used methods are Basic and Digest, as discussed in Chapter 12.

403 (Forbidden)

> Use this when your server will not let the client gain access to the resource and authentication will not help.
>
> For instance, you can return this when the user is already authenticated but is not allowed to request a resource.

404 (Not Found)

> Return this when the resource is not found. If possible, specify a reason in the message body.

405 (Not Allowed)

> Return this when an HTTP method is not allowed for this resource.
>
> Return an Allow header with methods that are valid for this resource (see Recipe 14.2).

406 (Not Acceptable)

> See Recipe 7.7.

409 (Conflict)

> Return this when the request conflicts with the current state of the resource. Include a body explaining the reason.

410 (Gone)

> Return this when the resource used to exist, but it does not anymore.
>
> You may not be able to return this code unless you have some bookkeeping data about deleted resources. If you do not keep track of deleted resources on the server side, return a 404 (Not Found) instead.

412 (Precondition Failed)
: See Recipe 10.4.

413 (Request Entity Too Large)
: Return this when the body of a POST of PUT request is too large.

: If possible, specify what is allowed in the body, and provide alternatives.

415 (Unsupported Media Type)
: Return this error when a client sends the message body in a format that the server does not understand.

Errors due to server errors: 5xx

The following list shows error codes that you may generate when the request fails because of some error on the server:

500 (Internal Server Error)
: This is the best code to return when your code on the server side failed due to some implementation bug.

503 (Service Unavailable)
: Return this when the server cannot fulfill the request either for some specific interval or for an undetermined amount of time.

: Two common conditions that prompt this error are failures with backend servers (such as a database connection failure) or when the client exceeded some rate limit set by the server.

: If possible, include a Retry-After response header with either a date or a number of seconds as a hint.

 HTTP status codes are normative, but the status messages are not. Those are the messages that HTTP 1.1 uses. Servers are free to use application-specific error message strings.

Message body for errors

Include a body in the error response for all errors except when the HTTP method is HEAD. In the body, include some or all of the following:

- A brief message describing the error condition
- A longer description with information on how to fix the error condition, if applicable
- An identifier for the error
- A link to learn more about the error condition, with tips on how to resolve it

Here is an example. This is an error that occurred when the client sent a request for an account transfer:

```
# Response
HTTP/1.1 409 Conflict
Content-Type: application/xml;charset=UTF-8
Content-Language: en
Date: Wed, 14 Oct 2009 10:16:54 GMT
Link: <http://www.example.org/errors/limits.html>;rel="help"

<error xmlns:atom="http://www.w3.org/2005/Atom">
  <message>Account limit exceeded. We cannot complete the transfer due to
  insufficient funds in your accounts</message>
  <error-id>321-553-495</error-id>
  <account-from>urn:example:account:1234</account-from>
  <account-to>urn:example:account:5678</account-to>
  <atom:link href="http://example.org/account/1234"
             rel="http://example.org/rels/transfer/from"/>
  <atom:link href="http://example.org/account/5678"
             rel="http://example.org/rels/transfer/to"/>
</error>
```

When generating the message body, consider following the recipes discussed Chapter 7.

3.14 How to Treat Errors in Clients

When implementing a client, there are two kinds of errors that the client needs to deal with. The first is network-level failures. The second is HTTP errors returned by servers. Programming libraries deal with the former class of errors and surface them via programming language-specific exception handling. The latter class is application specific and requires explicit coding.

Problem

You want to know how to interpret errors returned by the server.

Solution

See the following list for appropriate action for each error code:

400 (Bad Request)
: Look into the body of the error representation on hints for the root cause of the problem.

401 (Unauthorized)
: If the client is user-facing, prompt the user to supply credentials. In other cases, obtain the necessary security credentials. Retry the request with an Authorization header containing the credentials.

403 (Forbidden)
: This error means that the client is forbidden from accessing the resource with the request method. Do not repeat the request that caused this error.

404 (Not Found)

The resource is gone. If you stored data about the resource on the client side, clean up the data or mark it as deleted.

405 (Not Allowed)

Look for the `Allow` header for the methods that are valid for this resource, and make necessary code changes to limit access to only those methods.

406 (Not Acceptable)

See Recipe 7.7.

409 (Conflict)

Look for the conflicts listed in the body of the representation of `PUT`.

410 (Gone)

Treat this the same as `404 (Not Found)`.

412 (Precondition Failed)

See Recipe 10.4.

413 (Request Entity Too Large)

Look for hints on valid size in the body of the error.

415 (Unsupported Media Type)

See the body of the representation to learn the supported media types for the request.

500 (Internal Server Error)

Log this error, and then notify the server developers.

503 (Service Unavailable)

If the response has a `Retry-After` header, avoid retrying until that period of time. This error may be serverwide, and hence, you may need to implement appropriate back-off logic in your clients to avoid sending requests to the server for some period of time.

Discussion

Explicitly handling various error codes makes clients robust. In particular, watch out for HTTP client libraries that translate both network-level failures and HTTP errors into exception or error classes. These classes of errors need different treatments.

HTTP status codes are extensible, and servers can introduce new status codes. If a client does not understand an `Xmn` status code where `X` is 2, 3, 4, or 5, then it should treat it as an `X00` code. For example, if a server returns `599` and if the client does not understand what it is, treat it as `500`. The same goes for a status code like `245`.

Do not treat HTTP errors as I/O or network exceptions. Treat them as first-class application objects. See Recipe 1.5 for an example.

## CHAPTER 4

Designing URIs

URIs are identifiers of resources that work across the Web. A URI consists of a scheme (such as `http` and `https`), a host (such as `www.example.org`), a port number followed by a path with one or more segments (such as `/users/1234`), and a query string. In this chapter, our focus is on designing URIs for RESTful web services:

Recipe 4.1, "How to Design URIs"
> Use this recipe to learn some commonly practiced URI design conventions.

Recipe 4.2, "How to Use URIs As Opaque Identifiers"
> Use this recipe to learn some dos and don'ts to keep URIs as opaque identifiers.

Recipe 4.3, "How to Let Clients Treat URIs As Opaque Identifiers"
> Treating URIs as opaque identifiers helps decouple clients from servers. This recipe shows techniques that the server can employ to help clients treat URIs as opaque.

Recipe 4.4, "How to Keep URIs Cool"
> Since URIs are a key part of the interface between clients and servers, it is important to keep them "cool," i.e., stable and permanent. Use this recipe to learn some practices to help keep URIs cool.

4.1 How to Design URIs

URIs are opaque resource identifiers. In most cases, clients need not be concerned with how a server designs its URIs. However, following common conventions when designing URIs has several advantages:

- URIs that support convention are usually easy to debug and manage.
- Servers can centralize code to extract data from request URIs.
- You can avoid spending valuable design and implementation time inventing new conventions and rules for processing URIs.
- Partitioning the server's URIs across domains, subdomains, and paths gives you operational flexibility for load distribution, monitoring, routing, and security.

Problem

You want to know the best practices to design URIs for resources.

Solution

- Use domains and subdomains to logically group or partition resources for localization, distribution, or to enforce various monitoring or security policies.
- Use the forward-slash separator (/) in the path portion of the URI to indicate a hierarchical relationship between resources.
- Use the comma (,) and semicolon (;) to indicate nonhierarchical elements in the path portion of the URI.
- Use the hyphen (-) and underscore (_) characters to improve the readability of names in long path segments.
- Use the ampersand (&) to separate parameters in the query portion of the URI.
- Avoid including file extensions (such as *.php*, *.aspx*, and *.jsp*) in URIs.

Discussion

URI design is just one aspect of implementing RESTful applications. Here are some conventions to consider when designing URIs.

 As important as URI design is to the success of your web service, it is just as important to keep the time spent in URI design to a minimum. Focus on consistency of URIs instead.

Domains and subdomains

A logical partition of URIs into domains and subdomains provides several operational benefits for server administration. Make sure to use logical names for subdomains while partitioning URIs. For example, the server could offer localized representations via different subdomains, as in the following:

```
http://en.example.org/book/1234
http://da.example.org/book/1234
http://fr.example.org/book/1234
```

Another example is, partition based on the class of clients.

```
http://www.example.org/book/1234
http://api.example.org/book/1234
```

In this example, the server offers two subdomains, one for browsers and the other for custom clients. Such partitioning may let the server allocate different hardware or apply different routing, monitoring, or security policies for HTML and non-HTML representations.

Forward-slash separator

By convention, the forward slash (/) character is used to convey hierarchical relationships. This is not a hard and fast rule, but most users assume this when they scan URIs. In fact, the forward slash is the only character mentioned in RFC 3986 as typically indicating a hierarchical relationship. For example, all the following URIs convey a hierarchical association between path segments:

```
http://www.example.org/messages/msg123
http://www.example.org/customer/orders/order1
http://www.example.org/earth/north-america/canada/manitoba
```

Some web services may use a trailing forward slash for collection resources. Use such conventions with care since some development frameworks may incorrectly remove such slashes or add trailing slashes during URI normalization.

Underscore and hyphen

If you want to make your URIs easy for humans to scan and interpret, use the underscore (_) or hyphen (-) character:

```
http://www.example.org/blog/this-is-my-first-post
http://www.example.org/my_photos/our_summer_vacation/first_day/setting_up_camp/
```

There is no reason to favor one over the other. For the sake of consistency, pick one and use it consistently.

Ampersand

Use the ampersand character (&) to separate parameters in the query portion of the URI:

```
http://www.example.org/print?draftmode&landscape
http://www.example.org/search?word=Antarctica&limit=30
```

In the first URI shown, the parameters are `draftmode` and `landscape`. The second URI has the parameters `word=Antarctica` and `limit=30`.

Comma and semicolon

Use the comma (,) and semi-colon (;) characters to indicate nonhierarchical portions of the URI. The semicolon convention is used to identify matrix parameters:

```
http://www.example.org/co-ordinates;w=39.001409,z=-84.578201
http://www.example.org/axis;x=0,y=9
```

These characters are valid in the path and query portions of URIs, but not all code libraries recognize the comma and semicolon as separators and may require custom coding to extract these parameters.

Full stop, or period

Apart from its use in domain names, the full stop (.), or period, is used to separate the document and file extension portions of the URI:

```
http://www.example.org/my-photos/flowers.png
http://www.example.org/index.html
http://www.example.org/api/recent-messages.xml
http://www.example.org/blog/this.is.my.next.post.html
```

The last example in the previous list is valid but might introduce confusion. Since some code libraries use the period to signal the start of the file extension portion of the URI path, URIs with multiple periods can return unexpected results or might cause a parsing error.

Except for legacy reasons, there is no reason to use this character in URIs. Clients should use the media type of the representation to learn how to process the representation. "Sniffing" the media type from extensions can lead to security vulnerabilities. For instance, various versions of Internet Explorer are prone to security vulnerabilities because of its implementation of media type sniffing (*http://msdn.microsoft.com/en-us/library/ms775148(VS.85).aspx*).

Implementation-specific file extensions

Consider the following URIs:

```
http://www.example.org/report-summary.xml
http://www.example.org/report-summary.jsp
http://www.example.org/report-summary.aspx
```

In all three cases, the data is the same and the representation format may be the same, but the file extension indicates the technology used to generate the resource representation. These URIs will need to change if the technology used needs to change.

Spaces and capital letters

Spaces are valid URI characters, and according to RFC 3986, the space character should be percent-encoded to %20. However, the application/x-www-form-urlencoded media type (used by HTML form elements) encodes the space character as the plus sign (+). Consider the following HTML:

```
<!DOCTYPE HTML PUBLIC "-//W3C//DTD HTML 4.01 Transitional//EN">
<html lang="en">
  <head>
    <title>Search</title>
  </head>
  <body>
    <form method="GET" action="http://www.example.org/search"
      enc-type="application/x-www-form-urlencoded">
      <label for="phrase">Enter a search phrase</label>
      <input type="text" name="phrase" value=""/>
      <input type="submit" value="Search"/>
```

```
            </form>
          </body>
        </html>
```

When a user submits the search phrase "Hadron Supercollider," the resulting URI (using `application/x-www-form-urlencoded` rules) would be as follows:

```
http://www.example.org/search?phrase=Hadron+Supercollider
```

Code that is not aware of how the URI was generated will interpret the URI using RFC 3986 and treat the value of the search phrase as "Hadron+Supercollider."

This inconsistency can cause encoding errors for web services that are not prepared to accept URIs encoded using the `application/x-www-form-urlencoded` media type. This is not just a problem with common web browsers. Some code libraries also apply these rules inconsistently.

Capital letters in URIs may also cause problems. RFC 3986 defines URIs as case sensitive except for the scheme and host parts. For example, although `http://www.exam ple.org/my-folder/doc.txt` and `HTTP://WWW.EXAMPLE.ORG/my-folder/doc.txt` are the same, but `http://www.example.org/My-Folder/doc.txt` isn't. However, Windows-based web servers treat these URIs as the same when the resource is served from the filesystem. This case insensitivity does not apply to characters in the query portion. For these reasons, avoid using uppercase characters in URIs.

4.2 How to Use URIs As Opaque Identifiers

Treating URIs as opaque identifiers is, in most cases, trivial. It only requires you to make sure that each resource has a distinct URI. However, some practices illustrated in this recipe can lead to overloading URIs. In such cases, URIs may become generic gateways for unspecified information and actions. This can result in improperly cached responses, possibly even the leakage of secure data that should not be shared without appropriate authentication.

Problem

You want to know how to avoid situations that prevent URIs from being used as unique identifiers.

Solution

Use only the URI to determine which resource processes a request.

Do not tunnel repeated state changes over POST using the same URI or use custom headers to overload URIs. Use custom headers for informational purposes only.

Discussion

Designating URIs as unique resource identifiers is a straightforward exercise except when you overload some HTTP methods or use something other than the URI to determine how to process a request.

Here is an example that uses a custom HTTP header to determine what to return:

```
# Request
GET /news HTTP/1.1
Host: www.example.org
X-Filter: science;sports;weather

# Response
HTTP/1.1 200 OK
Content-Type: application/xml;charset=UTF-8

... message body ...
```

In this example, the URI http://www.example.org/news is overloaded by the contents of the X-Filter header. If another client makes a similar request but with a different value in this custom header (e.g., politics;economy;healthcare), the server will return the representation of a different resource.

Such practices are easy to avoid. In this example, the server should offer different URIs for different news filters.

Another common practice that uses URIs as gateways and not as unique identifiers is tunneling repeated state changes using POST. This is the default practice in several web frameworks including ASP.NET, JavaServer Pages, and some Ajax toolkits:

```
# Request
POST /ajax-endpoint HTTP/1.1
Host: www.example.org

<request>
  <filter>science</filter>
  <filter>sports</filter>
  <filter>weather</filter>
</request>

# Response
HTTP/1.1 200 OK
Content-Type: application/xml;charset=UTF-8

... message body ...

# Request
POST /ajax-endpoint HTTP/1.1
Host: www.example.org

<request>
  <filter>politics</filter>
  <filter>economy</filter>
```

```
    <filter>healthcare</filter>
  </request>

  # Response
  HTTP/1.1 200 OK
  Content-Type: application/xml;charset=UTF-8

  ... message body ...
```

Such practices are usually a result of treating HTTP as a transport protocol. As long as you avoid such practices, treating URIs as unique identifiers should be relatively easy.

4.3 How to Let Clients Treat URIs As Opaque Identifiers

No matter how you design your URIs, it is important that web services make it possible for clients to treat them as opaque identifiers to the extent possible. Clients should be able to use server-provided URIs to make additional requests without having to understand how the server's URIs are structured.

Problem

You want to know how to ensure clients treat URIs as opaque.

Solution

Whenever possible, provide URIs at runtime using links in the body of representations (see Recipes 5.1 and 5.2) or headers (see Recipe 5.3).

When it is not reasonable to provide a complete set of possible URIs, consider using URI templates (see Recipe 5.7), or establish out-of-band rules to let clients construct URIs programmatically.

Discussion

Neither the architectural constraints of REST nor HTTP require that clients treat URIs as opaque. But doing so reduces coupling between servers and clients. A server expecting clients to construct URIs from bits of information returned in representations or offline knowledge (e.g., documentation or reverse-engineering) indicates tight coupling. This coupling can break existing clients when the web service makes changes to the way it creates new URIs.

In most cases, the process of creating URIs belongs to the server, not the client. For example, consider a photo-sharing web service, returning a list of photos uploaded recently to the server.

```
  <?xml version="1.0" encoding="utf-8" ?>
  <photos>
    <photo>
      <id>nj1-1234</id>
      <user-id>987</user-id>
```

```
      <server-id>east-nj1</server-id>
    </photo>
    <photo>
      <id>nj4-1235</id>
      <user-id>988</user-id>
      <server-id>east-nj4</server-id>
    </photo>
    ...
  </photos>
```

Since no URIs are provided in this representation, anyone implementing a client for this web service must read documentation and write client code to programmatically create URIs to each photo.

```
http://east-nj1.photos.example.org/987/nj1-1234
http://east-nj4.photos.example.org/988/nj4-1235
```

These URIs contain implementation-level data such as server names, photo IDs, and user IDs. If the server makes architectural changes that result in changes in URIs for all new photos, clients will have to make changes in the way they create URIs.

 When your web service requires clients to create URIs based on the implementation details of your web service, those details will become part of your web service's public interface. Avoid or minimize leaking such implementation details to clients.

To decouple the client from these implementation details, the server can provide links in the representation.

```
<?xml version="1.0" encoding="utf-8" ?>
<photos xmlns:atom="http://www.w3.org/2005/Atom">
  <photo>
    <atom:link href="http://east-nj1.photos.example.org/987/nj1-1234"
         rel="alternate"
         title="Sunset view from our backyard"/>
    <atom:link href="http://east-nj1.photos.example.org/987"
         rel="http://www.example.org/rels/owner"/>
    <id>nj1-1234</id>
  </photo>
  <photo>
    <atom:link href="http://east-nj4.photos.example.org/988/nj4-1235"
         rel="alternate"/>
    <atom:link href="http://east-nj1.photos.example.org/988"
         rel="http://www.example.org/rels/owner"/>
    <id>nj4-1235</id>
  </photo>
  ...
</photos>
```

This representation uses links to encode implementation details into URIs directly. Each photo in this representation has a link with a URI to fetch the image file and another link to fetch the owner resource of each photo. To realize which link points to which, clients do not have to know how to manufacture URIs. They just need to understand the meaning of the values of the `rel` attribute.

 Note that requiring clients to treat URIs as opaque may require you to tradeoff against performance. Usually URIs are longer in length than database identifiers, and hence transporting URIs over the network increases the message size. This may matter when the representation needs to convey a large number of URIs.

In cases where it is impractical for web services to supply the client with a list of all the possible URIs in the representation (e.g., supporting ad hoc searching), use "semi-opaque" URI templates (see Recipe 5.7). You will also need to loosen/ignore opacity if you want to protect against request tampering by using digitally signed URIs (see Recipe 12.5) or to encrypt parts of the URI to shield sensitive information. For this purpose, clients and servers will need to exchange details of how to sign URIs out of band.

4.4 How to Keep URIs Cool

URIs should be designed to last a long time. Clients may store URIs in databases and configuration files, or may even hard-code them in code. In fact, the Web works under the assumption that URIs are permanent. This design principle is referred to with the axiom "Cool URIs don't change" (*http://www.w3.org/Provider/Style/URI*). When a server decides to change its URIs, clients will fail to function. Cool URIs are those that never change.

The effect of URI changes may seem insignificant when your web service is operating in a private and controlled network. However, URIs make up a vital part of the interface between clients and servers, and changes to URIs are bound to be disruptive. This recipe shows you how to keep URIs permanent.

Problem

You want to know how to support the axiom "Cool URIs don't change."

Solution

Design URIs based on stable concepts, identifiers, and information. Use rewrite rules on the server to shield clients from implementation-level changes. In cases where URIs must change (e.g., when merging two applications, major redesign, etc.), honor old URIs and issue redirects to clients with the new URI using 301 (Moved Permanently) responses or, in rare cases, by issuing a 410 (Gone) for URIs that are no longer valid.

URIs cannot be permanent if the concepts or identifiers used for URIs cannot be permanent for business, technical, or security reasons. See Recipe 5.6 for ways to deal with such cases.

Discussion

The permanence of URIs depends on stability and the permanence of concepts and identifiers used to create URIs. For example, the URI http://www.example.org/2009/11/my_trip_report for a document titled "My Trip Report" is stable as long as the server treats the title as unchangeable once the document has been published. Usually, unique identifiers used to store data of resources help design stable URIs. Such identifiers rarely change.

Even when the concepts/identifiers used to create URIs change, it may be possible to hide such changes by employing rewrite rules supported by web servers such as Apache mod_rewrite (*http://httpd.apache.org/docs/2.0/mod/mod_rewrite.html*) and Internet Information Services (IIS) server's URLRewrite (*http://www.iis.net/extensions/URLRewrite*). You can use these web server extensions to hide URI changes that may be caused by merging server applications, changing paths, etc.

If you are not able hide URI changes, respond to all requests to the old URI with a 301 (Moved Permanently) and the new URI in the Location header:

```
# Request
GET /users/1 HTTP/1.1
Host: www.example.org
Accept: application/json

# Response
HTTP/1.1 301 Moved Permanently
Location: http://www.example2.org/users/1
```

When a client receives the 301 (Moved Permanently) response, it should remove any copies of the old URI from the client's local storage and replace them with the new URI. This will reduce the number of redirects the client needs to follow.

 Do not disable support for redirects in client applications. Instead, consider a sensible limit on the number of redirects a client can follow. Also verify that the Location URI maps to a trusted domain or IP address. Disabling redirects altogether will break the client when the server decides to change URIs.

Once you set up redirection, monitor request traffic on the server for the old URIs. Maintain redirection services for old URIs until you are confident the majority of clients have updated their stored links to point to the new URI. When you cannot monitor the old URIs, establish and communicate an appropriate end-of-life policy for old URIs.

Once the traffic has fallen off or the preset time interval has passed, convert the 301 (Moved Permanently) responses to 410 (Gone) or 404 (Not Found). Also include a message body to indicate where the new (or related) resources may be found.

```
# Request
GET /users/ HTTP/1.1
Host: www.example.org
```

```
Accept: application/xml;charset=UTF-8

# Response
HTTP/1.1 410 Gone
Content-Type: application/xml;charset=UTF-8;
Expires: Sat, 01 Jan 2011 00:00:00 GMT

<error xmlns:atom="http://www.w3.org/2005/Atom">
  <atom:link rel="help" href="http://www.example2.org"/>
  <message xml:lang="en-US">This resource no longer exists.
  Related information may be found at http://www.example2.org</message>
</error>
```

Note that the previous example shows the 410 (Gone) response is marked with an Expires header value far into the future. For more on caching responses, see Chapter 9.

## CHAPTER 5

Web Linking

A link provides a means of navigation from one resource to another. There are many everyday examples of links. Travelers use street signs and maps to decide which way to travel. Books and articles use footnotes and references to direct readers to related material. In software, we use variables and pointers to create links between different parts of an application.

The World Wide Web is based on the same principle. HTML documents use anchors and forms to let users navigate between web pages, and they use `img`, `object`, and `link` elements to include references to related resources. Here is the body of a representation of a resource as an HTML document:

```
<html>
  <head>
    <link href="http://www.restful-webservices-cookbook.org/styles/main.css"
          rel="stylesheet" type="text/css"/>
    <link href="http://www.restful-webservices-cookbook.org/feed"
          rel="alternate feed" type="application/atom+xml"/>
  </head>
  <body>
    <p><img src="http://www.restful-webservices-cookbookorg/images/cover"
        align="left"/>Read <a href="http://www.restful-webservices-cookbook.org">
        RESTful Web Services Cookbook</a> to learn about building RESTful apps.
    </p>
  </body>
</html>
```

Each `link` element in this example points to a related resource. A browser can use the first `link` element to discover the stylesheet associated with this HTML document. A feed reader can use the second `link` to fetch a related Atom feed. The `img` element points to another related resource, an image file, that the browser can render on the screen. The anchor (`a`) element provides a way for the client to navigate to another page.

This chapter discusses the following recipes that show when and how to use links in RESTful web services:

Recipe 5.1, "How to Use Links in XML Representations"
Use this recipe to learn how to include links in general-purpose XML representations.

Recipe 5.2, "How to Use Links in JSON Representations"
Use this recipe to learn how to include links in JSON representations.

Recipe 5.3, "When and How to Use Link Headers"
Link headers provide a format-independent means to provide links. Use this recipe to learn when and how to use them.

Recipe 5.4, "How to Assign Link Relation Types"
Links without meaningful link relation types are not very useful. This recipe shows how to assign relation types to links.

Recipe 5.5, "How to Use Links to Manage Application Flow"
Use this recipe to learn how you can use links to manage application flow.

Recipe 5.6, "How to Deal with Ephemeral URIs"
Not all links can be permanent. This recipe shows scenarios where links may be ephemeral and how to deal with such cases.

Recipe 5.7, "When and How to Use URI Templates"
Use this recipe to learn how to use URI templates in cases where the server cannot construct complete URIs.

Recipe 5.8, "How to Use Links in Clients"
Use this recipe to learn how to implement clients to use links supplied by servers.

5.1 How to Use Links in XML Representations

HTML, XHTML, and Atom establish rules for including links in representations. Clients that understand the semantics of these formats can discover links in those representations. However, XML is a general-purpose format, and it is the server's responsibility to design a way to include links in XML-formatted representations and document that design to clients. Clients can refer to that design to learn how to find and use links included in representations.

Problem

You want to know how to include links in XML-formatted representations.

Solution

Use the link element defined in Atom. This element is declared in the *http://www.w3 .org/2005/Atom* namespace and has the following attributes:

`href`
> This contains the link's URI.

`rel`
> This attribute, which originally stood for "relation," indicates the type of the link.

`title` *(optional)*
> This is a human-readable title for the link. Clients can present this to end users if the end users are expected to activate the link.

`type` *(optional)*
> This is a hint to the media type of the representation that the server may return for the link's URI.

`hreflang` *(optional)*
> This is a hint to the content language of the representation that the server may return for the link's URI.

`length` *(optional)*
> This is a hint to the content length of the representation that the server may return for the link's URI.

The mere presence of a link in a particular element does not imply anything unless clients know how to find them and use them. Therefore, provide documentation on how clients can find links in XML representations.

Discussion

Atom's `link` element is flexible, is extensible, and is similar to links in HTML and XHTML documents. Here is an example of a link in the representation of a photo resource:

```
<photo xmlns:atom="http://www.w3.org/2005/Atom">
  ...
  <atom:link link href="http://east-nj1.photos.example.org/987/nj1-1234"
        type="image/jpeg"
        rel="alternate"
        title="Sunset view from our backyard"/>
</photo>
```

The intent of the link in this representation is to tell clients that the resource at the URI `http://east-nj1.photos.example.org/987/nj1-1234` is available as an alternate representation and that it may offer a JPEG-formatted representation.

The `href` and `rel` attributes are the most essential of all the link attributes. Although the value of the `href` attribute is necessary for the client to locate the URI of a resource, the `rel` attribute is the one that conveys the semantics of the link. It answers questions such as the following:

- What resource does the URI refer to?
- What is the significance of the link?

- What kind of actions can a client perform on the resource at the URI?
- What are the supported representation formats for requests and responses for that resource?

Other attributes are optional. Use them to provide hints when appropriate.

The value of `href` is an absolute URI. You can use relative URIs as long as you also include an `xml:base` attribute on the `link` element or one of its parent elements, as shown in the following example:

```
<addresses xmlns:atom="http://www.w3.org/2005/Atom" xml:base="http://www.example.org">
    <atom:link rel="http://www.example.org/rels/address"
        href="/address/1">
    <atom:link rel="http://www.example.org/rels/address"
        href="/address/2">
    <atom:link rel="http://www.example.org/rels/address"
        href="/address/3">
</addresses>
```

The value of the `xml:base` attribute is a URI that clients can use to resolve relative URIs in links.

 Since XML parsing libraries don't automatically resolve relative URIs against the `xml:base` attribute, absolute URIs are preferable.

Some applications use plain URIs to link resources together. Here are some examples:

```
<!-- Avoid these styles -->
<user>
  <uri>http://www.example.org/user/001</uri>
  <address>http://www.example.org/user/001/address/001</address>
</user>
```

Avoid such methods of communicating URIs because such URIs lack the flexibility and extensibility of Atom's `link` element. As discussed in Recipe 5.4, plain URIs with no link relation type do not communicate the semantics of URIs to clients.

5.2 How to Use Links in JSON Representations

As of writing this book, there is no standard approach for links in JSON representations. This recipe presents a mapping of Atom's definition of the `link` element to JSON, which retains the same flexibility and extensibility.

Problem

You want to know how to include links in JSON-formatted representations.

Solution

For each link, use a `link` property (or a `links` property to include several links as an array) whose value is a link object or a link object array. For each link object, include the `href` and `rel` properties. See Recipe 5.1 for the meaning of these properties.

Alternatively, use the link relation type as the name of the property with the link's URI as the value.

Discussion

Here are examples links using two alternative forms:

```
{
  "link" : {
    "rel" : "alternate",
    "href" : "http://east-nj1.photos.example.org/987/nj1-1234",
  }
}

{
  "links" : [
    {
      "rel" : "alternate",
      "href" : "http://east-nj1.photos.example.org/987/nj1-1234"
    },
    {
      "rel" : "http://www.example.org/rels/owner",
      "href" : "http://east-nj1.photos.example.org/987",
    }
  ]
}
```

The previous form follows Atom's `link` element. The following form defines the same links in a more compact form:

```
{
  "alternate" : "http://east-nj1.photos.example.org/987/nj1-1234"
  "owner" : "http://east-nj1.photos.example.org/987/nj1-1234"
}
```

No matter which form you adopt, it is important to capture the essence of Atom's `link` element. Make sure to at least convey a link relation type along with each URI. See Recipe 5.4 to learn why link relations types matter.

5.3 When and How to Use Link Headers

Link headers provide a format-independent means to convey links. Instead of embedding links inside the body of representations, you can communicate links via link headers.

Problem

You want to know how to communicate links via HTTP headers.

Solution

A link header provides a way to convey a link as an HTTP header. Here is the format of the `Link` header and an example:

```
# Link header format
Link: <{URI}>;rel="{relation}";type="{media type"};title="{title}"...

# An example
Link: <http://east-nj1.photos.example.org/987/nj1-1234>;rel="alternate"
```

Use link headers either when you want to convey links in a format-independent manner or when a representation format does not support links.

Discussion

Link headers are appropriate in the following cases:

- Representations that use binary format, such as images, rich-text documents, spreadsheets, etc.

- Representations in formats that do not allow the easy discovery of links (e.g., plain-text documents)

- When your client/server software needs to add links or read links without parsing the body of representations

Here is an example of the representation of a photo image resource with two links. The first link header refers to an alternative representation of the same photo resource, while the second one provides a link to the owner of the photo:

```
# Response
HTTP/1.1 200 OK
Content-Type: image/jpeg
Link: <http://east-nj1.photos.example.org/987/nj1-1234.xml>;
      rel="alternate;type="application/xml"
Link: <http://east-nj1.photos.example.org/987>;
      rel="http://www.example.org/rels/owner"

... bytes ..
```

The key benefits of a link header are that it is format independent and it is visible at the protocol level. On the other hand, links expressed inside representations are format dependent. In particular, general-purpose formats like XML and JSON do not define a processing model for discovering links. In other words, clients need to read the documentation provided by the server to learn how to discover links in XML or JSON representations. Link headers do not have the same limitation.

5.4 How to Assign Link Relation Types

Without meaningful semantics assigned to URIs in links, links by themselves are not very useful. A link relation type conveys the role or purpose of a link. Once clients and servers agree on the meaning of these types, clients can find and use URIs from links. It is essential that you assign very specific and meaningful relation types to links.

Problem

You want to know what relation type to use for a link.

Solution

The key purpose of a link relation type is to act as an identifier for the semantics associated with the link. There are two ways to assign a value for link relation types. When the purpose of a link matches one of the standard types described in Table 5-1, use that value. See Appendix E for a complete list of registered relation types. If none of the registered types match, define an extended link relation type using the following conventions:

- Express the link relation type as a URI, such as `http://www.example.org/rels/create-po`.

- Provide an informational resource as an HTML document at that URI, with the HTML document describing the semantics of the link relation type. Include details such as HTTP methods supported, representation formats supported for requests and responses, and business rules about using the link.

- If the link relation type is meant for public use, register that link relation as per the process outlined in Section 6.2 of Web Linking Internet-Draft.

Table 5-1. Some commonly used registered link relation types

Name	Purpose
self	Use this type to link to the preferred URI of the resource.
alternate	Use this type when providing a link to a URI for an alternative version of the same resource.
edit	Use this type to link to a URI that clients can use to edit the resource.
related	Use this type to link to a related resource.
previous and next	Use these types to link to the previous or next resource in an ordered series of resources.
first and last	Use these types to link to the first and last resources in an ordered series of resources, e.g., to the first and last resources in a collection.

Discussion

To keep links effective, you must choose unambiguous values for link relations. If the semantics of any type in Table 5-1 do not match your use case, take advantage of the extensible nature of link relation values to define application-specific values as URIs.

Link relations were first introduced in HTML. Section 6.12 of HTML 4.01 defines the `alternate`, `stylesheet`, `start`, `next`, `prev`, `contents`, `index`, `glossary`, `copyright`, `chapter`, `section`, `subsection`, `appendix`, `help`, and `bookmark` link relations. All these values are case insensitive. You can also use multiple values for each relation, such as `rel="alternate help"`. The HTML 5 specification defines additional link relations such as `archives`, `feed`, `pingback`, etc.

Atom Syndication Format, which also defines links, provides an extensible mechanism to define extended link relation types. Here is a sample representation that uses both registered and extended relation types:

```
<review xmlns="org:example:books" xmlns:atom="http://www.w3.org/2005/Atom">
  <atom:link rel="self" href="http://example.org/book/978-0374292881/review/189742"/>
  <atom:link rel="first" href="http://example.org/book/978-0374292881/review/9863"/>
  <atom:link rel="last" href="http://example.org/book/978-0374292881/review/49732"/>
  <id>urn:org:example:books:189742</id>
  <author>...</author>
  <content type="text/html">&lt;![CDATA[
    ...
  ]]&gt;</content>
  <atom:link rel="http://example.org/rels/book"
          href="http://example.org/book/978-0452286757"/>
  <atom:link rel="http://example.org/rels/author"
          href="http://example.org/authors/ayn_rand"/>
  <atom:link rel="http://example.org/rels/add-review"
          href="http://example.org/book/978-0452286757/reviews"/>
</review>
```

This representation pertains to a book review resource at URI `http://www.example.org/book/978-0374292881/review/189742` and uses the following link relation types:

`self`
> The purpose of this link relation type is to provide a link to the resource. Clients should be able to use the link's URI to fetch the resource.

`first` *and* `last`
> Links with these relation types refer to the first and last reviews of the book.

`http://www.example.org/rels/book`
> This extended relation type identifies the book associated with this review.

`http://www.example.org/rels/author`
> This extended relation type identifies the author of the book.

`http://www.example.org/rels/add-review`
> This purpose of the link with this relation type is to create new reviews for the book.

Always use URIs as the values of extended link relation types. In addition, consider providing HTML documentation at the URI of the extended link relation, describing the link relation with the following information:

- Purpose of the link relation
- The types of resources that use the link relation, and the types of resources at the target of the link
- Valid HTTP methods for the target URI
- Expected media types on request and response for the target URI

Here is an example:

```
<html>
  <head>
    <title>Link relation - http://www.example.org/rels/add-review</title>
  </head>
  <body>
    <h1>Link Relation: <code>http://www.example.org/rels/add-review</code></h1>

    <p>Use this link relation to add new book reviews. You may find links with this
    relation type in representations of book resources and review resources.</p>

    <p>You can use the link's URI to submit new reviews.</p>

    <p>Use a representation of media type <code>application/xml</code> and HTTP method
    <code>POST</code> to submit new reviews.</p>
  </body>
</html>
```

Such online documentation can help development-time discovery of link relation types.

 Use lowercase characters for all link relation types.

Note that registered link relation types such as self and alternate must be compared case insensitively, while extended relation types must be compared as URIs in a case-sensitive fashion. Using lowercase values for both types simplifies code used to extract links.

5.5 How to Use Links to Manage Application Flow

One of the key applications of hypermedia and links is the ability to decouple the client from learning about the rules the server uses to manage its application flow. The server can provide links containing application state, thereby using hypermedia as the engine of application state.

Problem

You want to know how to keep clients decoupled from the business logic used to implement the flow of the application.

Solution

Design each representation such that it contains links that help clients transition to all the next possible steps. If the server needs to carry forward state from one step to the next, encode the state in links as described in Recipe 1.3.

Discussion

Imagine a web service that manages an employee hiring process. This process has multiple steps, such as (a) enter candidate details, (b) check references, (c) conduct background security checks, and (d) make an offer. Each step must happen in sequence. You can use the resources and URIs shown in Table 5-2 to implement this sequence. The token {id} in these URIs is the candidate ID.

Table 5-2. URIs for employee hiring process

Method	URI	Purpose
POST	http://www.example.org/hires	Create a candidate resource.
POST	http://www.example.org/hires/{id}/refs	Submit reference comments.
POST	http://www.example.org/hires/{id}/bgchecks	Submit background check results.
POST	http://www.example.org/hires/{id}/hire	Make an offer.
POST	http://www.example.org/hires/{id}/no-hire	Do not make an offer.

Assume that this web service is governed by the following business rules:

- After entering candidate information, start the reference check.
- After receiving at least two positive references, start the background check.
- After getting background clearance, make an offer.

Given these rules and the URIs, you can implement a client for the employee hiring process. After each step, the client can check the rules to see whether it can move to the next step. However, this introduces coupling between the client and server's business rules, since the server, and not the client, should be responsible for managing those rules.

When your web service requires clients to learn and implement application flow rules, you are introducing yet another kind of coupling between your clients and servers. Just like the details to construct URIs, such flow rules also become part of your web service's public interface and therefore cannot be changed without breaking clients.

A better alternative is to let the server provide clients with "contextual" links containing URIs for possible next steps. When the client discovers a link, it can attempt a transition to the next step in the process. When the link is absent in the representation, the client can assume that the transition is not possible. This prevents the client from having to learn and hard-code application flow.

For an analogy, consider a user interacting with a browser-based web application. The browser, as instructed by the user, follows the links and forms without prior knowledge of the flow of the application. The purpose of links is to extend the same benefit to application clients. Here is a representation of the newly entered candidate resource created by the server:

```
# Request to enter candidate info
POST /hires HTTP/1.1
Host: www.example.org
Content-Type: application/json

{
  "name": "Joe Prospect",
  ...
}

# Response containing a link to post reference checks
HTTP/1.1 201 Created
Location: http://www.example.org/hires/099
Content-Location: http://www.example.org/hires/099
Content-Type: application/json

{
  "name": "Joe Prospect",
  "id": "urn:example:hr:hiring:099",
  ...
  "link" : { ❶
    "rel" : "http://www.example.org/rels/hiring/post-ref-result",
    "href" : "http://www.example.org/hires/099/refs"
  }
}
```

❶ Link to post reference check results

This representation has a link to submit new reference check results. Since there is no other link, the client cannot yet initiate the background check process or make an offer.

After entering two positive reference check results, the server can return a representation to indicate that the client can start the background check:

```
# Request to enter first reference comment
POST /hires/099/refs HTTP/1.1
Host: www.example.org
Content-Type: application/json

{
  "text" : "Joe is a ...",
  "by" : "...",
```

```
    "on" : "2009:10:12T16:05:00Z"
  }

# Response
HTTP/1.1 200 OK
Content-Location: http://www.example.org/hires/099
Content-Type: application/json

{
  "name": "Joe Prospect",
  "id": "urn:example:hr:hiring:099",
  ...
  "link" : {
    "rel" : "http://www.example.org/rels/hiring/post-ref-result",
    "href" : "http://www.example.org/hires/099/refs"
  }
}

# Request to enter second reference comment
POST /hires/099/refs HTTP/1.1
Host: www.example.org
Content-Type: application/json

{
  "text" : "Worked with Joe, ...",
  "by" : "...",
  "on" : "2009:10:12T17:00:00Z"
}

# Response
HTTP/1.1 200 OK
Content-Location: http://www.example.org/hires/099
Content-Type: application/json

{
  "name": "Joe Prospect",
  "id": "urn:example:hr:hiring:099",
  "refs": ...,
  ...
  "links" : [{ ❶
      "rel" : "http://www.example.org/rels/hiring/add-ref-result",
      "href" : "http://www.example.org/hires/099/refs"
    },
    { ❷
      "rel" : "http://www.example.org/rels/hiring/add-background-check",
      "href" : "http://www.example.org/hires/099/bgchecks"
    }]
}
```

❶ Link to post reference check results

❷ Link to post background check results

At this point, the client can either enter more reference checks or move on to submit background check results. If the results are acceptable based on the server's business policies, the server can include a link to make an offer.

```
# Request to submit background check results
POST /hires/099/bgchecks HTTP/1.1
Host: www.example.org
Content-Type: application/json
{
  "text" : "...",
  "by" : "...",
  "on" : "..."
}

# Successful background check
HTTP/1.1 200 OK
Content-Location: http://www.example.org/hires/099
Content-Type: application/json;charset=UTF-8

{
  "prospect" : {
    "name": "Joe Prospect",
    "id": "urn:example:hr:hiring:099",
    "refs": ...,
    "link" : { ❶
      "rel" : "http://www.example.org/rels/hiring/make-offer",
      "href" : "http://www.example.org/hires/099/hire"
    }
  }
}
```

❶ Link to make an offer

In this manner, the server guides the client through an employee hiring process without forcing the client to implement any more logic than it should.

The mere presence of a link will not still decouple the client from having to know how to prepare the data and make a request for the transition. As discussed in Recipe 5.4, servers will have to establish and document how to find links and the semantics of all extended link relation types.

5.6 How to Deal with Ephemeral URIs

As discussed in Recipe 4.4, the integrity of the Web is based on the permanence (or "coolness") of URIs. However, there are cases when URIs are temporary. For example, a URI may be valid only for a single use or may expire after a fixed period of time. Here are some situations that rely on ephemeral URIs:

- A web service provides a security token to its clients, like the token you may receive for accessing a teller's counter at a bank. Clients can use this token to gain access to a resource for a short period of time.

- An insurance quote web service generates quotes. Each quote is specific to a given client and is valid for 72 hours, after which the quote expires, and the client will have to fetch a new quote.
- Upon registering a user on a website, the server emails a secret token to the user and expects the user to enter the token in an HTML form on the server in order to validate the user's email address.

Problem

You want to know how to support short-lived URIs.

Solution

Communicate ephemeral URIs via links. Assign extended relation types for those links and document how long such URIs are valid and what the client should do after the expiry. When a client submits a request for an expired URI, return an appropriate 4xx error code with instructions in the body on any actions the client can take.

Discussion

When a server provides a URI for a resource, by default clients expect URIs to be permanent. Since servers cannot generate ephemeral URIs beforehand, they can use links to communicate those URIs at runtime. But that is just one part of the problem. The other part of the problem is how to inform clients that those URIs are ephemeral. Clearly documenting link relations can help solve this part of the problem.

For instance, if the problem is to let the client make a purchase within two minutes after making a bid, the server could include a link for the purchase. The link may contain an encrypted state that becomes invalid after two minutes as an extra measure of security:

```
# Request
POST /bid/ASBV_04_10_2009_1 HTTP/1.1
Host: www.example.org
Content-Type: application/xml;charset=UTF-8

...

HTTP/1.1 200 OK
Content-Type: application/xml;charset=UTF-8

<purchase-req xmlns:atom="http://www.w3.org/2005/Atom">
  <amount currency="USD">...</amount>
  ...
  <atom:link rel="http://www.example.org/purchase-req/auth"
        href="http://www.example.org/auth/ASBV_04_10_2009_1/09_31?_k=a1191fd35d23"/>
</purchase-req>
```

In this case, the server needs to document that the URI with link relation type `http://www.example.org/purchase-req/auth` is valid only for two minutes. If a client activates the URI after its expiry, the server returns an error:

```
# Request
POST /auth/ASBV_04_10_2009_1/09_31?_k=a1191fd35d23
Host: www.example.org
Content-Type: application/xml;charset=UTF-8

...

HTTP/1.1 403 Forbidden
Content-Type: application/xml;charset=UTF-8
Date: Sat, 17 Oct 2009 20:16:18 GMT

<error xmlns:atom="http://www.w3.org/2005/Atom">
  <message xml:lang="en">Authorization expired. Resubmit the bid.</message>
  <atom:link rel="http://www.example.org/purchase-req/bid"
        href="http://www.example.org/auth/ASBV_04_10_2009_1?retry"/>
</error>
```

See Recipe 5.8 for details on how to implement clients to deal with ephemeral URIs.

5.7 When and How to Use URI Templates

The recipes in this chapter so far assume that the server has all the information necessary to generate a valid and complete URI for each link. When this is not the case, the server can provide URI templates to clients.

Problem

You want to know how to let clients include additional information in URIs before submitting requests to the server.

Solution

A URI template is a string consisting of tokens marked off between matching braces ({ and }). Clients substitute these tokens (including the matching braces) with URI-safe strings to convert the template into a valid URI.

To keep token substitution and matching simple, limit the tokens to the following parts of URIs:

- Path segments, as in `http://www.example.org/segment1/{token1}/segment2`
- Values of query parameters, as in `http://www.example.org/path?param1 ={p1}&param2={p2}`
- Values of matrix parameters, as in `http://www.example.org/path;param1 ={p1};param2={p2}`

To include a URI template in a representation, use the following:

- For the XML family of representation, use a `link-template` element defined in your own application XML namespace. For the sake of consistency, define the same set of attributes on this element as that of the `link` element.

  Note that the `href` element in the `link` element defined by the Atom Syndication Format does not permit using URI templates.

- For JSON representations, use `link-template` or `link-templates` properties to convey URI templates.

Discussion

URI templates provide a way for servers to return semi-opaque URIs to clients and allow clients to fill in the missing pieces to generate valid URIs. The idea of URI templates is not new. Section 6.8.1.1 of WSDL 2.0 uses braces to specify replacement tokens. WADL uses the same notation to specify resource IDs in URI path segments. There was also an effort to formalize the syntax used for URI templates as an Internet-Draft.[*]

Here is an example URI template that can be used for searching people:

```
http://www.example.org/people?k={keyword}&
    p={page-number}&r={results-per-page}
```

This template has three tokens: one for search keywords, one for the starting page number, and one for the number of results per page. A client can replace these tokens with actual values to generate a valid URI.

```
http://www.example.org/people/k=sports&p=1&r=10
```

 Because of the presence of brace characters, a URI template is not a valid URI until you replace all the tokens, including the braces, with URI-safe characters.

Here are snippets of representations containing URI templates:

```
<!-- XML representations -->
<link-template href="http://www.example.org/customers/{customer-id}"
               title="View customer detail"
               rel="http://www.example.org/rels/detail"/>
<link-template href="http://www.example.org/search/k={keyword}&p={page-number}&
               r={results-per-page}"
               title="Search results"
               rel="http://www.example.org/rels/search"/>

// JSON representations
```

---

[*] At the time of writing this book, this Internet-Draft has expired. Check *http://tools.ietf.org/html/draft-gregorio-uritemplate* for any updates.

```
"link-templates" : [{
    "rel" : "http://www.example.org/rels/detail",
    "href" : "http://www.example.org/customers/{customer-id}",
    "title" : "View customer detail"
},
{
    "rel" : "http://www.example.org/rels/search",
    "href" : "http://www.example.org/search/k={keyword}&p={page-number}&r=
        {results-per-page}",
    "title" : "Search results"
}]
```

The href values in these link-template elements are URI templates. The first template requires the client to replace {customer-id} with a valid value. The second template requires the client to replace {keyword}, {page-number}, and {results-per-page}.

Since URI templates are semi-opaque and contain tokens that clients need to substitute, you need a way to tell clients what values are valid for each token. The simplest way to do so is to document the tokens used in your URI templates, as in Table 5-3.

Table 5-3. URI template: /search/k={keyword}&p={page-number}&r={results-per-page}

Token	Purpose
{keyword}	A comma- or space-separated list of search terms.
{page-number}	Page number of search results. The first page starts at 0.
{results-per-page}	Results per page.

5.8 How to Use Links in Clients

A web browser is the best example of a client that uses links for browsing. The server presents the current state of the application in the form of HTML with links. Users can either invoke links immediately or bookmark them for later use. The HTML presented in the page helps the user determine whether a particular link is bookmarkable (i.e., it can be used later) or whether the user needs to act on certain links immediately. You need to implement clients to operate in the same manner.

Problem

You want to know to how to implement a client using links supplied by the server.

Solution

To support URIs and URI templates provided by the server, extract URI and URI templates from links based on known link relation types. These links along with other resource data constitute the current state of the application.

If the application is long running, store the URIs and the relation type along with other representation data.

Make flow decisions based on the presence or absence of links. Store the knowledge of whether a representation contains a given link.

Check the documentation of the link relation to learn any associated business rules regarding authentication, permanence of the URI, methods and media types supported, etc.

Discussion

When a server is using links to communicate its URIs in a representation, implement clients to take advantage of those links. This requires extracting the current state of the application from links (in particular URIs and link relation types), storing them, and making choices based on the presence or absence of links of known relation types.

Consider the employee hiring process discussed in Recipe 5.5 from the client's point of view. Most likely, the client application would be long running. It may be a desktop application or a web application with a web-based user interface. Someone using the client does some out-of-band work such as sending requests for background checks. Whenever there is new information, the user invokes the client and drives it to the next step. In between the steps, the client needs to store the state of the resource and all the valid transitions (i.e., links) in its database.

For instance, revisit the request to enter the prospective employee information and the server's response.

```
# Request to enter candidate info
POST /hires HTTP/1.1
Host: www.example.org
Content-Type: application/json

{
  "name": "Joe Prospect",
  ...
}

# Response containing a link to post reference checks
HTTP/1.1 201 Created
Location: http://www.example.org/hires/099
Content-Location: http://www.example.org/hires/099
Content-Type: application/json

{
  "name": "Joe Prospect",
  "id": "urn:example:hr:hiring:099",
  ...
  "link" : {
    "rel" : "http://www.example.org/rels/hiring/post-ref-result",
    "href" : "http://www.example.org/hires/099/refs"
  }
}
```

When a client receives this representation, it needs to extract and store the following:

- Employee details such as name, ID, and other information
- The current state of the resource that the hiring process is ready for reference checks

When the user conducts reference checks, and is ready to enter those details, the client needs to recognize the current state of the resource and provide a user interface for the user. In this case, this involves presenting a user interface to enter reference checks.

After entering two positive reference checks, the current state of the resource changes to the following:

```
# Response
Content-Location: http://www.example.org/hires/099
Content-Type: application/json

{
  "name": "Joe Prospect",
  "id": "urn:example:hr:hiring:099",
  "refs": ...,
  ...
  "links" : [{
      "rel" : "http://www.example.org/rels/hiring/add-ref-result",
      "href" : "http://www.example.org/hires/099/refs"
    },
    {
      "rel" : "http://www.example.org/rels/hiring/add-background-check",
      "href" : "http://www.example.org/hires/099/bgchecks"
    }]
}
```

The current state of the resource now includes two links: one to add further reference checks and one to add background check results. The client's user interface needs to offer a choice to the user to either add a new reference check or enter background check results. At this point, the user likely follows business policies to start background checks and reopens the client after getting those results. The client then re-creates the user interface with the same choices to enter the results of the reference check or background check.

As you see from this example, when a server uses links, the client needs to act like a browser to use those links. Although this may seem cumbersome, this approach decouples the client from the server and helps the client and server evolve independently of each other.

## CHAPTER 6

Atom and AtomPub

The Atom Syndication Format (RFC 4287) and the Atom Publishing Protocol (also called as AtomPub, RFC 5023) define resources such as entries and feeds, their representations, and a protocol to operate on those resources. Atom was designed with human-readable content such as HTML and plain text in mind. It works best for resources that are primarily text-based and intended for people to read such as blogs, discussion forums, commenting systems, etc. AtomPub describes semantics that allow clients to create and modify Atom-formatted resources. AtomPub also introduces service and category resources to aid application discovery.

Atom and AtomPub have been used for a number of application scenarios. Although Atom is used commonly for blog feeds, it is possible to extend this format to application data such as user profiles, search results, albums, and so on. For instance, Google Data Protocol APIs extend Atom for a number of Google's products. Such usages bring up the questions of when using Atom and AtomPub is appropriate. Even when you find that Atom and AtomPub are not suitable for your web service, you may find using links, service documents, and supporting media resources and categories useful. This chapter presents the following recipes to help answer these questions:

Recipe 6.1, "How to Model Resources Using Atom"
Use this recipe to learn how to model resources and collections using Atom.

Recipe 6.2, "When to Use Atom"
Use this recipe to determine whether Atom is an appropriate format for your resource representations.

Recipe 6.3, "How to Use AtomPub Service and Category Documents"
Use this recipe to learn how to use AtomPub service and category documents.

Recipe 6.4, "How to Use AtomPub for Feed and Entry Resources"
Use this recipe to learn how to use AtomPub to manage Atom-formatted resources.

Recipe 6.5, "How to Use Media Resources"
Use this recipe to learn how to use AtomPub to manage media resources.

6.1 How to Model Resources Using Atom

A key advantage of using Atom for resources is interoperability. A wide range of tools (feed readers such Google Reader, Bloglines, and NewsGator, as well as most browsers and email clients) and programming libraries (Apache Abdera, ROME Project, Windows Communication Foundation, etc.) are available. Using Atom as a representation format for resources involves modeling resources as Atom entries and feeds and mapping application-specific data fields to elements and attributes specified by Atom.

Problem

You want to know how to support the Atom format for your resource representations.

Solution

To use Atom, model resources as entries and collections as feeds. The representation of an entry is an XML document with the **entry** element defined in Atom as the root element. The representation of a feed is an XML document with the **feed** element as the root element. A **feed** document consists of several **entry** elements. These elements are defined in the *http://www.w3.org/2005/Atom* namespace. The most commonly used prefix for this namespace is **atom**. See Appendix D for an overview of the elements defined in the Atom format.

Discussion

Atom is an XML format that is based on two types of resources: entry documents and feed documents. To best illustrate how to design representations using Atom, consider an XML-formatted representation of a book:

```
# Request
GET /books/1 HTTP/1.1
Host: www.example.org

# Response
HTTP/1.1 200 OK
Content-Type: application/xml;charset=UTF-8

<book xmlns:atom="http://www.w3.org/2005/Atom">
  <isbn>0-9767736-6-X</isbn>
  <title>Johnny Web and the Atomic Circle</title>
  <atom:link href="http://www.example.org/books/1"/>
  <date-published>2010-01-01</date-published>
  <cover-art href="http://www.example.org/books/1/cover" type="image/jpeg"/>
  <author href="http://www.example.org/books/1/authors/1">R. W. Smith</author>
  <description>
    A lively tale of a young boy who discovers a secret
    scientific fraternity with a dark past and hidden purpose.
  <description>
</book>
```

Here is the same resource expressed as an Atom entry document:

```
# Request
GET /books/1 HTTP/1.1
Host: www.example.org

# Response
HTTP/1.1 200 OK
Content-Type: application/atom+xml;type=entry;charset=UTF-8

<atom:entry xmlns:atom="http://www.w3.org/2005/Atom">
  <atom:id>urn:isbn:0-9767736-6-X</atom:id> ❶
  <atom:title>Johnny Web and the Atomic Circle</atom:title> ❷
  <atom:link href="http://www.example.org/books/1" rel="edit"/>
  <atom:link href="http://www.example.org/books/1/cover.png" ❸
             rel="enclosure" type="image/png"/>
  <atom:published>2010-01-01T00:00:00Z</atom:published> ❹
  <atom:author> ❺
    <atom:name>R. W. Smith</atom:name>
    <atom:uri>http://www.example.org/books/1/authors/1</atom:uri>
  </atom:author>
  <atom:updated>2010-12-13T18:30:02Z</atom:updated>
  <atom:content type="text"> ❻
    A lively tale of a young boy who discovers a secret scientific fraternity
    with a dark past and hidden purpose.
  </atom:content>
</atom:entry>
```

❶ ISBN identifier of the book

❷ Title of the book

❸ Link to the cover art

❹ Date published

❺ Author of the book

❻ Description of the book

The media type of this representation is `application/atom+xml`, which is registered with the IANA by Atom.

 Atom registers the media type `application/atom+xml` for feed documents. AtomPub, discussed in Recipe 6.4, defines entry documents as representations with the media type `application/atom +xml;type=entry`. In AtomPub, you can use `application/atom+xml` or `application/atom+xml;type=entry` as the media type when the representation is an Atom entry document.

This representation contains several mandatory elements along with application data such as the author, title, description, link to cover art, etc. Both the representations shown previously contain the same information, but they differ in the way the server encodes them as representations. Some notable differences are as follows:

- The ISBN identifier of the book is mapped to the `atom:id` element.
- The link to the cover art is mapped to an `atom:link` element.
- Metadata such as the title of the book and its date of publication is mapped to corresponding Atom elements.
- The data for the author of the book is mapped to the `atom:author` element.

Such a mapping exercise can remain meaningful as long as the application's semantics for resources closely match those specified by Atom.

You can extend this example to use an Atom feed document to represent a collection of books:

```
GET /books HTTP/1.1
Host: www.example.org

HTTP/1.1 200 OK
Content-Type: application/atom+xml;charset=UTF-8

<atom:feed xmlns:atom="http://www.w3.org/2005/Atom"> ❶
  <atom:title>Sci-Fi Books</atom:title>
  <atom:link href="http://www.example.org/books" rel="self"
    hreflang="en" type="application/atom+xml"/>
  <atom:updated>2013-12-13T18:30:02Z</atom:updated>
  <atom:author>
    <atom:name>Example Inc.</atom:name>
  </atom:author>
  <atom:id>urn:uuid:5f49aa74-e920-425d-a150-8907494905e7</atom:id>
  <atom:entry> ❷
    <atom:id>urn:isbn:0-9767736-6-X</atom:id>
    <atom:title>Johnny Web and the Atomic Circle</atom:title>
    <atom:link href="http://www.example.org/books/1" rel="alternate"/>
    <atom:link href="http://www.example.org/books/1/cover.png"
               rel="enclosure" type="image/png"/>
    <atom:published>2010-01-01T00:00:00Z</atom:published>
    <atom:author>
      <atom:name>R. W. Smith</atom:name>
      <atom:uri>http://www.example.org/books/1/authors/1</atom:uri>
    </atom:author>
    <atom:updated>2010-12-13T18:30:02Z</atom:updated>
    <atom:content type="text">
      A lively tale of a young boy who discovers a secret scientific fraternity
      with a dark past and hidden purpose.
    </atom:content>
  </atom:entry>
  <atom:entry> ❸
    <atom:id>urn:isbn:0-9767736-9-X</atom:id>
    <atom:title>Johnny Web Meets the Wolfman</atom:title>
    <atom:link href="http://www.example.org/books/2" rel="alternate"/>
    <atom:link href="http://www.example.org/books/2/cover.png"
               rel="enclosure" type="image/png"/>
```

```
<atom:published>2011-02-21T00:00:00Z</atom:published>
<atom:author>
  <atom:name>R. W. Smith</atom:name>
  <atom:uri>http://www.example.org/books/1/authors/1</atom:uri>
</atom:author>
<atom:updated>2010-12-13T18:30:02Z</atom:updated>
<atom:content type="text">
  Young Johnny goes to college and sets out to solve the mystery behind the
  strange noises coming from Professor Sirius' basement lab.
</atom:content>
    </atom:entry>
  </atom:feed>
```

❶ Collection of books represented as a feed

❷ A book represented as a member entry of the feed

❸ Another book represented as a member entry of the same feed

In this representation, the feed document has two entries, each corresponding to a book. If there are more entries and if the server needs to paginate the feed, the server can use links with relations such as previous, next, first, and last. These relations are specified by the RFC 5005. See Appendix E for a list of registered link relation types, and see Recipe 3.7 for an example of using links for pagination.

Any client software that understands the Atom format can process or display the feed of books without custom coding. For example, you can use a feed reader to subscribe to updates of all upcoming books when the publisher offers the collection of latest books as an Atom feed document. See Recipe 6.2 for a more detailed discussion on applicability of Atom.

6.2 When to Use Atom

The default content model of Atom feeds and entries consists of text, HTML, or XHTML content and summary, an identifier, links, authorship, categories, etc. This content model is best suited for publishing and syndicating snippets of information as feeds. However, since this format captures essential concepts that benefit most applications, it can be applied to a wide variety of scenarios and not just for content feeds. This recipe helps you determine whether Atom is a good fit for your web service.

Problem

You want to know if the Atom-format is appropriate for your web service.

Solution

Use Atom when the information model or metadata of resources naturally maps to the syntax and semantics of Atom feeds and entries. Even when the information model of resources does not map to Atom, consider offering Atom feeds with entries consisting of short text, HTML, or XHTML summaries of resources and links to them. Users can learn about those resources by relying on feed-capable tools such as feed readers.

Discussion

The Atom format has strong semantics for lists of snippets of information. Atom specifies elements for identifying the resource, related links, and metadata such as authors. However, it has relatively weak semantics for carrying data within `atom:content` and `atom:summary` elements. For example, consider the following Atom entry:

```
<atom:entry xmlns:atom="http://www.w3.org/2005/Atom">
  <atom:title>Johnny Web Series Goes Anime</atom:title>
  <atom:id>urn:blog:1234</atom:id>
  <atom:link rel="self" href="http://www.example.org/blog/2009/11/01"/>
  <atom:updated>2009-11-11T11:11:11Z</atom:updated>
  <atom:author>
    <atom:name>J. W. Smith</atom:name>
  </atom:author>
  <atom:content type="xhtml">
   <div xmlns="http://www.w3.org/1999/xhtml">
     <h1>Johnny Web Series goes Anime</h1>
     <p>After months of negotiation and lots of hush-hush shuttle diplomacy,
     I am pleased to announce we&apos;ve reached a deal to bring the entire
     Johnny Web book series out as an anime television show.</p>
     <p>The first production is scheduled for early next year. &quot;Atomic
     Circle&quot; will be the book used for the first season.
     Others will follow.</p>
     <p>I&apos;ll keep you posted here on the latest developments.
     As Johnny always sez:</p>
     <blockquote>
       <p>Ursus Major!</p>
     </blockquote>
   </div>
  </atom:content>
</atom:entry>
```

This is an example of a blog entry. The bulk of the information is contained in the `atom:content` element as XHTML markup. Clients that understand Atom can interpret the contents of the Atom entry document.

Now consider the following representation of a production schedule. This representation relies on the extensible nature of `atom:entry` elements (see Appendix D for various ways to use `atom:content`). Client applications should use this production information to track and manage the production schedule for a television project:

```
<atom:entry xmlns:atom="http://www.w3.org/2005/Atom">
  <atom:title>Johnny Web Sample Production Schedule</atom:title>
  <atom:id>urn:example:sked:1111</atom:id>
  <atom:link rel="self" href="http://www.example.org/ps/1111"/>
  <atom:updated>2011-11-11T11:11:11Z</atom:updated>
  <atom:author><name>J. W. Smith</name></atom:author>
  <atom:content type="application/xml"> ❶
    <production-schedule>
```

```
      <story-development>
        <days>5</days>
        <planned-start>2012-01-01</planned-start>
      </story-development>
      <pencil-roughs>
        <days>2</days>
        <planned-start>2012-01-10</planne-start>
      </pencil-roughs>
      <layouts-and-ink>
        <days>3</days>
        <planned-start>2012-01-15</planned-start>
      </layouts-and-ink>
    </production-schedule>
  </content>
</atom:entry>
```

❶ Production schedule as a child element of the `atom:content` element

Although the previous representation is a valid Atom entry, standard Atom clients will not know how to process the custom XML in the `atom:content` element. Custom application clients that understand the embedded XML document can, however, read this data, with some extra overhead. For custom clients, first parsing the entry document only to extract an additional XML document from the `atom:content` is added work that does little to improve the efficiency of the client code.

For non-HTML data that is targeted at machine clients, Atom format is less useful, and it is often simpler to design a more compact XML representation of the resource:

```
<production-schedule xmlns:atom="http://www.w3.org/2005/Atom">
  <atom:link rel="self" href="http://www.example.org/ps/1111"/>
  <story-development>
    <days>5</days>
    <planned-start>2012-01-01</planned-start>
  </story-development>
  <pencil-roughs>
    <days>2</days>
    <planned-start>2012-01-10</planne-start>
  </pencil-roughs>
  <layouts-and-ink>
    <days>3</days>
    <planned-start>2012-01-15</planned-start>
  </layouts-and-ink>
</production-schedule>
```

Consider the following criteria in the order of their importance before choosing Atom for the representation of a resource:

- Whether the data model and semantics of the resource maps to an Atom feed or entry
- Whether the metadata (such as `atom:author`, `atom:category`, and `atom:contributor`) is meaningful for the resource
- Interoperability with Atom-capable tools

Here is another example. The server offers a user's address book as a resource with each address consisting of a postal address, an email, a few telephone numbers, etc., formatted as XHTML.

Atom is well suited for this example since the server can represent the XHTML content along with the metadata of each address as a resource:

```
<atom:feed xmlns:atom="http://www.w3.org/2005/Atom"> ❶
  <atom:title>John Doe's Address Book</title>
  <atom:link href="http://www.example.org/user/001/ab" rel="self"
    hreflang="en" type="application/atom+xml"/>
  <atom:updated>2013-12-13T18:30:02Z</atom:updated>
  <atom:author>
    <atom:name>John Doe</atom:name>
  </atom:author>
  <atom:id>urn:uuid:94dcfd50-dd4b-11de-8a39-0800200c9a66</atom:id>
  <atom:entry> ❷
    <atom:id>urn:uuid:b550ca30-dd4b-11de-8a39-0800200c9a66</atom:id>
    <atom:title>John's home address</atom:title>
    <atom:link href="http://www.example.org/user/ab/1" rel="alternate"/>
    <atom:published>2009-01-05T10:00:00Z</atom:published>
    <atom:author>
      <atom:name>John</atom:name>
    </atom:author>
    <atom:updated>2009-05-10T13:30:00Z</atom:updated>
    <atom:content type="xhtml">
      <div> <!-- XHTML of the address -->  </div>
    </atom:content>
  </atom:entry>
  <atom:entry> ❸
    <atom:id>urn:uuid:b550ca30-dd4b-11de-8a39-0800200c9a66</atom:id>
    <atom:title>Jane</atom:title>
    <atom:link href="http://www.example.org/user/ab/2" rel="alternate"/>
    <atom:published>2009-01-05T10:00:00Z</atom:published>
    <atom:author>
      <atom:name>Jane Doe</atom:name>
    </atom:author>
    <atom:updated>2009-01-10T13:30:00Z</atom:updated>
    <atom:content type="xhtml">
      <div> <!-- XHTML of the address -->  </div>
    </atom:content>
  </atom:entry>
```

❶ Address book represented as an `atom:feed` document

❷ Address represented as an `atom:entry` element containing XHTML

❸ Another address represented as an `atom:entry` element containing XHTML

Now consider the same address book for processing by a desktop address book application. To implement such a desktop client, the server needs to provide addresses in a format suitable for data and not presentation. Here is an example:

```
<atom:feed xmlns:atom="http://www.w3.org/2005/Atom"> ❶
  <atom:title>John Doe's Address Book</title>
```

```
<atom:link href="http://www.example.org/user/001/ab" rel="self"
  hreflang="en" type="application/atom+xml"/>
<atom:updated>2013-12-13T18:30:02Z</atom:updated>
<atom:author>
  <atom:name>John Doe</atom:name>
</atom:author>
<atom:id>urn:uuid:94dcfd50-dd4b-11de-8a39-0800200c9a66</atom:id>
<atom:entry>
  <atom:id>urn:uuid:b550ca30-dd4b-11de-8a39-0800200c9a66</atom:id>
  <atom:title>John's home address</atom:title>
  <atom:link href="http://www.example.org/user/ab/1" rel="alternate"/>
  <atom:published>2009-01-05T10:00:00Z</atom:published>
  <atom:author>
    <atom:name>John</atom:name>
  </atom:author>
  <atom:updated>2009-05-10T13:30:00Z</atom:updated>
  <atom:content type="application/xml">
    <address> ❷
      <street>...</street>
      <city>...</city>
      <postal-code>...</postal-code>
      <phone type="home">...</phone>
    </address
  </atom:content>
</atom:entry>
<atom:entry>
  <atom:id>urn:uuid:b550ca30-dd4b-11de-8a39-0800200c9a66</atom:id>
  <atom:title>Jane</atom:title>
  <atom:link href="http://www.example.org/user/ab/2" rel="alternate"/>
  <atom:published>2009-01-05T10:00:00Z</atom:published>
  <atom:author>
    <atom:name>Jane Doe</atom:name>
  </atom:author>
  <atom:updated>2009-01-10T13:30:00Z</atom:updated>
  <atom:content type="application/xml">
    <address> ❸
      <street>...</street>
      <city>...</city>
      <postal-code>...</postal-code>
      <phone type="home">...</phone>
    </address>
  </atom:content>
</atom:entry>
```

❶ Address book feed for a desktop client

❷ First address formatted as application-specific XML element

❸ Second address formatted as application-specific XML element

This form makes the Atom format less useful.

Finally, consider a list of stock quotes with each stock listing containing ticker name, volume, and hourly, daily, weekly, and yearly high and low values. The data model for such a resource cannot be mapped to an Atom entry without extensions to describe volume, highs and lows. Atom is not the best fit for such resources.

6.3 How to Use AtomPub Service and Category Documents

AtomPub introduces additional resources such as service documents and media resources. Service documents help clients discover collections offered by a web service. Servers can use media resources to associate media such as audio and video files, images or any arbitrary document with an Atom entry. Recipe 6.5 discusses media resources.

Problem

You want to know how to use AtomPub service and category documents.

Solution

Use a service document resource to group collections into workspaces. The representation of this resource is an XML document with `service` as the root element defined in the *http://www.w3.org/2007/app* namespace. The most commonly used namespace prefix for this namespace is `app`. The media type of this representation is `application/atomsvc+xml`.

A service consists of one or more workspaces (`app:workspace`). Each workspace consists of several collections (`app:collection`) listing URIs of all feeds, media types that they accept (`app:accept`), and categories (`app:category`).

A category resource lists categories of resources in a collection. Its representation is an XML document with `category` as the root element. It consists of `atom:category` elements. The media type of this representation is `application/atomcat+xml`.

See the "Discussion" section next for complete examples.

Discussion

The purpose of service documents is to let clients find the collections available on a server, and a workspace is a convenience mechanism to group related collections. Once the client knows a URI of the service document, it can find the URIs of all the collections in that service. Here is an example:

```
# Request
GET /bookservice HTTP/1.1
Host: www.example.org

# Response
HTTP/1.1 200 OK
Content-Type: application/atomsvc+xml;charset=UTF-8

<app:service xmlns="http://www.w3.org/2007/app" ❶
             xmlns:atom="http://www.w3.org/2005/Atom">
```

```
    <app:workspace> ❷
     <atom:title>CDs by Independent Artists and Reviews</atom:title>
     <app:collection href="http://www.example.org/cds" > ❸
       <atom:title>CDs</atom:title>
       <app:categories href="http://www.example.org/cds/categories"/>
       <app:accept>image/png</accept>
       <app:accept>image/jpeg</accept>
       <app:accept>image/gif</accept>
     </app:collection>
     <app:collection href="http://www.example.org/reviews"> ❹
       <atom:title>Reviews</atom:title>
     </app:collection>
    </app:workspace>
   </app:service>
```

❶ A service document

❷ A workspace

❸ A CD collection

❹ A reviews collection

This is a representation of a service document consisting of a single workspace. A workspace is a logical grouping of collections. This workspace has two collections: one for CDs and the other for reviews.

The CDs collection has the URI http://www.example.org/cds. Along with Atom entries, this collection offers PNG, JPEG, and GIF images. See Recipe 6.5 to learn how to manage such media resources. Clients can fetch the categories resource to discover the categories of resources offered by this collection.

```
# Request
GET /cds/categories HTTP/1.1
Host: www.example.org

# Response
HTTP/1.1 200 OK
Content-Type: application/atomcat+xml;charset=UTF-8

<app:categories xmlns:app="http://www.w3.org/2007/app"
                xmlns:atom="http://www.w3.org/2005/Atom"
                fixed="yes" scheme="http://www.example.org/audio">
  <atom:category term="jazz"/>
  <atom:category term="hip hop"/>
  <atom:category term="classical"/>
</app:categories>
```

The second collection in this workspace is a reviews collection to manage reviews. See Appendix B of RFC 5023 for the schema for service and category documents.

6.4 How to Use AtomPub for Feed and Entry Resources

The Atom Publishing Protocol (RFC 5023) is an application protocol for editing Atom documents. It describes, among other things, how to create, update, and delete Atom entries. It also supports editing associated nontextual media such as images, archive files, etc. If you are publishing your resources using the Atom format and those resources are editable, consider supporting AtomPub.

Problem

You want to know how to use the AtomPub protocol.

Solution

Allow clients to create new resources by submitting an Atom entry document as the body of a `POST` request using the URI of the Atom feed as a factory. Clients can subsequently use the link with the `edit` relation type to modify (using `PUT`) or delete (using `DELETE`) the resource.

Add a parameter `type=entry` to the media type when the representation is an Atom entry document.

Discussion

AtomPub uses a subset of HTTP to create, retrieve, update, and delete resources. Resources in AtomPub are Atom entries, Atom feeds, and media resources (see Recipe 6.5). AtomPub uses `POST` to create new resources, `GET` to retrieve representation, `PUT` to update a resource, and `DELETE` to delete a resource. Here is a typical sequence of operations:

```
# Request to create a resource
POST /books HTTP/1.1 ❶
Content-Type: application/atom+xml;type=entry;charset=UTF-8

<atom:entry>
  <atom:id>urn:isbn:0-9767736-7-X</atom:id>
  <atom:title>Johnny Web Goes Out West</atom:title>
  <atom:published>2012-04-01T00:00:00Z</atom:published>
  <atom:author>
    <atom:name>R. W. Smith</atom:name>
    <atom:uri>http://example.org/books/1/authors/1</atom:uri>
  </atom:author>
  <atom:updated>2012-04-01T18:30:02Z</atom:updated>
  <atom:content type="text">
    Space hero Johnny Web tries
    to enjoy a vacation at a dude
    ranch only to be swept up in
    a criminal plot to sell unregulated
    solar power to off-worlders.
  </atom:content>
</atom:entry>
```

```
# Response
HTTP/1.1 201 Created
Location: http://www.example.org/books/13

# Request to update ❷
PUT /books/13 HTTP/1.1
Host: www.example.org
Accept: application/atom+xml
If-Match: "h1g2f3d4s5a"

<atom:entry>
  ...
</atom:entry>

# Response
HTTP/1.1 200 OK
Content-Type: application/atom+xml;type=entry;charset=UTF-8
Content-Length: XXX
ETag: "m1n2b3v4c5x6z"

<atom:entry>
  ...
</atom:entry>

# Request to delete ❸
DELETE /books/13 HTTP/1.1
Host: www.example.org
If-Match: "m1n2b3v4c5x6z"

# Response
HTTP/1.1 204 No Content
```

❶ Use POST to create a new resource.

❷ Use PUT to update a resource.

❸ Use DELETE to delete a resource.

Note that AtomPub registers the edit relation type with IANA. Clients can use the URI of a link with this relation type to retrieve, update, or delete the resource.

AtomPub also specifies the Slug header. Clients can use this header with POST requests to provide a text value that servers can use for the URI assigned to the new resource. See Recipe 1.9 for an example.

6.5 How to Use Media Resources

One of the types of resources that AtomPub introduces is a media resource. A media resource is anything other than an Atom entry document and can be used to represent documents, images, audio and video files, etc. Since the media resource is not an Atom entry document, AtomPub associates a media link resource for each media resource.

A media link resource is nothing but an Atom entry that describes the media resource and links to it.

Problem

You want to know how to deal with media such as images, audio/video files, etc., associated with Atom entries.

Solution

Atom uses a media link entry with each media resource. Since media resources may be binary resources, you can use a media link entry to provide metadata for each media resource.

If a collection (i.e., feed) supports media resources, list the supported media types in the service document as described in Recipe 6.3.

Let clients create media resources by submitting a POST request to the collection. Create the media resource and a media link resource. Return the URI of the media link resource via the Location header. In the representation of the media link resource, provide the URI of the newly created media resource via the src attribute of the atom:content element.

If the server supports editing media resources, include a link with relation edit-media in the Atom entry. Clients can use this link to retrieve, update, or delete the media resource.

Discussion

AtomPub supports read/write operations on media resources (i.e., images, audio, video files, etc.) through the use of a media resource and an associated media link entry resource. The media resource is the actual media. The media link entry is an Atom entry that contains metadata about the media resource. The media link entry appears in the associated Atom feed along with other Atom entries.

When a client adds a media file using AtomPub, the server creates both the media resource and the media link entry. Here is an example:

```
# Request
POST /cds HTTP/1.1
Host: www.example.org
Content-Type: image/png
Slug: Epocalyptica
Content-Length: nnn

... binary data ...

# Response
HTTP/1.1 201 Created
Content-Type: application/atom+xml;charset=UTF-8
Location: http://www.example.org/cds/112-epocalyptica ❶
```

```
Content-Location: http://www.example.org/cds/112-epocalyptica
```

```
<atom:entry xmlns:atom="http://www.w3.org/2005/Atom">
  <atom:title>Epocalyptica</atom:title>
  <id>urn:uuid:1225c695-cfb8-4ebb-aaaa-80da344efa6a</id>
  <atom:updated>2009-04-01T04:01:00Z</atom:updated>
  <atom:author><atom:name>Jay Doe</atom:name></atom:author>
  <atom:summary type="text">Epocalyptica</atom:summary>
  <atom:content type="image/png"
                src="http://www.example.org/cds/112-epocalyptica.png"/> ❷
  <atom:link rel="self" href="http://www.example.org/cds/112-epocalyptica"/>
  <atom:link rel="edit-media"
             href="http://www.example.org/cds/112-epocalyptica.png"/> ❸
  <atom:link rel="edit"
             href="http://www.example.org/cds/112-epocalyptica"/> ❹
</atom:entry>
```

❶ Media link resource

❷ Media entry resource containing metadata of the media

❸ Link to edit the media

❹ Link to edit metadata of the media

The purpose of the media resource URI (the one with the `edit-media` relation type) is to modify the actual media file, as shown in the following example:

```
# Request
PUT /cds/112-epocalyptica.png HTTP/1.1
Host: www.example.org
Content-Type: image/png
Content-Length: nnn

...binary data...

# Response
HTTP/1.1 200 OK
```

Clients can use the media link entry URI (the one with the `edit` relation) to modify the metadata associated with the media file. Here is an example that adds summary content to media link entry associated with media resource:

```
# Request
PUT /cds/112-epocalyptica HTTP/1.1
Content-Type: application/atom+xml;charset=UTF-8
If-Match: "z9x8c7v6b5n4m3"

<atom:entry xmlns:atom="http://www.w3.org/2005/Atom">
  <atom:title>Epocalyptica</atom:title>
  <atom:id>urn:uuid:1225c695-cfb8-4ebb-aaaa-80da344efa6a</atom:id>
  <atom:updated>2009-04-01T04:01:00Z</atom:updated>
  <atom:author><name>Jay Doe</name></atom:author>
  <atom:summary type="text">Coolest album ever</atom:summary>
  <atom:content type="image/png"
                src="http://www.example.org/cds/112-epocalyptica.png"/>
```

```
    <atom:link rel="self"
               href="http://www.example.org/cds/112-epocalyptica"/>
    <atom:link rel="edit-media"
               href="http://www.example.org/cds/112-epocalyptica.png"/>
    <atom:link rel="edit"
               href="http://www.example.org/cds/112-epocalyptica"/>
</atom:entry>

# Response
HTTP/1.1 204 No Content
```

This example shows how to deal with arbitrary media content and how to manage the metadata of the media. You can apply this pattern for a wide variety of use cases that involve nontextual resources and their metadata. Some examples include movie trailer videos, reports, presentations, spreadsheets, scanned documents, etc.

## CHAPTER 7

Content Negotiation

Content negotiation, or *conneg* as it is sometimes called, is the process of selecting the best representation of a resource for a client when there are multiple representations (or *variants*) available. Although content negotiation is often associated with the practice of indicating media type preferences, content negotiation is also used to indicate preferences for localizing by language, character encoding, and compression.

HTTP specifies two types of content negotiation. These are server-driven negotiation and agent-driven negotiation. *Server-driven negotiation* uses request headers to select a variant, and *agent-driven negotiation* uses a distinct URI for each variant.

This chapter discusses the following recipes that deal with content negotiation:

Recipe 7.1, "How to Indicate Client Preferences"
Use this recipe to decide which Accept-* headers to include when requesting a resource and with what values.

Recipe 7.2, "How to Implement Media Type Negotiation"
Use this recipe to learn how to implement servers that correctly interpret the Accept request header for media type negotiation.

Recipe 7.3, "How to Implement Language Negotiation"
Use this recipe to learn how to implement language negotiation using the Accept-Language header.

Recipe 7.4, "How to Implement Character Encoding Negotiation"
Use this recipe to learn how to determine the requested character encoding for a representation.

Recipe 7.5, "How to Support Compression"
HTTP allows clients to indicate their preference for compressed representations via the Accept-Encoding request header. Use this recipe to decide how to process this header on the server.

Recipe 7.6, "When and How to Send the Vary Header"
Use this recipe to learn how to use the Vary header.

Recipe 7.7, "How to Handle Negotiation Failures"
> Use this recipe to determine when and how to return an error when the preferred variant is not available.

Recipe 7.8, "How to Use Agent-Driven Content Negotiation"
> Agent-driven negotiation is an alternative for a client to ask for a specific representation of a resource. Use this recipe to learn when and how to use this.

Recipe 7.9, "When to Support Server-Driven Negotiation"
> Use this recipe to learn the pros and cons of supporting multiple representations.

7.1 How to Indicate Client Preferences

When you are implementing a client, it is important for the client to indicate its preferences and capabilities to the server. These include representation formats it can process, languages it prefers, character encodings it can deal with, and its support for compression. Even when you know out of band the format, character encoding, language, and type of compression for a given representation in a response, clearly indicating the client's preferences and capabilities can help the client in the face of change. If not, when a server decides to offer an alternative representation for a resource, any default preferences your HTTP library may be using may prompt the server to return a different representation and break the client. It is better to ask for a specific representation instead of getting a default one, because the default representation can change.

Problem

You want to know how to allow a client to indicate its capabilities, such as supported media types, languages, etc.

Solution

When making a request, add an `Accept` header with a comma-separated list of media type preferences. If the client prefers one media type over the other, add a q parameter with each media type. This parameter indicates a relative preference for each media type listed in `Accept-*` headers. It is most commonly used with the `Accept` header. If the client can process only certain formats, add `*; q=0.0` in the `Accept` header to indicate to the server it cannot process anything other than the media types listed in the `Accept` header.

If the client can process characters of a specific character set only, add an `Accept-Charset` header with the preferred character set. If not, avoid adding this header.

Add an `Accept-Language` header for the preferred language of the representation.

If the client is able to decompress representations compressed using encodings such as `gzip`, `compress`, or `deflate`, add an `Accept-Encoding` header listing the supported encodings. If not, skip this header.

Discussion

In HTTP, the purpose of the `Accept-*` header is to let the client express its preferences for response representation. The server, based on its own capabilities, evaluates client preferences and determines an appropriate representation to return. Since the server determines the outcome of this process, this technique is called *server-driven negotiation*.

For example, consider a client with the following preferences:

- The client prefers a French representation but can accept English.
- The client can process an Atom-formatted representation with media type `application/atom+xml`, can accept an XML-formatted representation with media type `application/xml` representation, but cannot accept anything else.
- The client knows how to process `gzip`-compressed representations.

The client can indicate these preferences with the following request headers:

```
# Request headers
Accept: application/atom+xml;q=1.0, application/xml;q=0.6, */*;q=0.0
Accept-Language: fr;q=1.0, en;q=0.5
Accept-Encoding: gzip
```

In these headers, the part after the semicolon is the q parameter. The value of this header parameter is a floating-point number usually with one digit after the decimal, although HTTP 1.1 allows using up to three digits after the decimal. Clients can use this parameter to indicate the relative preference of each option in a range of 0.0 (i.e., unacceptable) to 1.0 (i.e., most preferred). For instance, the previous `Accept` header indicates that the client cannot process anything other than Atom- and XML-formatted representations. The default value of the q parameter is 1.0.

 Not all servers support q parameters. Such servers may select the first supported media type from the `Accept` header.

Note that servers may not always support content negotiation completely or correctly. Clients should be prepared to receive a representation that does not meet the `Accept-*` headers. Recipe 3.2 discusses how to use entity headers such as `Content-Type` to determine how to process response representations.

Accept-* headers such as Accept and Accept-Language express ranges of media types, languages, etc.

Content-* headers, on the other hand, express a specific media type, language, etc.

7.2 How to Implement Media Type Negotiation

Whether the server supports one media type or several media types for any resource, correctly interpreting the Accept header is necessary to improve interoperability.

Problem

You want to know how to decide which media type to use for a representation in a response.

Solution

If the request has no Accept header, return a representation using the default format for the requested resource.

If the request has an Accept header, parse the header and sort the values of media types by the q parameters in descending order. Then select a media type from the list that the server supports. Include a Vary response header as described in Recipe 7.6.

If the server does not support any of the media types in this list, use Recipe 7.7 to determine an appropriate response.

Discussion

Consider this Accept header:

```
Accept: application/atom+xml;q=1.0, application/xml;q=0.6, text/html
```

This includes two media types with different q parameter values and a third media type with no q parameter value. Since the default value of the q parameter is 1.0, this header is equivalent to the following:

```
Accept: application/atom+xml;q=1.0, application/xml;q=0.6, text/html;q=1.0
```

From such a header, the server's first choice should be either application/atom+xml or text/html, and the second choice should be application/xml. If the server supports all three, it can return either Atom- or HTML-formatted representations. Given the value of the Accept header, either choice should be acceptable to the client:

```
# Response
HTTP/1.1 200 OK
Content-Type: application/atom+xml;charset=UTF-8

... representation ...
```

Although implementing this logic is simple, certain situations can break interoperability with clients. Consider the following.

In the beginning, assume that the server supports `application/xml` for all its representations. Since it is not serving any other representation, it chooses to ignore the `Accept` header and returns XML-formatted representations for all requests. Then, because of client demand, it adds support for `application/json` and decides to rely on the value of the `Accept` header. This results in the following:

```
# Original request
GET /movie/gone_with_the_wind HTTP/1.1
Host: www.example.org
Accept: application/json

# Server can only support XML
HTTP/1.1 200 OK
Content-Type: application/xml;charset=UTF-8

... xml ...

# Same request now
GET /movie/gone_with_the_wind HTTP/1.1
Host: www.example.org
Accept: application/json

# Response - server supports JSON as well as XML
HTTP/1.1 200 OK
Content-Type: application/json

... json ...
```

This breaks compatibility because a working client no longer works. When you are faced with such situations, serve the new representation using a new URI. Here is an example:

```
# Same request now
GET /movie/gone_with_the_wind?format=json HTTP/1.1
Host: www.example.org
Accept: application/json

HTTP/1.1 200 OK
Content-Type: application/json

... json ...
```

This technique is called *agent-driven negotiation*. See Recipe 7.8.

7.3 How to Implement Language Negotiation

HTTP's support for language negotiation can help with limited localization support for web services. Language selection is just one aspect of localization. Apart from translation of human-readable text in representations, localization often involves the regional and cultural adaptation of information.

Problem

You want to know how to decide the language to use for the human-readable text in a representation.

Solution

If the request has no `Accept-Language` header, return a representation with all human-readable text in a default language.

If the request has an `Accept-Language` header, parse the header, sort the media types by the q parameters, and select the first language in the list that the server can support. Include a `Vary` response header as described in Recipe 7.6.

If the server does not support any languages in the list and the `Accept-Language` header does not contain `*; q=0.0`, use a default language for that resource.

Discussion

The protocol for language negotiation is similar to media type negotiation. The client expresses its intent by supplying an `Accept-Language` header with acceptable languages and their q header parameter values, and the server decides which one to use for the response.

```
# Request
GET /movie/gone_with_the_wind HTTP/1.1
Host: www.example.org
Accept-Language: en,en-US,fr;q=0.6

# Response
HTTP/1.1 200 OK
Content-Type: application/xml;charset=UTF-8
Content-Language: en
Vary: Accept-Language

<movie>
  <title>Gone with the Wind</title>
  <year>1936</year>
  ...
</movie>
```

This approach is best suited when representations in different languages differ only in terms of the language used for any human-readable text in the representation, as in the following representation:

```
# Request
GET /movie/gone_with_the_wind HTTP/1.1
Host: www.example.org
Accept-Language: en,en-US,fr;q=0.6
```

```
# Response
HTTP/1.1 200 OK
Content-Type: application/xml;charset=UTF-8
Content-Language: fr
Vary: en

<movie>
  <title>Autant en emporte le vent</title>
  <year>1936</year>
  ...
</movie>
```

If the differences between representations are more significant, use other means of localization such as the client's IP address or region/language-specific URIs.

7.4 How to Implement Character Encoding Negotiation

If the client asks (via the Accept-Charset header) for textual representations to be encoded in a particular character encoding, encoding the response using that encoding promotes interoperability.

Problem

You want to know what character encoding to use for textual representations in responses.

Solution

If the request has no Accept-Charset header, return a representation using UTF-8 encoding.

If the request has an Accept-Charset header, parse the header, sort the character sets by the q parameters, and select the character set that the server can support for encoding.

If the server does not support any requested character sets and the Accept-Charset header does not contain *; q=0.0, return a representation using UTF-8 encoding.

In all these cases, if the media type is textual and allows a charset parameter, include the charset parameter in the Content-Type header indicating the character encoding that the server used. Also include a Vary response header as described in Recipe 7.6.

Discussion

Most platforms and programming languages support UTF-8. UTF-8 is the default encoding for both application/xml and application/json media types. Always use UTF-8 encoding unless the client asks for a different encoding.

Avoid using `text/xml` since its default encoding is `US-ASCII`.

7.5 How to Support Compression

Servers can optionally serve compressed representations to clients using encodings such as `gzip`, `deflate`, or `compress`. In HTTP, this technique is generally called *content encoding*.

Problem

You want to know when to enable compression of representations.

Solution

If the server is capable of compressing-response body, select the compression technique from the `Accept-Encoding` header. Include a `Vary` response header as described in Recipe 7.6. If no encoding in this header matches the server's supported encodings, ignore this header. The q parameter processing is similar to other `Accept-*` headers.

If the request has no `Accept-Encoding` header, do not compress representations.

Discussion

Clients may or may not support content encodings such as `gzip` or `deflate`. It is important to return compressed responses only when the client sends an `Accept-Encoding` header with a compression format that the server supports. Here is an example:

```
# Request
GET /movie/gone_with_the_wind HTTP/1.1
Host: www.example.org
Accept-Encoding: gzip

# Response
HTTP/1.1 200 OK
Content-Type: application/xml;charset=UTF-8
Content-Encoding: gzip
Vary: Accept-Encoding

... gzipped bytes ...
```

In most cases, you should be able to configure your HTTP servers to automatically apply a given encoding for responses. For instance, placing the following line in your Apache HTTP server configuration tells the server to apply `deflate` encoding to all `application/xml` representations:

```
AddOutputFilterByType DEFLATE application/xml
```

7.6 When and How to Send the Vary Header

When a server uses content negotiation to select a representation, the same URI can yield different representations based on `Accept-*` headers. The `Vary` header tells clients which request headers the server used when selecting a representation.

Problem

You want to know how to use the `Vary` header to indicate clients how the server chose a particular representation.

Solution

Include a `Vary` header whenever multiple representations are available for a resource. The value of this header is a comma-separated list of request headers the server uses when choosing a representation. If the server uses information other than the headers in the request, such as the client's IP address, time of the day, user personalization, etc., include a `Vary` header with a value of *.

Discussion

The server can use the `Vary` header to inform clients of the results of server-driven content negotiation. The value of the `Vary` header is a set of request headers and not response headers. For instance, consider the following sequences of requests and responses:

```
# Request for English representation
GET /status HTTP/1.1
Host: www.example.org
Accept-Language: en;q=1.0,*/*;q=0.0

# Response
HTTP/1.1 200 OK
Content-Language: en
Vary: Accept-Language

...

# Request for German representation
GET /status HTTP/1.1
Host: www.example.org
Accept-Language: de;q=1.0,*/*;q=0.0

# Response
HTTP/1.1 200 OK
Content-Language: de
Vary: Accept-Language

...

# Request for French representation
```

```
GET /status HTTP/1.1
Host: www.example.org
Accept-Language: fr;q=1.0,*/*;q=0.0

# Response
HTTP/1.1 200 OK
Content-Language: fr
Vary: Accept-Language
```

Although the request URI is the same, clients and intermediaries can differentiate between the responses by looking at the value of the request headers listed in Vary header. Caches use this header as part of cache keys to maintain variants of a resource. Clients can use this information to know the criteria the server used for content negotiation.

7.7 How to Handle Negotiation Failures

Servers are free to serve any available representation for a given resource. However, clients may not be able to handle arbitrary media types. Except for browsers, most HTTP clients can deal with only one or two formats.

Problem

You want to know whether to serve a default representation, or return an error, when the server is unable to serve a representation preferred by the client.

Solution

When the server cannot serve a representation that meets the client's preferences and if the client explicitly included a */*;q=0.0, return status code 406 (Not Acceptable) with the body of the representation containing the list of representations.

If the server is unable to support requested Accept-Encoding values, serve the representation without applying any content encoding.

Discussion

Here is an example of a request from a client that can process no media type except application/json:

```
# Request
GET /user/001/followers HTTP/1.1
Accept: application/json,*/*;q=0.0 ❶

# Response
406 Not Acceptable ❷
Content-Type: application/json
Link: <http://www.example.org/errors/mediatypes.html>;rel="help" ❸

{
    "message" : "This server does not support JSON. See help for alternatives."
}
```

❶ The client cannot process anything other than JSON.

❷ The server does not support JSON.

❸ A link with help on supported formats.

In this example, the server recognizes JSON but is unable to serve a representation of the resource in that format. Since the client request includes a q=0.0 for every other media type except application/json, a failure is acceptable for the client.

Note that the server uses a JSON-formatted representation for the error message. It is quite reasonable for the server to implement error messages in commonly used formats. If not, return the error message in human-readable HTML format.

```
# Request
GET /user/001/followers HTTP/1.1
Accept: application/json,*/*;q=0.0

# Response
406 Not Acceptable
Content-Type: text/html;charset=UTF-8
Link: <http://www.example.org/errors/mediatypes.html>;rel="help"

<html>
  <head>
    <title>JSON Not Supported</title>
  </head>
  <body>
    <p>This server does not support JSON. See <a
    href="http://www.example.org/errors/mediatypes.html">help</a> for alternatives.</p>
  </body>
</html>
```

7.8 How to Use Agent-Driven Content Negotiation

Although server-driven negotiation is built into HTTP, it has limitations:

- Content negotiation does not include elements such as currency units, distance units, date formats, and other regional flavors for any human-readable text in representations. For instance, you cannot always determine currency and date formats based on the language preference.

- In some cases, because of complex localization requirements, the server may decide to maintain different resources for different locales.

- Common web browsers use a broad range of media types for the Accept headers. For instance, some installations of the Firefox browser send Accept: text/html, application/xhtml+xml,application/xml;q=0.9,*/*;q=0.8. This makes it difficult to view content-negotiated representations in browsers.

For these, use agent-driven negotiation. Agent-driven negotiation is useful when the client cannot communicate its preferences using Accept-* headers.

Problem

You want to know how to implement agent-driven negotiation.

Solution

Provide a URI for each representation.

Discussion

Agent-driven negotiation simply means providing a distinct URI for each variant and allowing the client to use that URI to select the desired representation. In agent-driven negotiation, client uses out-of-band information from the server to determine which URI to use. If the representation exists, the server returns it. If it does not, it returns a 404 (Not Found) response code.

> Since the client determines the outcome of this process, this technique is called *agent-driven negotiation*. The term *agent* refers to user agents, and the most common user agents are browsers.

Although it is possible to implement agent-driven negotiation for all Accept-* headers, in practice it is most commonly used for media types and languages.

There are several ways for the server to assign URIs for each language and media type of a resource. Some commonly used approaches include the following:

Query parameters

Append the language and or media type as query parameters to a base URI, with the values of these query parameters using a shorthand notation for media types. Examples include format for language negotiation and lang to support media type negotiation. Here are some examples:

```
http://www.example.org/status?format=json
http://www.example.org/status?format=xml
http://www.example.org/status?format=csv
```

URI extensions

Append a dot (the . character), and shorthand media type to a base URI. Examples include status.atom for an application/atom+xml representation and status.json for an application/json representation.

Subdomains

Create subdomains to support language-specific representations. Examples include en.wikipedia.org to serve English-language representations of Wikipedia entries and de.wikipedia.org to serve German-language representations of Wikipedia entries.

When using agent-driven negotiation, the server can choose to advertise alternatives using links with the `alternate` link relation type. Here is an example:

```
<status xmlns:atom="http://www.w3.org/2005/Atom">
  <atom:link rel="self" href="http://www.example.org/status?format=xml&lang=en"/> ❶
  <atom:link rel="alternate" type="application/json"
        href="http://www.example.org/status?format=json&lang=fr"/> ❷
  ...
</status>
```

❶ A link to the resource

❷ A link to a variant

7.9 When to Support Server-Driven Negotiation

Content negotiation is not always appropriate. Although some popular web services and web service frameworks support general-purpose formats such as XML, JSON, and Atom for every resource, consider the cost of supporting multiple formats in your web services.

Problem

You want to know if server-driven negotiation is right for your web service.

Solution

Support multiple variants when only your clients need them or whether each variant contains the same information. If the information content is different, use a distinct URI for each.

Discussion

Content negotiation is only cheap to implement when your development framework supports it. In other cases, content negotiation takes time and effort to implement, test, and manage. Most client applications can deal only with a single format. In such cases, supporting multiple formats may be unnecessary. Before deciding to support multiple representations for each resource, consider the following:

- In some cases, the application flow may be different for each representation format. This is particularly true for HTML representations. User interface constraints may require HTML representations to follow a different application flow from the one used for, say, XML-formatted representations. In this case, server-driven negotiation for both HTML and XML formats is not realistic.

- Unambiguously returning a variant based on the `Accept` header with several media types with different q is not trivial. Not all development frameworks support this.

- Language negotiation may be simplistic for global services. In some cases, legal and business requirements may be regional, and agent-driven negotiation may be the best approach.
- Caches may not handle content-negotiated responses well. Some caches may ignore or limit the number of variants they store for any given resource.

Given these, carefully consider the requirements before supporting server-driven content negotiation in your server applications.

## CHAPTER 8

Queries

Querying for information is a common application of the HTTP method GET. Queries usually involve three components. They are filtering, sorting, and projections. *Filtering* is the process of selecting a subset of entities based on some filter criteria. *Sorting* influences how the server arranges the results in the response. Finally, a *projection* is the process of selecting certain fields in each entity to be included in the results. For example, a query submitted to a movies server may involve filtering the movies by genre, then sorting the movies by their release dates in reverse chronological order, but then selecting only the title, the year, and a brief description of each movie in the response to the client.

Query design is relatively simple as far as URIs and representations are concerned. For clients to run queries, the server's responsibilities include designing URIs to support filtering, sorting, and projections; designing representations; and setting appropriate caching headers. This chapter deals with such protocol-visible aspects of query design, covering the following recipes:

Recipe 8.1, "How to Design URIs for Queries"
    This recipe shows how to design URIs for queries.

Recipe 8.2, "How to Design Query Responses"
    This recipe shows how to model query results as representations of collection resources.

Recipe 8.3, "How to Support Query Requests with Large Inputs"
    Use this recipe to learn how to process queries with large inputs.

Recipe 8.4, "How to Store Queries"
    Use this recipe to implement stored queries.

8.1 How to Design URIs for Queries

Problem

You want to know how to design URIs to support queries.

Solution

Use query parameters to let clients specify filter conditions, sort fields, and projections. Treat the query parameters as optional with sensible defaults. To support commonly used queries, use predefined named queries. Document the purpose of each parameter using Recipe 14.1.

Discussion

Using query parameters to design queries is a common convention. Depending on your use cases, you may need to support query parameters for one or all of the following:

- To select data from among the resources available
- To specify sort criteria
- To list the fields of resources to be included in the response

For instance, consider a URI that identifies reviews of a book.

```
http://www.example.org/book/978-0374292881/reviews
```

When a client submits a GET request, the server returns a collection of reviews. The server may apply a default query for this URI and treat it as equivalent to the following:

```
http://www.example.org/book/978-0374292881/reviews?sortbyDesc=created&limit=5
```

This URI includes a query to return the latest five reviews sorted in reverse chronological order of the creation date of each review. There are several types of queries possible for this example:

```
# Select all reviews where the author of the review contains "Jane"
http://www.example.org/book/978-0374292881/reviews?author=Jane

# Select all 5-star-rated reviews
http://www.example.org/book/978-0374292881/reviews?rating=5

# Select all reviews posted after August 15, 2009
http://www.example.org/book/978-0374292881/reviews?after=2009-08-15

# Select all reviews posted after August 15, 2009, and sort the
# results in the ascending order by date posted
http://www.example.org/book/978-0374292881/reviews?after=2009-08-15&sortbyAsc=date
```

All these URIs include filter and sort conditions as query parameters. You can further refine the output of this query, say, to return only the title of each review:

```
http://www.example.org/book/978-0374292881/reviews?after=2009-08-15&
    sortbyAsc=date&fields=title
```

In this URI, the query parameter `fields` is used to specify a projection. Alternatively, if most clients only need review summaries sorted in reverse chronological order of the creation date, the server can predefine the query to include a projection for the title, the rating, and a link for each review:

```
http://www.example.org/book/978-0374292881/reviews?after=2009-08-15&
    view=summary
```

The value of the parameter `view` is a predefined query. Predefined queries give you a chance to optimize the server implementation to serve commonly used queries and guarantee faster response times. For instance, in this example, the server can cache review summaries of the most popular books in memory.

 Consider predefined queries for commonly used queries.

Finally, you can extend queries to let clients run ad hoc queries. Here are some examples:

```
# Get all movies with titles containing "war" released after the year 2000
#    with at least 100 comments. Sort the results by year
http://www.example.org/movies$contains('war')$compare(year>2000)
    $compare(count(comments)>100)?$sortby=year

# Use the value of the query parameter as part of a SQL WHERE clause
http://www.example.org/movies?query=
    '.title%20like%20'war'%20and%20year%20%3E%202000%20order%20by%20year'

# Use an XPath expression to select movie titles
http://www.example.org/movies[year>2000&genre='war']/title
```

Such queries are flexible for clients to use since clients can treat servers as databases. However, they may reduce the ability for the server to optimize the data storage and backend caching, thereby reducing performance. These queries may also tightly couple the URIs to how data is stored.

 Avoid ad hoc queries that use general-purpose query languages such as SQL or XPath.

Some servers use HTTP range requests for queries. Here is an example:

```
# Request
GET /book/978-0374292881/reviews HTTP/1.1
Host: www.example.org
Range: query:after=2009-08-15&sortbyAsc=date
```

```
# Request
GET /report/June2009 HTTP/1.1
Host: www.example.org
Range: xpath://title
```

However, HTTP does not define range requests for anything other than byte ranges, as in the following example:

```
# Request to fetch a part of the representation
GET /docs/reportsJune2009.pdf HTTP/1.1
Host: www.example.org
Accept: application/pdf
Range: bytes=10241-20480

# Response
HTTP/1.1 206 Partial Content
Content-Type: application/pdf
Content-Range: bytes=102341-20480

...
```

Caches may ignore range requests when used for anything other than byte ranges. In contrast, query parameters are simpler to implement and support.

 Avoid range requests for implementing queries.

8.2 How to Design Query Responses

This recipe discusses how to use a collection as a resource for implementing queries.

Problem

You want to know how to design representations for query responses.

Solution

Design the response of a query as a representation of a collection resource. See Recipe 3.7 to learn how to design collection representations. Set the appropriate expiration caching headers as described in Recipe 9.1.

If the query does not match any resources, return an empty collection.

Discussion

A collection is a convenient way to model representations of queries. Here is the result of a query to get, at most, five reviews of a book posted after August 15, 2009, sorted in reverse chronological order of the creation date of each review:

```
# Request
GET /book/978-0374292881/reviews?after=2009-08-15&sortbyDesc=created&limit=5 HTTP/1.1
Host: www.example.org

# Response
HTTP/1.1 200 OK
Content-Type: application/xml;charset=UTF-8
Cache-Control: max-age=86400
Content-Language: en

<reviews total="23" ❶ xmlns:atom="http://www.w3.org/2005/Atom"
  xml:base="http://www.example.org/book/978-0374292881">
  <atom:link rel="self"
    href="/reviews?after=2009-08-15&sortbyDesc=created&limit=5"/> ❷
  <atom:link rel="next"
    href="/reviews?after=2009-08-15&sortbyDesc=created&limit=5&start=5"/> ❸
  <review>
    <atom:link rel="self" href="/book/review/03213"/>
    <created>2007-08-02</created>
    <title>Oversimplified?</title>
    <body>...</body>
  </review>

  <!-- four more -->
  ...
</reviews>
```

❶ Total number of reviews that match the query

❷ Link to a URI that returns the first five reviews that match the query

❸ Link to a URI that returns the next five reviews that match the query

This is a representation containing five reviews and a link to the next five reviews, designed as per Recipe 3.7. You can let clients refine the output of this query, say, to return only the links to all reviews:

```
# Request
GET /book/978-0374292881/reviews?after=2009-08-15&sortbyDesc=created&limit=5&
    fields=link HTTP/1.1
Host: www.example.org

# Response
HTTP/1.1 200 OK
Content-Type: application/xml;charset=UTF-8
Content-Language: en

<reviews total="23" xmlns:atom="http://www.w3.org/2005/Atom"
  xml:base="http://www.example.org/book/978-0374292881">
  <atom:link rel="self" href="/reviews?after=2009-08-15&sortbyAsc=date"/>
  <atom:link rel="next" href="/reviews?after=2009-08-15&sortbyAsc=date&next=5"/>
  <atom:link rel="http://www.example.org/rels/review" href="/book/review/03213"/>
  <atom:link rel="http://www.example.org/rels/review" href="/book/review/03493"/>
  <atom:link rel="http://www.example.org/rels/review" href="/book/review/04501"/>
  <atom:link rel="http://www.example.org/rels/review" href="/book/review/04731"/>
```

```
    <atom:link rel="http://www.example.org/rels/review" href="/book/review/04934"/>
  </reviews>
```

In this representation, the server uses an extended link relation type to identify that the link's URI is a review. The client can obtain the review representation using the URI.

Each permutation and combination of query parameters results in a different URI. This may reduce cache efficiency since, at the protocol level, each URI corresponds to a different resource. To reduce the number of URIs possible, consider using predefined queries as described in the previous recipe.

8.3 How to Support Query Requests with Large Inputs

Although HTTP does not pose any limit on the length of URIs, some implementations do. Browsers like Internet Explorer limit the length to 2,083 characters. The Apache web server, by default, limits the length of the request line (e.g. GET /jobs?params..... HTTP/1.1) to 8,190 bytes (see the documentation of Apache's LimitRequestLine directive). Microsoft's Internet Information Services (IIS) uses a default value of 16,384 for the cumulative number of bytes used to represent the request line and headers (see the documentation of IIS's MaxClientRequestBuffer). Squid limits URIs to 8,192 bytes. Such limits usually exist for security reasons, such as circumventing buffer overruns. These limits may prevent you from encoding a large number of filter conditions into URIs.

Problem

You want to know how to support queries involving large numbers of query parameters that, when included URIs, cause URIs to exceed the typical length restrictions posed by various HTTP-level software.

Solution

Use HTTP POST to support large queries.

Discussion

Using POST for queries weakens HTTP's uniform interface since GET is defined for safe and idempotent information retrieval. However, this is a necessary trade-off to address a practical limitation. For instance, consider a server that lets clients search for job postings based on the location of the job, qualifications, experience level, type of the job, keywords, company names, etc. This list of conditions is long. When a client encodes those conditions into a URI via query parameters, the length of the URI or the request line may exceed the limits mentioned previously. Use POST to support such queries:

```
# Request
POST /jobs HTTP/1.1
```

```
Host: www.example.org
Content-Type: application/x-www-form-urlencoded

keywords=web,ajax,php&industry=software&experience=5&...
```

The query is encoded as an `application/x-www-form-urlencoded` string in the body of this request. The server responds with a representation of the search results:

```
# Response
HTTP/1.1 200 OK
Content-Type: application/xml;charset=UTF-8

<postings xmlns:atom="http://www.w3.org/2005/Atom" xml:base="http://www.example.org">
  <posting>
    <atom:link rel="self" href="/job/499"/>
    ...
  </posting>
  <posting>
    <atom:link rel="self" href="/job/1863"/>
    ...
  </posting>
  ...
</postings>
```

Given that this operation is safe and idempotent, using the `POST` method is a misuse of HTTP's uniform interface. A consequence of this implementation is a loss of cacheability.

 Adding a `Cache-Control` or `Expires` header does not help since caches treat responses of the `POST` method as not cacheable.

Another limitation of this technique is latency during pagination. To browse the search results, the client needs to repeat the `POST` request:

```
# Request to get the results starting from 10
POST /jobs HTTP/1.1
Host: www.example.org
Content-Type: application/x-www-form-urlencoded

start=10&amp;keywords=web,ajax,php&amp;industry=software&amp;experience=5&amp;...

# Response
HTTP/1.1 200 OK
Content-Type: application/xml;charset=UTF-8

<postings xmlns:atom="http://www.w3.org/2005/Atom" xml:base="http://www.example.org">
  <posting>
    <atom:link rel="self" href="/job/5323"/>
    ...
  </posting>
  <posting>
    <atom:link rel="self" href="/job/435"/>
```

```
      ...
   </posting>
   ...
</postings>
```

Since these results are not cacheable, any client-side user interface controls to browse the results back and forward cause the server, and not a cache, to respond to each request. This introduces extra latency for the client and reduced scalability for the server. If such queries are frequently needed in your web service, use Recipe 8.4 to store queries on the server.

8.4 How to Store Queries

Stored queries can help make queries submitted using POST cacheable. Recipe 8.3 uses POST to process queries that have a large number of parameters. This recipe shows you how to store those queries on the server so that clients can use GET to execute stored queries.

Problem

You want to know to how to store large query requests so that clients can use GET to execute them.

Solution

When a client makes a query request using POST, create a new resource whose state contains the query criteria. Return response code 201 (Created) with a Location header referring to a resource created. Implement a GET request for the new resource such that it returns query results.

If the same or another client repeats the same query request using POST, find the resource that matches the request, and redirect the client to the URI of that resource.

Discussion

You can make query results cacheable by storing the query criteria permanently in a data store, and you can assign a URI for stored query. The client can use this URI to repeat the query. By transforming POST-based queries into GET requests for resources, caches can serve cached representations of query results to clients.

In response to the query request, the server stores the query and assigns the URI http://www.example.org/query/1 to it:

```
# Request
POST /jobs HTTP/1.1
Host: www.example.org
Content-Type: application/x-www-form-urlencoded

keywords=web,ajax,php&amp;industry=software&amp;experience=5&amp;...
```

```
# Response
HTTP/1.1 201 Created
Content-Type: application/xml;charset=UTF-8
Location: http://www.example.org/query/1
Content-Length: 0
```

The client can use the created resource to fetch query results:

```
# Request
GET /query/1 HTTP/1.1
Host: www.example.org
```

```
# Response
HTTP/1.1 200 OK
Content-Type: application/xml;charset=UTF-8
Date: Wed, 28 Oct 2009 07:22:34 GMT
Cache-Control: max-age:3600
Expires: Wed, 28 Oct 2009 08:22:34 GMT

<postings xmlns:atom="http://www.w3.org/2005/Atom" xml:base="http://www.example.org">
  <posting>
    <atom:link rel="self" href="/job/499"/>
    ...
  </posting>
  <posting>
    <atom:link rel="self" href="/job/863"/>
    ...
  </posting>
  ...
</postings>
```

Moreover, since the query is stored, the server can support the pagination of query results via GET, and not through POST as is done in Recipe 8.3:

```
# Request
GET /query/1?start=10 HTTP/1.1
Host: www.example.org
```

Stored queries thus compensate for some of the limitations of using POST for queries. The downside is having to permanently store queries as resources. Furthermore, unless the possible number of queries is small, the server may end up accumulating a large number of less frequently used queries that may require frequent cleanup.

 Also note that making queries cacheable does not guarantee that the results will be served from the cache in the future. If the possible number of such queries is high, since each URI calls for a different cached copy of the response, the cache hit ratio will be low. The cache may fill up quickly, and it may discard less frequently used URIs.

## CHAPTER 9

Web Caching

Caching is one of the most useful features built on top of HTTP's uniform interface. You can take advantage of caching to reduce end user perceived latency, to increase reliability, to reduce bandwidth usage and cost, and to reduce server load. Caches can be anywhere. They can be in the server network, content delivery networks (CDNs), or in the client network (usually called *forward proxies*).

It is common to use the word *cache* to refer to either an object cache such as memcached (*http://memcached.org/*) or HTTP caches such as Squid (*http://www.squid-cache.org/*) or Traffic Server (*http://incubator.apache.org/projects/trafficserver.html*). Both of these kinds of caches improve performance and have key roles to play in the overall web service deployment architecture. But there is an important difference between these two. HTTP caches such as Squid do not require clients and servers to call any special programming API to manage data in the cache. This is not the case with object caches. For instance, in order to use memcached, you must use memcached's programming API to store, retrieve, and delete objects. HTTP caches are based on the same uniform interface that clients and servers use. Therefore, as long as you are using HTTP as defined, you should be able to add a caching layer without making code changes.

 Since a cache can be both an HTTP client and a server, in caching-related discussions, the term *origin server* is used to differentiate between caching servers and the servers that host your server code.

Here is the list of recipes discussed in this chapter:

Recipe 9.1, "How to Set Expiration Caching Headers"
Expiration caching headers control if and how long a cache can serve a cached copy of a representation to its clients. Use this recipe to learn how to set these headers.

Recipe 9.2, "When to Set Expiration Caching Headers"
Only certain responses in HTTP are cacheable. Use this recipe to determine when to set expiration caching headers.

9.1 How to Set Expiration Caching Headers

Caches operate efficiently when they can serve as many responses as possible without contacting the origin server. Expiration caching is designed to reduce the number of requests received by the origin server as well as reduce the bandwidth used by your application.

Expiration caching is based on `Cache-Control` and `Expires` headers. These headers instruct clients and caches to keep a copy of the representation returned by the server for a specific length of time. Caches can fulfill any subsequent requests within or even beyond that time window by serving a cached copy of the representation without contacting the origin server.

Problem

You want to know how to enable caching for your resource representations.

Solution

Based on the frequency of updates, determine a time period during which caches can serve a representation. This time period is the *freshness lifetime*. After this time, caches will consider cached representation stale.

When serving a representation, include a `Cache-Control` header with a `max-age` value (in seconds) equal to the freshness lifetime. The `Cache-Control` header is an HTTP 1.1 header. To support legacy HTTP 1.0 caches, also include an `Expires` header with the expiration date-time. The expiration time is a time at which the server generated the representation plus the freshness lifetime. Also include a `Date` header with a date-time of the time at which the server returned the response. Including this header helps clients compute the freshness lifetime as the difference between the values of the `Expires` and `Date` headers.

If you determine that caches must not serve cached copies, add a `Cache-Control` header with the value `no-cache`. In this case, also add a `Pragma: no-cache` header to support legacy HTTP 1.0 caches.

See the following list for `Cache-Control` directives and their applicability:

public

> This is the default. You can also use this directive when the request is authenticated but you still want to allow shared caches to serve cached responses.

private

> Use this directive when the response is private to the client or the user. When this directive is present, any client-side cache (e.g., the browser cache or a forward proxy) can cache the representation, but shared caches such as those at the server or along the network must not cache it.
>
> Add this directive when serving representations based on client or user authentication.

no-cache and no-store

> Add these directives to prevent any cache from storing or serving a cached response.

max-age

> Use the freshness lifetime in seconds as the value of this directive.

s-maxage

> This directive is similar to max-age but is meant only for shared caches. When an origin server sets both a max-age and s-maxage directive, caches use the s-maxage header. In practice, setting a max-age directive alone is sufficient.

must-revalidate

> Use this directive to require caches to check the origin server before serving stale representations.

proxy-revalidate

> This directive is similar to the must-revalidate directive except that it applies only to shared caches.

Discussion

A server can control expiration caching via two HTTP headers: the Expires (HTTP 1.0) header and the Cache-Control (HTTP 1.1) header. Here is an example that instructs a cache to serve the representation for an hour:

```
# Response
HTTP/1.1 200 OK
Date: Sun, 09 Aug 2009 00:56:14 GMT  ❶
Last-Modified: Sun, 09 Aug 2009 00:56:14 GMT ❷
Expires: Sun, 09 Aug 2009 01:56:14 GMT ❸
Cache-Control: max-age=3600,must-revalidate ❹
Content-Type: application/xml; charset=UTF-8

...
```

❶ The date-time value the server generated the response

❷ The date-time value the representation was last modified by the server

❸ Expiration date-time value

❹ Expiration lifetime and other directives

This message has a `Cache-Control` header with the `max-age` directive set to 3600 seconds. Also note the `Expires` and `Date` headers. The difference between the values of these headers is 3600 seconds. After one hour, because of the presence of the `must-revali date` directive, caches will make a conditional request to the server to revalidate the response before serving it again to clients (see Recipe 10.3).

When a client makes another request for the same resource before the expiry of one hour, provided the cache still has a copy of the response, it will fulfill the request by serving a stored copy of the representation without contacting the origin server:

```
# First request
GET /person/joe HTTP/1.1
Host: www.example.org

# First response
HTTP/1.1 200 OK
Date: Sun, 09 Aug 2009 00:44:14 GMT
Last-Modified: Sun, 09 Aug 2009 00:40:14 GMT
Expires: Sun, 09 Aug 2009 01:44:14 GMT
Cache-Control: max-age=3600,must-revalidate

...

# Second request after 10 minutes
GET /person/joe HTTP/1.1
Host: www.example.org

# Second response - returned by cache
HTTP/1.1 200 OK
Date: Sun, 09 Aug 2009 00:54:14 GMT
Last-Modified: Sun, 09 Aug 2009 00:40:14 GMT
Expires: Sun, 09 Aug 2009 01:44:14 GMT
Cache-Control: max-age=3600,must-revalidate
Age: 600

...
```

The **Age** header in this response is added by a cache. It indicates how long ago the cache retrieved the representation from the origin server. By looking at this header in this response, the client can determine that it received a 10-minute-old copy. If the value of this header is greater than `max-age`, then the representation is stale.

The key to optimal expiration caching is calculating a reasonable freshness lifetime value for the resource representation. If you have historical information such as update logs for the representations, use them to establish a base lifetime. If you do not have such information, start with a reasonable guess, and adjust this value as you get more information. Usually that information comes in the form of discovering that a client is unable to see a recently updated representation.

Adding either no-cache or no-store directives will prevent any cache from serving cached responses. Do not use these unless you must. Usually using a small value of max-age as opposed to adding no-cache or no-store directives helps clients fetch cached copies for at least a short duration of time without compromising freshness severely.

Caches like Squid support two extension directives to the Cache-Control header. These are stale-if-error and stale-while-revalidate. Servers can use stale-if-error to tell caches that they can continue to serve a stale response until the specified time interval.

```
# Response
HTTP/1.1 200 OK
Cache-Control: max-age=3600, stale-if-error=600
```

...

In this case, the response becomes stale after an hour. But if the cache encounters errors while contacting the origin server after the expiry, it can continue to serve a stale response for 10 more minutes.

The following example illustrates stale-while-revalidate:

```
# Response
HTTP/1.1 200 OK
Cache-Control: max-age=3600, stale-while-revalidate=600
```

...

This extension allows the cache to revalidate the response asynchronously while serving a stale response for up to 10 minutes. See Recipe 10.3 to learn about revalidation.

9.2 When to Set Expiration Caching Headers

Not every response in HTTP is cacheable. HTTP specifies what is cacheable and what is not, and caches may only implement parts of the HTTP's caching protocol. This recipe lists what is cacheable and what is not.

Problem

You want to know when to include expiration caching headers on responses.

Solution

Set expiration caching headers for responses of GET and HEAD requests for all successful response codes. Although POST is cacheable, caches consider this method as noncacheable. You need not set expiration headers on other methods.

In addition to successful responses with the 200 (OK) response code, consider adding caching headers to the 3xx and 4xx response codes listed here. This will help reduce the amount of error-triggering traffic from clients. This is called *negative caching*.

- 300 (Multiple Choices)

  The representation with this status code may not change often. Making this response cacheable may reduce server load.

- 301 (Moved Permanently)

  Clients that store URIs in databases may not update them when the resource moves permanently. In such cases, caches can serve the redirect response without contacting the origin server.

- 400 (Bad Request)

  When the server returns this code, clients are not supposed to repeat the request. But some clients may because of software bugs or malintent.

- 403 (Forbidden)

  Add this if the server is permanently refusing to serve the resource.

- 404 (Not Found)

  The resource does not exist, and there is no need for the server to attempt to generate a representation only to fail.

- 405 (Method Not Allowed)

  Clients may repeat such requests because of software bugs in the client.

- 410 (Gone)

  The resource no longer exists, and hence the error response can be served by caches for as long as possible.

Discussion

As per HTTP 1.1, responses from the methods GET, HEAD, and POST are cacheable. Moreover, caches can store and serve any response to GET and HEAD requests unless you explicitly prevent this by using caching directives such as Cache-Control: no-cache. Even if you include caching headers, caches will not cache responses from POST requests.

Furthermore, when a client submits a HEAD request, most caches forward the request as a GET request to the origin server, store it if the response is cacheable, and then return a response to the client with no body:

```
# Request from the client
HEAD /person/joe HTTP/1.1
Host: www.example.org

# Request from the cache to the origin server
GET /person/joe HTTP.1.1
Host: www.example.org
```

```
# Response from the origin server to the cache
HTTP/1.1 200 OK
Cache-Control: max-age=3600
Date: Sun, 09 Aug 2009 00:56:14 GMT
Last-Modified: Sun, 09 Aug 2009 00:56:14 GMT
Expires: Sun, 09 Aug 2009 01:56:14 GMT

...body...

# Response from the cache to the client
HTTP/1.1 200 OK
Cache-Control: max-age=3600
Date: Sun, 09 Aug 2009 00:56:14 GMT
Last-Modified: Sun, 09 Aug 2009 00:56:14 GMT
Expires: Sun, 09 Aug 2009 01:56:14 GMT

...
```

Consequently, if you mark GET responses cacheable, caches will be able to respond to both GET and HEAD requests.

It may be worth noting that it is common for a cache to negative cache 404 (Not Found) and similar response status codes by assigning their own (usually short-term) freshness to these responses, even when the response from the origin has no explicit freshness information. The motivation for this is usually to handle error conditions quickly without contacting the origin server.

9.3 When and How to Use Expiration Headers in Clients

The previous two recipes discussed expiration caching headers from the server's point of view. This recipe discusses them from the client's point of view.

Problem

You want to know whether you must explicitly implement support for caching in your client.

Solution

Unless you are building a shrink-wrapped client application that users install and run, avoid implementing support for expiration caching within the client application. Instead, deploy a forward proxy cache in the client network, and avoid implementing your own caching layer in the client code.

Discussion

In general, clients should stay independent of expiration caching. In theory, it is possible to build client applications that support HTTP's caching protocol. For example, common browsers implement expiration caching and store representations in memory and/or the filesystem. In practice, building and maintaining a cache within a client application is a nontrivial task. It involves correctly implementing expiration directives such as `no-store`, `no-cache`, and `must-revalidate`, and honoring the `Vary` header. Placing a cache within the same runtime can introduce memory and CPU contention between the client application code and the caching code. This can make tuning the client more difficult. Moreover, any errors in implementation could lead to security vulnerabilities in the client.

In comparison, placing a forward proxy cache between your clients and servers is less complex. It does not involve any development activity, and you can have the benefits of a well-tested and robust caching infrastructure without building one. It also leaves room for expansion since you can set up a cluster of forward proxy servers to be shared by all clients.

 Avoid programmatic caching, even if your client library supports such an approach. Instead, delegate all caching activities to a forward proxy.

If both clients and servers are within the same network, a forward proxy may be unnecessary. The server can deploy a cache that can be shared by all clients. But if your clients are interacting with third-party web services in other networks, using a forward proxy can help reduce round-trip times between clients and servers.

9.4 How to Support Caching for Composite Resources

Problem

You want to know how to enable expiration caching for composite resources.

Solution

Base caching decisions on the part of the data that has the strongest freshness requirements. Set expiry headers based on how frequently such data changes.

Discussion

Implementing caching for composite resources is trickier than other kinds of resources. Such resources contain data that overlaps with other resources that may have differing expiration times. One example is a customer snapshot resource containing customer information, contact details, a summary of the latest purchase orders from the customer, and any pending requests for quotes. Since the server may have offered customer information, contact details, purchase orders, and quotes as resources, changes to any of those resources can render the composite resource stale.

Composites are a good example of a trade-off between convenience and cache efficiency. Composites are convenient for clients to use but costly for the server to serve fresh. In this example, there are three pieces of information, each of which may change at different frequencies and possibly via different sources:

- Customer, with name, contact information, and other details. This data may not change often. When serving this data as a resource, the server can set a large expiry interval (e.g., seven days).

- Collection of purchase orders for each customer. This data may change nightly as it gets imported from another backend system, and the server can set the Last-Modified header to the date-time at midnight and set an expiry of 24 hours.

- Collection of pending quotes for each customer. This data may be business critical, and the server may want to set an expiry of five minutes for this data.

Now assume that this composite is for use by an employee who manages customer relations, and that employee using a client needs to be aware of new quote requests within five minutes.

In this case, the choice for the server is obvious. Since the pending quote information is the most critical, the server can use that to guide the computation of the Last-Modified and ETag headers:

```
# Request
GET /snapshot/1234 HTTP/1.1
Host: www.example.org

# Response
HTTP/1.1 200 OK
Content-Type: application/xml;charset=UTF-8
Date: Sun, 25 Oct 2009 18:08:22 GMT
Last-Modified: Sun, 25 Oct 2009 16:54:10 GMT
Cache-Control: max-age=300
ETag: "81a540e69b4c29a80586284be0d3f296"

<snapshot xmlns:atom="http://www.w3.org/2005/Atom">
  <customer>
    <id>1234</id>
    <atom:link rel="self" href="http://www.example.org/customer/1234">
    <name>...</name>
    <address>...</address>
  </customer>
  <orders>
    <atom:link rel="http://www.example.org/rels/orders/recent"
          href="http://www.example.org/orders?customerid=1234&sortby=date_desc&"/>
    <order>
      <id>...</id>
      ...
    </order>
  </orders>
  <quotes>
    <atom:link rel="http://www.example.org/rels/quotes/recent"
```

```
        href="http://www.example.org/quotes?customerid=1234&sortby=date_desc&"/>
    ...
  </quotes>
</snapshot>
```

This example shows a trade-off. To guarantee that the user of this resource is able to see quotes within five minutes, the server chooses a shorter expiry interval for the entire representation. This is an inefficient use of the cache since even less frequently changing data will become stale after five minutes. A fix is to break the composite into three resources. But this will force the client to make multiple requests to fetch the data. In other words, the server needs to consider competing interests and make a trade-off. This situation can occur whenever the representation of a resource is coarse-grained, consisting of data that could potentially be offered as independent resources.

9.5 How to Keep Caches Fresh and Warm

One of the challenges of supporting caching is keeping caches fresh (up-to-date) and warm (nonempty) even when clients are not making requests. For instance, consider a photo-sharing service. After a user uploads photos, all caches will be empty for those photos, and hence the server will have to generate representations of photos. Similarly, when you introduce a new cache, it will be empty and will only fill up over time as clients start making requests. When a cache is fresh, it contains the latest possible representations. A warm cache avoids the cold-start problem. However, proactively keeping caches fresh and warm is outside the realm of HTTP. The techniques presented in this recipe are just hints.

Problem

You want to know how to ensure that caches have the fresh representations and are operating efficiently.

Solution

Whenever possible, synchronize expiry with the frequency of updates. When this is not possible, implement background processes to watch for database updates, and schedule unconditional GET requests (see Recipe 10.6) to refresh caches. Make sure to account for database replication delays while scheduling such requests.

If you are using Squid, use the HTTP cache channels extension to propagate resource updates to caches.

If you want to purge cached representations, check the documentation of your cache. For instance, Squid provides an extension to purge representations from the cache (see *http://wiki.squid-cache.org/SquidFaq/OperatingSquid*). Note that you can purge representations only from the caches that are in your control. There may be several downstream caches that may continue to hold cached copies.

Discussion

In HTTP, caches are required to invalidate representations when a client submits PUT, POST, or DELETE requests. Consequently, when a client submits a GET or HEAD request for the same resource, the cache will obtain a fresh representation from the origin server. Although this approach is not efficient (because the cache cannot stay warm), it guarantees that clients see fresh representations.

In reality, it is possible that your network has several applications that read and write to the same data stores. Write operations by any of those applications bypass HTTP caches and servers, thus leaving caches with stale representations. Consider the following examples:

- The server may have a nightly job that updates summary data tables to reflect the day's work. This update may happen directly at the database level and not be tied at all to any HTTP requests. However, you may have one or more of these resources in caches. Once the nightly update occurs, responses stored in the cache become stale.
- Widely distributed data stores may perform periodic replication throughout the day. Changes to data may not be reflected in all caches.
- Large applications may have one or more clients or services that use custom protocols to update data. Anyone using these services will be able to make changes to the database without using HTTP. Caches will not see resource updates.

In all these cases, you need a way to make sure any changes to the backend data stores are eventually reflected in caches. One way to solve this problem is to implement triggers to monitor all database updates. You can then run a scheduler to submit unconditional GET requests (see Recipe 10.6) through the cache to the server. By the time a client makes a request for those resources, their representations will be in the cache. For instance, you may schedule such a task every morning so that the previous day's updates will be in the cache when the business day starts.

Another possible solution is to take advantage of Cache-Control extensions such as HTTP cache channels. This extension defines a "channel" to which cache services can subscribe in order to receive notifications of resource updates. As of writing this book, the Squid web cache supports this extension. Here is an example of a server offering a URI to check for resource updates:

```
# Request
GET /orders HTTP/1.1
Host: www.example.org

# Response
HTTP/1.1 200 OK
Cache-Control: max-age=600,channel="http://www.example.org/channels/orders"
Date: Sun, 09 Aug 2009 00:56:14 GMT
Last-Modified: Sun, 09 Aug 2009 00:56:14 GMT
Expires: Sun, 09 Aug 2009 01:56:14 GMT
```

```
Content-Type: application/xml;charset=UTF-8

...
```

Caching services that understand this extension can use the URI `http://www.exam
ple.org/channels/orders` to subscribe to events published by the server. See *http://iet
freport.isoc.org/idref/draft-nottingham-http-cache-channels* for more details.

## CHAPTER 10

Conditional Requests

Conditional requests in HTTP help address two problems. For GET requests, conditional requests help clients and caches validate that a cached representation can still be considered fresh. For unsafe requests such as PUT, POST, and DELETE, conditional requests provide concurrency control.

Not supporting conditional GET requests reduces performance, but in the face of concurrency, not making unsafe requests such as POST, PUT, and DELETE conditional may affect the integrity of the application. In the absence of adequate concurrency control checks, the server is susceptible to "lost updates" and "stale deletes." When a client submits a request to modify or delete a resource, it does so based on what it thinks is the current state of the resource. But under concurrent conditions, the current state of the resource is not static. Either the server, through some backend means, or other clients may have updated or deleted the resource.

Concurrency control ensures the correct processing of data under concurrent operations by clients. There are two ways to implement concurrency control:

Pessimistic concurrency control
> In this model, the client gets a lock, obtains the current state of the resource, makes modifications, and then releases the lock. During this process, the server prevents other clients from acquiring a lock on the same resource. Relational databases operate in this manner.

Optimistic concurrency control
> In this model, the client first gets a token. Instead of obtaining a lock, the client attempts a write operation with the token included in the request. The operation succeeds if the token is still valid and fails otherwise.

HTTP, being a stateless application control, is designed for optimistic concurrency control. The essence of optimistic concurrency control is as follows:

1. The server gives a token to the client with each representation of the resource.

2. The server implements resource modifications such that these tokens change with every change to the resource. In other words, the server's version of tokens change whenever the state of the resource changes.

3. With each request to modify or delete a resource, the client supplies the token back to the server. A request containing such a token is called a *conditional request*.

4. The server checks whether the client-supplied token is still valid. If it is not, then there is a concurrency failure, and the server aborts the request.

Clients, servers, and caches can use a similar technique to implement conditional GET requests. Conditional GET requests can extend the life of stale representations. This chapter describes the following recipes to implement conditional requests:

Recipe 10.1, "How to Generate Last-Modified and ETag Headers"
Use this recipe to learn how to generate Last-Modified and ETag headers.

Recipe 10.2, "How to Implement Conditional GET Requests in Servers"
Use this recipe to learn how to implement support for conditional GET requests in servers.

Recipe 10.3, "How to Submit Conditional GET and HEAD Requests from Clients"
Use this recipe to learn how to make conditional GET requests from clients.

Recipe 10.4, "How to Implement Conditional PUT Requests in Servers"
Use this recipe to implement optimistic concurrency control in servers for PUT requests.

Recipe 10.5, "How to Implement Conditional DELETE Requests in Servers"
Use this recipe to implement optimistic concurrency control in servers for DELETE requests.

Recipe 10.6, "How to Make Unconditional GET Requests from Clients"
Use this recipe to learn how to retrieve fresh representations for development and debugging purposes.

Recipe 10.7, "How to Submit Conditional PUT and DELETE Requests from Clients"
Use this recipe to learn how to implement clients to supply If-Unmodified-Since and If-Match headers as tokens for concurrency control checks.

Recipe 10.8, "How to Make POST Requests Conditional"
Use this recipe to learn how servers can use links to exchange concurrency control tokens for POST requests.

Recipe 10.9, "How to Generate One-Time URIs"
Use this recipe to learn how to generate a URI that is conditional on the state of the resources it is used to modify or that can be used just once.

10.1 How to Generate Last-Modified and ETag Headers

Servers use `Last-Modified` and `ETag` response headers to drive conditional requests. Clients use the following request headers to make requests conditional:

- `If-Modified-Since` and `If-None-Match` for validating cached representations
- `If-Unmodified-Since` and `If-Match` as preconditions for concurrency control

If the names of these headers seem confusing, remember the intent. For GET requests, the client's intent is to ask for a fresh representation only *if* the representation was *modified since* the date-time specified and/or *if none* of the supplied entity tags *matches*.

For concurrency control, the intent is to request to perform an operation only *if* the representation was *not modified* since the date-time specified and/or *if* the supplied entity tags *match*.

Both these sets of request headers allow clients to supply "preconditions" with requests.

The efficacy of processing conditional requests depends on how quickly the server can validate the `Last-Modified` and `ETag` headers. This recipes discusses how to generate these headers.

Problem

You want to know how to generate `Last-Modified` and `ETag` headers to support caching and conditional requests for your resource representations.

Solution

If you have control on the data store used for storing resources, modify the storage schema for each resource to include a timestamp for the modified date-time and/or a sequence number to keep track of a version.

In the case of relational databases, use database triggers to automatically update these fields whenever the data is modified.

If you cannot modify the storage schema or if your data store does not permit maintaining timestamps or sequence numbers, use some function of the resource data to generate a value for the `ETag` header. Store this value and a timestamp in a separate table or data store such that the server does not need to reload the entire representation to compute this.

If the representation size is not large, use the representation body to generate an MD5 hash value for the `ETag`. Alternatively, use some field of the data that changes every time the resource is updated.

Make sure to use a different ETag value for each representation of the resource.

Discussion

Most web servers let you add ETag and Last-Modified headers automatically for static content. For application resources, you need to generate them programmatically.

Of these headers, Last-Modified has a one-second resolution and hence is considered a "weak" validator. An entity tag is a strong validator since its value can be changed every time the server modifies the representation. An entity tag is like an object's hash code. You can use entity tags to compare representations of a resource.

You do not need to use both Last-Modified and ETag headers to support conditional requests. Use either or both consistently to support conditional requests.

If you are designing a new web service, include a timestamp and a version counter in your data store. Most relational databases let you use some database-specific triggers to automatically update and increment these values whenever the data changes. This is usually the most efficient approach since the server does not need to load all the resource data from the database to check these values.

Some web frameworks autogenerate ETag headers after letting your code generate the representation. They do so by computing a hash of the entire representation. This may not perform well if the data for the representation takes time to load from the database.

In case the data for the resource spawns multiple tables, you may need to pick the latest last-modified timestamps from those tables and use a hash of the corresponding version numbers.

The techniques you need to employ for nonrelational data stores vary from implementation to implementation.

 When you use version numbers for generating ETag values, ensure that this header value is representation specific. For instance, if two representations of a resource vary by the media type, use the media type value along with the version identifier to make the ETag values representation specific.

10.2 How to Implement Conditional GET Requests in Servers

Conditional GET requests give the server an opportunity to skip the response body if the representation has not changed since the last time it served the representation. Conditional requests involve the client sending If-Modified-Since and If-Match headers based on the Last-Modified and ETag headers from a previous request. Conditional requests do not cut down on the number of requests from the client, but they can reduce the number of times a server needs to send a fresh representation to the client.

Problem

You want to know how to implement conditional GET requests.

Solution

Design the server to keep track of last modification date-time values and/or entity tags. Include the last-modified date-time as the `Last-Modified` header and the entity tag as the `ETag` header when serving representations.

When responding to GET and HEAD requests from the client, if the client has sent an `If-None-Match` header, compare its value with the `ETag` of the representation on the server. If the client has sent an `If-Unmodified-Since`, compare its value with the last-modified time of the representation on the server.

If either checks are false or if the client sent neither of these headers, return the latest copy of the representation to the client including new `ETag` and/or `Last-Modified` headers. If not, return HTTP status code 304 (`Not Modified`) to the client with no message body.

Discussion

The process of using conditional GET requests to extend the life of a cached copy is called *validation*. To support this, the server must return expiration headers along with conditional headers to clients and implement validation by returning 304 (`Not Modified`) to extend the life of a cached response.

 The following example illustrates how clients can take advantage of a caching proxy server to store cached response and let the cache handle validation automatically. See Recipe 10.3 if your client stores a copy of a representation in its local storage and would like to check whether its locally stored copy can still be considered fresh.

Here is a representation that includes `ETag` and `Last-Modified` headers along with expiry caching headers:

```
# Response
HTTP/1.1 200 OK
Date: Sun, 09 Aug 2009 00:56:14 GMT
Last-Modified: Sun, 09 Aug 2009 00:56:14 GMT
Expires: Sun, 09 Aug 2009 01:56:14 GMT
Cache-Control: max-age=3600,must-revalidate
E-Tag: "3f4a74db207d0447d46710a64971e777"
Content-Type: application/xml; charset=UTF-8

...
```

In this example, the value of the ETag header is an entity tag. If you make two GET requests and receive two different values for the ETag header, this implies that the representation changed.

 The values of the ETag, If-Match, and If-None-Match headers are quoted strings.

The server's intent in this example is to let a cache serve a stored representation for an hour and, upon expiry, validate the representation by making a conditional GET request. The following sequence illustrates the process of validation:

```
# First request
GET /person/joe HTTP/1.1
Host: www.example.org

# First response
HTTP/1.1 200 OK ❶
Date: Sun, 09 Aug 2009 00:44:14 GMT
Last-Modified: Sun, 09 Aug 2009 00:40:14 GMT
Expires: Sun, 09 Aug 2009 01:44:14 GMT
Cache-Control: max-age=3600,must-revalidate ❷

...

# Second request after 10 minutes
GET /person/joe HTTP/1.1
Host: www.example.org

# Second response - returned by cache
HTTP/1.1 200 OK
Date: Sun, 09 Aug 2009 00:54:14 GMT
Last-Modified: Sun, 09 Aug 2009 00:40:14 GMT
Expires: Sun, 09 Aug 2009 01:44:14 GMT
Cache-Control: max-age=3600,must-revalidate
Age: 600 ❸

...
```

❶ Response generated by the server

❷ Response may be cached for 3600 seconds but must be revalidated after that time period

❸ A 600-second-old response served by the cache

Requests made by clients after the expiry of one hour cause the cache to revalidate the cached response.

```
# Third request after an hour
GET /person/joe HTTP/1.1 ❶
Host: www.example.org
```

```
# Request sent by the cache to the origin server
GET /person/joe HTTP/1.1 ❷
Host: www.example.org
If-Modified-Since: Sun, 09 Aug 2009 00:40:14 GMT
If-None-Match: "3f4a74db207d0447d46710a64971e777"

# Response generated by the server
HTTP/1.1 304 Not Modified ❸
Date: Sun, 09 Aug 2009 01:54:14 GMT
Last-Modified: Sun, 09 Aug 2009 00:56:14 GMT
Expires: Sun, 09 Aug 2009 02:54:14 GMT
Cache-Control: max-age=3600,must-revalidate
E-Tag: "3f4a74db207d0447d46710a64971e777"
Content-Type: application/xml; charset=UTF-8

# Response returned by the cache
HTTP/1.1 200 OK ❹
Date: Sun, 09 Aug 2009 00:54:14 GMT
Last-Modified: Sun, 09 Aug 2009 00:40:14 GMT
Expires: Sun, 09 Aug 2009 01:44:14 GMT
Cache-Control: max-age=3600,must-revalidate

...
```

❶ Request by the client after expiry

❷ Request by the cache to the origin server to validate the cached response

❸ Response by the origin server indicating that the response has not been modified

❹ Response by the cache to the client containing a cached copy

The server does not see the second request since the response has not expired and the cache still has a copy. The third request does reach the server for validation. The third response by the server says that the representation has not changed. It also extends the freshness lifetime for another hour.

> In this example, the server's responsibility is to compare the values of the If-Modified-Since and/or If-None-Match headers with their current values and return either 200 (OK) with a resource representation or 304 (Not Modified).

10.3 How to Submit Conditional GET and HEAD Requests from Clients

When a client stores representations locally, it can use conditional GET or HEAD requests to find whether the locally stored representation is still fresh.

Problem

You want to know how to implement conditional GET and HEAD requests in your clients.

Solution

When a server returns `Last-Modified` and/or `ETag` headers, store them along with the representation data.

When making GET and HEAD requests for the same resource in the future, include the following headers to make these requests "conditional":

- `If-Modified-Since` header with a value of the stored `Last-Modified` header
- `If-None-Match` header with a value of the stored `ETag` header

Discussion

Supporting conditional requests involves storing `Last-Modified` and `ETag` headers and then replaying them with future requests to the server. Consider the following request:

```
# Request
GET /person/joe HTTP/1.1
Host: www.example.org

# Response
HTTP/1.1 200 OK
Date: Sun, 09 Aug 2009 02:55:46 GMT
Last-Modified: Sun, 09 Aug 2009 00:56:14 GMT
Expires: Sun, 09 Aug 2009 03:55:46 GMT
Cache-Control: max-age=3600,must-revalidate
E-Tag: "3f4a74db207d0447d46710a64971e777"
Content-Type: application/xml; charset=UTF-8

<person xmlns="org:example:people" xmlns:atom="http://www.w3.org/2005/Atom">
  <name>John Doe</name>
  <address>
    <street>1 Main Street</street>
    <city>Seattle</city>
    <atom:link rel="self" href="http://www.example.org/person/john/address"/>
    <state>WA</state>
  </address>
  <atom:link rel="self" href="http://www.example.org/person/john"/>
</person>
```

This is not a conditional request because of the request does not include `If-Modified-Since` of `If-None-Match`.

If you are storing this representation for future use by the client, you are likely to include the name of the person, the address, and the URI of the resource in the storage. Also include the values of `Last-Modified` and/or `ETag` in the same storage for each representation so that you can make conditional requests.

At a later time, you can check to see whether the server changed the representation by including If-Modified-Since and/or If-None-Match headers with the request:

```
# Request
GET /person/joe HTTP/1.1
If-Modified-Since: Sun, 09 Aug 2009 00:56:14 GMT
If-None-Match: "3f4a74db207d0447d46710a64971e777"

# Response
HTTP/1.1 304 Not Modified
Date: Sun, 09 Aug 2009 03:10:03 GMT
Last-Modified: Sun, 09 Aug 2009 00:56:14 GMT
Expires: Sun, 09 Aug 2009 04:10:03 GMT
Cache-Control: max-age=3600,must-revalidate
E-Tag: "3f4a74db207d0447d46710a64971e777"
```

The response from the server implies that the client's copy of the representation is still fresh. This response also extends the freshness lifetime for another hour from the time the server returned the response.

 Do not send conditional requests unless you have a copy of the representation stored locally on the client.

10.4 How to Implement Conditional PUT Requests in Servers

Lax implementation or lack of concurrency control for PUT requests can cause "lost updates." This recipe shows how to use Last-Modified and/or ETag headers to implement conditional PUT requests in servers for optimistic concurrency control.

Problem

You want to know how to implement concurrency control for PUT requests.

Solution

If the resource does not exist yet and if the server supports resource creation via PUT, create a new resource at the URI specified by the client. If the server does not support resource creation, return 404 (Not Found) status to the client.

If the resource exists, take the following steps:

- If the client does not include If-Unmodified-Since and/or If-Match headers, return 403 (Forbidden). Explain why in the body of the response.
- If the supplied If-Unmodified-Since or If-Match headers do not match the actual modified date-time and ETag values of the representation on the server, return error code 412 (Precondition Failed).

- If the clients submits a conditional PUT request and if the supplied conditions match, update the resource, and return 200 (OK) or 204 (No Content).

  You can optionally include updated Last-Modified and/or ETag headers provided the response also includes a Content-Location header with the URI of the updated resource.

See Figure 10-1 for an overview of the checks that the server needs to make.

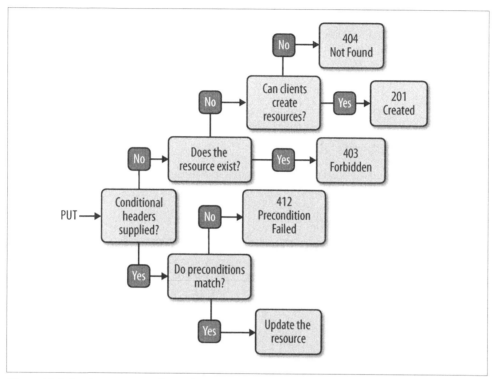

Figure 10-1. Implementing conditional PUT requests

To make this work, make sure to include Last-Modified and/or ETag headers whenever the server is returning a representation to a client.

Discussion

The steps to implement conditional PUT requests are similar to those of conditional GET requests (see Recipe 10.2). The key difference is the use of If-Unmodified-Since and/or If-Match headers in place of If-Modified-Since and/or If-None-Match headers.

Here is a conditional PUT request submitted by a client:

```
# Process this request if and only if the included conditional tags match
PUT /reviews/notes_from_underground HTTP/1.1
Host: www.example.org
```

```
If-Unmodified-Since: Sun, 09 Aug 2009 00:56:14 GMT
If-Match: "3f4a74db207d0447d46710a64971e777"
```

If the server is expecting conditional headers but finds none in the request, it must return response code 403 (Forbidden). If it finds conditional headers in the request, it must compare them with the current values of Last-Modified and/or ETag values. If they match, the server can process the update, and return 200 (OK). If not, the server must return response code 412 (Precondition Failed). See Recipe 10.7 for some example response messages for these response codes.

 If the server sends both Last-Modified and ETag headers on requests, process the PUT request only if both the If-Unmodified-Since and If-Match headers match the current values. Even if one of them fails to match, return 412 (Precondition Failed).

Here is an example that illustrates why making PUT requests conditional is important. Consider a wiki-like server that manages content, where clients can modify and/or delete content. Assume that there are two clients, A and B, that would like to modify a resource in the following sequence. Client A obtains a representation of the resource. A user of client A starts editing the resource in a text editor locally:

```
# Request from client A
GET /reviews/notes_from_underground HTTP/1.1
Host: www.example.org

# Response
HTTP/1.1 200 OK
Content-Type: application/xml;charset-UTF-8

...
```

Client B gets a representation of the same resource, and a user of client B starts editing the resource locally:

```
# Request from client B
GET /reviews/notes_from_underground HTTP/1.1
Host: www.example.org

# Response
HTTP/1.1 200 OK
Content-Type: application/xml;charset-UTF-8

...
```

The user of client B finishes her edits and submits the changes by making a PUT request to the server:

```
# Request from client B
PUT /reviews/notes_from_underground HTTP/1.1 ❶
Host: www.example.org

# Response
```

```
HTTP/1.1 200 OK
Content-Type: application/xml;charset-UTF-8

...
```

❶ First update

A few seconds later, user of client A finishes her edits and submits the changes with
another PUT request:

```
# Request from client A
PUT /reviews/notes_from_underground HTTP/1.1 ❶
Host: www.example.org

# Response
HTTP/1.1 204 OK
Content-Type: application/xml;charset-UTF-8

...
```

❶ Second update overwrites the first update

As a result of this sequence, client A overwrites changes made by client B. Client B's
update has been lost! Neither client A nor client B is aware of the lost update. As far
these clients are concerned, both PUT operations succeeded. It is only later that B's user
will find that her updates are lost. Unless you implement the server to log every change
explicitly, you cannot debug the server to detect this lost update.

Making PUT requests conditional prevents the lost update. Here is the request from
client B:

```
# Request from client B
PUT /reviews/notes_from_underground HTTP/1.1 ❶
Host: www.example.org
If-Unmodified-Since: Sun, 09 Aug 2009 00:56:14 GMT
If-Match: "3f4a74db207d0447d46710a64971e777"

# Response
HTTP/1.1 204 No Content
Content-Location: http://www.example.org/reviews/notes_from_underground
Content-Type: application/xml;charset-UTF-8
Last-Modified: Sun, 09 Aug 2009 01:10:14 GMT
If-Match: "5dcb920acfd4f3943dbc1672756d7f43"
```

❶ First conditional update succeeds

The response includes a Content-Location header and updated Last-Modified and
ETag values that the client can use in future requests.

The update by client A will fail if the client's request is conditional and the server
correctly identifies conflicts:

```
# Request from client A
PUT /reviews/notes_from_underground HTTP/1.1 ❶
Host: www.example.org
If-Unmodified-Since: Sun, 09 Aug 2009 00:56:14 GMT
```

```
If-Match: "3f4a74db207d0447d46710a64971e777"

# Response
HTTP/1.1 412 Precondition Failed
Content-Type: application/xml;charset-UTF-8

<error>
  <message>The review you are trying to update has changed.</message>
  <description>You are trying to  update a resource based on stale information.
  Get a new copy of this review, resolve any differences, and retry.</description>
</error>
```

❶ Second conditional update fails

10.5 How to Implement Conditional DELETE Requests in Servers

Conditional DELETE requests can help block clients from deleting resources based on stale information. For example, a client may not want to delete a user resource if another client changes the state of the user from "inactive" to "active."

Problem

You want to now how to implement concurrency control for DELETE requests.

Solution

If the client submits an unconditional DELETE request, return error code 403 (Forbidden). If the supplied conditions do not match, return error code 412 (Precondition Failed). In either case, explain the reason for the failure to the client in the body of the representation.

If the clients submits a conditional DELETE request and the supplied conditions match, delete the resource.

See Figure 10-2 for an overview of the checks that the server needs to make.

Discussion

A client may decide to delete a resource assuming that it is ready to be deleted. In the meantime, another client may update the same resource, invalidating the first client's assumption. Using conditional DELETE prevents this. When the server makes the DELETE request conditional, the server can verify that the client's decision to delete the resource is based on the most recent state of the resource. The server can do this by comparing the client-supplied If-Unmodified-Since and If-Match headers with their current values.

```
# Process this request if and only if the included conditional tags match
DELETE /reviews/notes_from_underground HTTP/1.1
```

```
Host: www.example.org
If-Unmodified-Since: Sun, 09 Aug 2009 00:56:14 GMT
If-Match: "3f4a74db207d0447d46710a64971e777"

# Response
HTTP/1.1 204 No Content
```

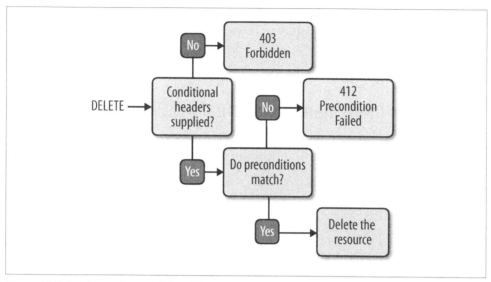

Figure 10-2. Implementing conditional DELETE requests

10.6 How to Make Unconditional GET Requests from Clients

HTTP 1.1 allows clients to modify expiration caching and ask for fresh representations. You can use this recipe to get a fresh representation of a resource after you receive a 412 (Precondition Failed) or even after a successful PUT or PATCH to get the latest representation.

Problem

You want to know how to implement a client to get the freshest representation available from a server.

Solution

Include Cache-Control: no-cache and Pragma: no-cache headers in the GET request.

Discussion

Suppose the client makes a conditional PUT request to update a resource. But the supplied conditions do not match, and the server returns 412 (Precondition Failed).

```
# Process this request if and only if the included conditional tags match
PUT /reviews/notes_from_underground HTTP/1.1
Host: www.example.org
If-Unmodified-Since: Sun, 09 Aug 2009 00:56:14 GMT
If-Match: "3f4a74db207d0447d46710a64971e777"

...

# Response
HTTP/1.1 412 Precondition Failed
Content-Length: 0
```

The client can now make an unconditional GET request to obtain a fresh representation of the resource.

```
# Request
GET /status HTTP/1.1
Cache-Control: no-cache ❶
Pragma: no-cache

# Response
HTTP/1.1 200 OK
Date: Sun, 09 Aug 2009 05:20:10 GMT
Last-Modified: Sun, 09 Aug 2009 05:20:10 GMT ❷
ETag: "a3d3005f4a1632c88e8889af985e6294"
Expires: Sun, 09 Aug 2009 15:56:14 GMT
Cache-Control: max-age=36000,public
Content-Type: application/xml; charset=UTF-8

...
```

❶ Cache-Control: no-cache and Pragma: no-cache headers make client requests unconditional.

❷ The server responds with a fresh representation along with the applicable Last-Modified and ETag.

The no-cache directive in the request asks any intermediate caches to not serve a cached representation but pass the request to the origin server.

Note that some caches may be configured to ignore the no-cache directive. In such cases, caches may return a Warning header.

```
# Request
GET /status HTTP/1.1
Cache-Control: no-cache
Pragma: no-cache

# Response
Date: Sun, 09 Aug 2009 00:56:14 GMT
Last-Modified: Sun, 09 Aug 2009 00:56:14 GMT
Expires: Sun, 09 Aug 2009 10:56:14 GMT
Cache-Control: max-age=36000,public
Content-Type: application/xml; charset=UTF-8
Age: 1021
Warning: 110
```

The value of the Warning header is an integer code, which in this example indicates that the response is stale. For further details of this header, refer to HTTP 1.1.

 Do not make unconditional GET requests unless necessary. Unconditional requests downgrade performance and increase latency.

10.7 How to Submit Conditional PUT and DELETE Requests from Clients

Problem

You want to know how to support concurrency control for PUT and DELETE requests in clients.

Solution

When the client is creating a new resource using PUT or the server has not returned If-Modified-Since and/or ETag headers from a previous GET or PUT request to the resource, make PUT requests as usual.

If the client has If-Modified-Since and/or ETag headers from a previous request to the resource, when making PUT and DELETE requests, include the following headers to make these requests "conditional":

- An If-Unmodified-Since header with the same value as the Last-Modified header, to indicate that the server should process the request if and only if the server has not modified the resource since the time specified in this header
- An If-Match header, with the same value as the ETag header, to indicate that the server should process the request if and only if the supplied header value matches the current ETag value

If the server returns status code 412 (Precondition Failed), submit an unconditional GET request (Recipe 10.6) to obtain fresh Last-Modified and ETag headers, verify that the decision to update or delete the resource is still valid per the fresh representation, and then repeat the PUT or DELETE request with those headers.

Discussion

Here is an example of a client making a conditional PUT request:

```
# Request
PUT /reviews/notes_from_underground HTTP/1.1
Host: www.example.org
If-Unmodified-Since: Sun, 09 Aug 2009 00:56:14 GMT
If-Match: "3f4a74db207d0447d46710a64971e777"
```

```
...

# Response
HTTP/1.1 200 OK
Date: Sun, 16 Aug 2009 01:00:23 GMT
Content-Location: http://www.example.org/reviews/notes_from_underground
Last-Modified: Sun, 16 Aug 2009 01:00:23 GMT
E-Tag: "5bbae963eb30e03cf1fd218a9dc92a5b"
Content-Type: application/xml; charset=UTF-8

...
```

In this request, the value of If-Unmodified-Since is the value the Last-Modified header that the client obtained during a previous request (see Recipe 10.3). Similarly, the value of the If-Match header is the value of the ETag header. If the client does not already have these headers for its copy of the representation or if the server returns response code 412 (Precondition Failed), submit a new unconditional request GET request to obtain those as described in Recipe 10.6.

```
# Unconditional GET request
GET /reviews/notes_from_underground HTTP/1.1
Host: www.example.org
Cache-Control: no-cache
Pragma: no-cache

# Response
HTTP/1.1 200 OK
Content-Type: application/xml;charset-UTF-8
Date: Sun, 16 Aug 2009 01:00:23 GMT
Last-Modified: Sun, 09 Aug 2009 00:55:46 GMT
ETag: "3f4a74db207d0447d46710a64971e777"

...
```

 Obtaining these headers by making a HEAD request is not sufficient. For the clients, these headers correspond to the current state of the resource. Getting the headers alone via a HEAD request will not help the client know the current state of the resource. It needs to get the body along with the headers.

The client must follow the same process for DELETE requests. A 412 (Precondition Failed) to either request implies that the client is making its decision to update or delete a resource based on stale information.

```
# Conditional request
PUT /reviews/notes_from_underground HTTP/1.1
Host: www.cxample.org
If-Unmodified-Since: Sun, 09 Aug 2009 00:56:14 GMT
If-Match: "3f4a74db207d0447d46710a64971e777"

# Response
HTTP/1.1 412 Precondition Failed
```

```
Content-Type: application/xml;charset=UTF-8

<error>
  <message>The review you are trying to update has changed.</message>
  <description>You are trying to  update a resource based on stale information.
  Get a new copy of this review, resolve any differences, and retry.</description>
</error>
```

10.8 How to Make POST Requests Conditional

Unlike PUT or DELETE, the outcome of a POST request to a resource may not result in any changes to the resource at the request URI. The server may create a new resource (with response code 201) or identify the outcome with a different URI (with response code 303). For these cases, the client will not have a representation and the conditional headers stored locally. This recipe shows how to use links to make such POST requests conditional. You can apply this recipe to make POST requests conditional and nonrepeatable (i.e., used "once-only").

Problem

You want to implement POST such that the server can detect and prevent duplicate submission by clients.

Solution

Let clients use a one-time URI supplied by the server via a link for each POST request. Use Recipe 10.9 to generate the one-time URI. This URI contains a token generated by the server that is valid for just one usage of the POST request. Store all used tokens in a transaction log on the server.

When the client submits a POST request, verify whether the token exists in the transaction log. If it does, return response code 403 (Forbidden). Explain why in the body. If not, process the request to return 201 (Created) or 303 (See Other) depending on the outcome. Also store the token in the transaction log.

Discussion

Consider a bank transfer application, where the server needs to transfer a given sum of money from one account to another. The server can employ a controller resource to implement this transfer.

```
# Request
POST /transfers ❶
Host: example.org
Content-Type: application/xml;charset=UTF-8

<transfer>
  <source>urn:example:org:account:1</source>
  <target>urn:example:org:account:2</target>
```

```
    <currency>USD</currency>
    <amount>100.00</amount>
    <note>Testing transfer</note>
  </transfer>

# Response
HTTP/1.1 201 Created ❷
Content-Type: application/xml;charset=UTF-8
Location: http://www.example.org/transactions/1
Content-Location: http://www.example.org/transactions/1

<transfer xmlns:atom="http://www.w3.org/2005/Atom">
  <source>urn:example:org:account:1</source>
  <target>urn:example:org:account:2</target>
  <atom:link href="http://www.example.org/transactions/1" rel="self"/>
  <currency>USD</currency>
  <amount>100.00</amount>
  <note>Testing transfer</note>
</transfer>
```

❶ The client submits a POST request based on what it thinks is the current state of the two bank account resources.

❷ The server cannot verify whether the client's request is based on the current state of the account resources.

In this example, the resource identified by the URI http://www.example.org/trans fers is a controller resource. The outcome of the POST request in this example is the modification of two account resources and the creation of a new resource. To make this request conditional, the server must use a token whose value is a function of the current state of the two account resources. The server can use Recipe 10.9 to generate the following URI:

```
http://www.example.org/transfers;t=e6e3c89d4dfe7f3a818734a6237ccfc5
```

Unlike http://www.example.org/transfers, this URI includes a token that is a function of the two resources being modified. The client can use the URI to request for a transfer. The server can verify that the token in the URI still corresponds to the current state of the account resources before proceeding to create an account transfer.

```
# Request
POST /transfer;t=e6e3c89d4dfe7f3a818734a6237ccfc5 HTTP/1.1 ❶
Host: example.org
Content-Type: application/xml;charset=UTF-8

<transfer>
  <source>urn:example:org:account:1</source>
  <target>urn:example:org:account:2</target>
  <currency>USD</currency>
  <amount>100.00</amount>
  <note>Testing transfer</note>
</transfer>

# Response
```

```
HTTP/1.1 201 Created ❷
Content-Type: application/xml;charset=UTF-8
Location: http://www.example.org/transactions/1
Content-Location: http://www.example.org/transactions/1

<transfer xmlns:atom="http://www.w3.org/2005/Atom">
  <source>urn:example:org:account:1</source>
  <target>urn:example:org:account:2</target>
  <atom:link href="http://www.example.org/transactions/1" rel="self"/>
  <currency>USD</currency>
  <amount>100.00</amount>
  <note>Testing transfer</note>
</transfer>
```

❶ The client submits a conditional POST request with a URI that is based on the current state of the two bank account resources.

❷ The server can verify whether the client's request is based on the current state of the account resources.

The server can detect duplicate requests by checking that the token exists in the server's transaction log.

```
# Request
POST /transfer;t=e6e3c89d4dfe7f3a818734a6237ccfc5 HTTP/1.1 ❶
Host: example.org
Content-Type: application/xml;charset=UTF-8

<transfer>
  <source>urn:example:org:account:1</source>
  <target>urn:example:org:account:2</target>
  <currency>USD</currency>
  <amount>100.00</amount>
  <note>Testing transfer</note>
</transfer>

# Response
HTTP/1.1 403 Forbidden ❷
Content-Type: application/xml;charset=UTF-8
Date: Sat, 17 Oct 2009 20:16:18 GMT

<error xmlns:atom="http://www.w3.org/2005/Atom">
  <message xml:lang="en">Transfer already created.</message>
</error>
```

❶ The client submits a conditional POST request.

❷ The server detects a conflict.

This time, the server checks the transaction log to see that the token has already been used. It returns 403 (Forbidden) instead of creating a duplicate. This technique is sometimes called *POST once exactly*.

10.9 How to Generate One-Time URIs

This recipe discusses how to generate URIs that can be used for conditional POST requests.

Problem

You want to generate a URI that clients can use to implement conditional POST requests.

Solution

If the purpose of the URI is to create a new resource, generate a token based either on a sequence number or on a concatenation of a timestamp and a random number. If the purpose of the URI is to modify one or more resources, also include the entity tags and identifiers of those resources in the token. Encode that token in the URI.

Discussion

Consider the bank account transfer example from Recipe 10.8. To request the transfer, the server needs to supply a URI that is a function of the current state of the two bank accounts. Here is a resource that can generate such a URI:

```
# Request
GET /transfer-token?from=urn:example:org:account:1&
  to=urn:example:org:account:2 HTTP/1.1 ❶
Host: www.example.org

# Response
HTTP/1.1 200 OK
Cache-Control: no-cache
Link: <http://www.example.org/transfers;t=e6e3c89d4dfe7f3a818734a6237ccfc5>;
    rel="http://www.example.org/rel/transfer" ❷

<accounts> ❸
  <account>
    <id>urn:example:org:account:1</id>
    <balance>200.00</balance>
  </account>
  <account>
    <id>urn:example:org:account:2</id>
    <balance>100.00</balance>
  </account>
</accounts>
```

❶ Request to get a URI to make a conditional request

❷ Conditional URI

❸ Current state of the resources

The resource in the request is like a token-dispensing machine. The client supplies the accounts involved in the transfer, and the server returns a link with a URI to initiate the transfer. The server also includes the current state of the accounts.

 The client must base its decision to use the link on the state returned in the response. This link is valid only for the current state of the account resources.

There are several ways to generate such a URI. The following URI contains a token whose value is an MD5 hash of the concatenation of a random number, current date-time value, and entity tags of the two bank accounts:

```
http://www.example.org/transfers;t=e6e3c89d4dfe7f3a818734a6237ccfc5
```

To prevent URI tampering, consider including digital signatures as well in the URI. The server does not need to store this token for later verification since it can recompute the token from the current entity tags of the resources. If the hashes do not match, the server can conclude that the URI used by the client is no longer valid. Such one-time tokens are called *nonce*s. Nonce stands for "number used once."

 You can also use one-time URIs to detect replay attacks. Replay attacks involve a malicious entity eavesdropping to capture requests and responses and replaying requests masquerading as a genuine client.

When using one-time URIs for such purposes, ensure that the token used is randomly generated so that the malicious entity cannot guess future token values.

If the purpose of the URI is to create a new resource using POST, generate the token based on the current date-time value and a random number. Here is a one-time URI issued to create a new address resource. The token in this URI is an MD5 hash of a random number and the current time.

```
# Request
GET /user/smith/address-token HTTP/1.1 ❶
Host: www.example.org

# Response
HTTP/1.1 204 No Content
Cache-Control: no-cache
Link: <http://www.example.org/user/smith;t=360e22a55267f0a525b1d49ddc9eed71>;
    rel="http://www.example.org/rel/transfer" ❷
```

❶ Request to get a URI to make a conditional request to create a resource

❷ Conditional URI

In this case, there is no need to supply any inputs to generate the URI. To verify that the URI has not been used before, the server needs to maintain a transaction log. When the client submits the URI to create a new resource using POST, first check whether the token exists in a transaction log on the server. If not, process the request, and store the token in the transaction log.

 In the case of web applications, you can also encode the token as hidden form fields in HTML forms. This is a common pattern to detect duplicate form submissions.

## CHAPTER 11

Miscellaneous Writes

This chapter addresses some problems that are often seen as challenging or outside the realm of REST's uniform interface constraint. Use cases for recipes in this chapter involve operations such as making copies, taking snapshots, moving and merging, processing batch requests, and supporting transactions. Although such use cases may not be common in every RESTful web service, this chapter shows how to combine HTTP's uniform interface with resources and links to address such problems.

The key principle used in this chapter is to always think in terms of application use cases and not generalize the problem or the solution any further than necessary. For instance, a use case may involve changing the category of an album. In the server's implementation, such a change may require changing the URI of the album. You may generalize this problem into that of "moving" a resource from one location to another. Since there is no such method as MOVE in HTTP, you may conclude that this problem is beyond the scope of HTTP. However, a problem like "changing the category" could easily be addressed by using Recipe 11.3 without needing to extend HTTP. The same goes for other problems such as batch processing, copying, and even transactions. Here is the list of recipes discussed in this chapter:

Recipe 11.1, "How to Copy a Resource"
Use this recipe to learn how to make a copy of a resource.

Recipe 11.2, "How to Merge Resources"
Use this recipe to learn how to merge two or more resources.

Recipe 11.3, "How to Move a Resource"
Use this recipe to learn how to move a resource.

Recipe 11.4, "When to Use WebDAV Methods"
Use this recipe to learn when to use WebDAV extension methods.

Recipe 11.5, "How to Support Operations Across Servers"
Use this recipe to learn how to support operations across server boundaries.

Recipe 11.6, "How to Take Snapshots of Resources"
Use this recipe to implement a simple versioning mechanism for resources so that clients can browse through changes made to a given resource.

Recipe 11.7, "How to Undo Resource Updates"
Use this recipe to learn how to undo changes made to a resource.

Recipe 11.8, "How to Refine Resources for Partial Updates"
Use this recipe to learn how to refine resources and adjust their granularity to allow the use of PUT for partial updates.

Recipe 11.9, "How to Use the PATCH Method"
Use this recipe to learn how to use the PATCH method for making partial updates.

Recipe 11.10, "How to Process Similar Resources in Bulk"
Use this recipe to learn how to create, update, or delete similar resources in bulk.

Recipe 11.11, "How to Trigger Bulk Operations"
Use this recipe to learn how to employ an application-specific resource to trigger batch operations.

Recipe 11.12, "When to Tunnel Multiple Requests Using POST"
Use this recipe to learn why batch processing by tunneling multiple HTTP requests via a single HTTP POST request is not recommended.

Recipe 11.13, "How to Support Batch Requests"
Use this recipe to learn how to use POST for batch processing.

Recipe 11.14, "How to Support Transactions"
Use this recipe to learn how to deal with transactions when designing RESTful web services.

11.1 How to Copy a Resource

This recipe shows how to make a copy of a resource without leaking the server's implementation details.

Problem

You want to know how to make a copy of an existing resource.

Solution

Design a controller resource that can create a copy. The client makes a POST request to this controller to copy the resource. To make the POST conditional, provide a one-time URI to the client using Recipe 10.9.

After the controller creates the copy, return response code 201 (Created) with a Location header containing the URI of the copy.

Discussion

Consider a web service that manages photo albums. The client would like to duplicate an album and then make some changes to the newly created copy. To support this, the server can design a controller resource to make the copy and include a link to this controller resource in the album representation. Here is a request to fetch a representation of the album resource:

```
# Request
GET /albums/2009/10/1011 HTTP/1.1
Host: www.example.org

# Response
HTTP/1.1 200 OK
Content-Type: application/xml;charset=UTF-8

<album xmlns:atom="http://www.w3.org/2005/Atom">
  <id>urn:example:album:1011</id>
  <atom:link rel="self" href="http://www.example.org/albums/2009/10/1011"/>
  <atom:link rel="http://www.example.org/rels/duplicate"
             href="http://www.example.org/albums/2009/10/1011/duplicate;
                   t=a5d0e32ddff373df1b3351e53fc6ffb1"/> ❶
  ...
</album>
```

❶ A link with a URI to copy a resource

The URI for the controller resource includes a token to make the request conditional. The server can use the token to ensure that repeating the POST does not cause extraneous duplicate albums.

Assuming that the client knows the semantics of the link relation type `http://www.exam ple.org/rels/duplicate`, it can use the URI `http://www.example.org/albums/2009/08/ hiking/duplicate;t=a5d0e32ddff373df1b3351e53fc6ffb1` to create a copy of the album.

```
# Request
POST /albums/2009/08/1011/duplicate;t=a5d0e32ddff373df1b3351e53fc6ffb1 HTTP/1.1 ❶
Host: www.example.org

# Response
HTTP/1.1 201 Created
Content-Type: application/xml;charset=UTF-8
Location: http://www.example.org/2009/08/1014 ❷
Content-Location: http://www.example.org/2009/08/1014

<album xmlns:atom="http://www.w3.org/2005/Atom">
  <id>urn:example:album:1014</id>
  <atom:link rel="self" href="http://www.example.org/albums/2009/08/1014"/>
  ...
</album>
```

❶ Request to copy a resource

❷ Copy of the original resource

In this implementation, the server makes the copy and provides a new URI to the copied resource. The client is completely isolated from the server's implementation details.

11.2 How to Merge Resources

Problem

You want to know how to merge two or more resources.

Solution

Design an application-specific controller resource to merge resources. The client submits a GET request to this URI with URIs or identifiers of the resources to be merged to this controller as query parameters. The server returns a Last-Modified, and an ETag header along with a summary of the resources to be merged in the body of the representation. In the entity tag, include a sequence number or a concatenation of a timestamp and a random number.

Upon verifying the summary, the client makes a POST request supplying If-Unmodified-Since and If-Match headers to the same URI to cause the merge.

After merging, the server stores the If-Match header value in a transaction log and returns response code 201 (Created) with a Location header containing the URI of the merged resource. In the future, if a client submits a POST request with the same If-Match value, the server returns 412 (Precondition Failed).

Discussion

A merge involves two or more resources presented to the server. To keep clients loosely coupled, the details of merging two documents should be left up to the server. Here is a request by the client to get a URI to merge two albums into a new album:

```
# Request
GET /albums/merge?src=urn%3Aexample%3Aalbum%3A1011&
  dest=urn%3Aexample%3Aalbum%3A1012 HTTP/1.1 ❶
Host: www.example.org

# Response
HTTP/1.1 200 OK
Cache-Control: no-cache
Content-Type: application/xml;charset=UTF-8
Last-Modified: Sun, 08 Nov 2009 04:47:03 GMT ❷
ETag: "d88a39e41c314f57917da04c920fd608"

<albums> ❸
 <album>
   <id>urn:example:album:1011</id>
   <atom:link rel="self" href="http://www.example.org/albums/2009/08/1011"/>
   ...
 </album>
```

```
<album>
  <id>urn:example:album:1012</id>
  <atom:link rel="self" href="http://www.example.org/albums/2009/08/1012"/>
  ...
</album>
</albums>
```

❶ Request to get the current state of resources being merged

❷ `Last-Modified` and `ETag` for the representation

❸ State of resources being merged

In this example, the client supplies the identifiers of two resources to merge, and the server returns a summary of the resources to be merged. You may alternatively use URIs as parameters for merging.

 This step essentially manifests a new composite resource (see Recipe 2.4) for the resources being merged.

On the client side, you need to verify that the state of albums in the previous response is the same as the one the client has locally before submitting a request to merge.

```
# Request
POST /albums/merge?src=urn%3Aexample%3Aalbum%3A1011&
  dest=urn%3Aexample%3Aalbum%3A1012 HTTP/1.1 ❶
Host: www.example.org
If-Unmodified-Since: Sun, 08 Nov 2009 04:47:03 GMT ❷
If-Match: "d88a39e41c314f57917da04c920fd608"

# Response
HTTP/1.1 201 Created
Location: http://www.example.org/albums/2009/08/1091
Content-Location: http://www.example.org/albums/2009/08/1091
Content-Type: application/xml;charset=UTF-8
Last-Modified: Sun, 08 Nov 2009 05:30:10 GMT
ETag: "48be3ab269550ee00a84eb5a1a44f330"

<album>
  <id>urn:example:album:1091</id>
  <atom:link rel="self" href="http://www.example.org/albums/2009/08/1091"/>
  ...
</album>
```

❶ Request to merge resources

❷ Preconditions

The server creates a new merged resource. During this process, depending on what the server's use cases demand, the server may also delete the original resources.

11.3 How to Move a Resource

Problem

You want to know how to move a resource.

Solution

Include a link or a link template to a controller that can move the resource. Let the client use POST to submit a request to move. Use Recipe 10.8 to make the POST request conditional.

After processing the request, return response code 201 (Created) or 303 (See Other) depending on the outcome.

Discussion

What a move means is completely application specific. It could mean copying a resource to a different location on the same or a different server and deleting the original. Alternatively, it could also mean changing the state of a resource without changing its location. In either case, to maintain loose coupling, the client should not concern itself about what a move means and how the server implements it.

Consider a photo album. The album is part of a friends folder. The client would like to move the album to the family folder. The server organizes its URIs based on the album's category. A move operation results in a change in the album's URI.

Moving a resource is not much different from copying. In this case, the server can provide a URI or a URI template to let the client supply criteria for a destination resource:

```
# Request
GET /albums/friends/2009/08/1011 HTTP/1.1
Host: www.example.org

# Response
HTTP/1.1 200 OK
Content-Type: application/xml;charset=UTF-8

<album xmlns:atom="http://www.w3.org/2005/Atom">
  <id>urn:example:album:1011</id>
  <atom:link rel="self" href="http://www.example.org/albums/2009/08/1011"/>
  <link-template rel="http://www.example.org/rels/move"
     href="http://www.example.org/albums/friends/2009/08/1011/move;
         t=dc4128786d463dc7e40c18457d1826fa?group={category}"/> ❶
  <category>friends</category>
  ...
</album>
```

❶ A link with a URI template to change the category of a resource

In this representation, the server uses a URI template for the client to specify a category for the resource to be moved into.

```
# Request
POST /albums/friends/2009/08/1011/move;t=dc4128786d463dc7e40c18457d1826fa?
    group=family HTTP/1.1 ❶
Host: www.example.org
Content-Length: 0

# Response
HTTP/1.1 201 Created
Content-Type: application/xml;charset=UTF-8
Location: http://www.example.org/family/2009/08/1021 ❷
Content-Location: http://www.example.org/family/2009/08/1021

<album>
  <id>urn:example:album:1021</id>
  <atom:link rel="self" href="http://www.example.org/family/albums/2009/08/1021"/>
  <category>family</category>
  ...
</album>
```

❶ Request to change the category

❷ New resource

The result of this request is a new resource at URI http://www.example.org/albums/family/2009/08/1021. The server can return either a 410 (Gone) or a 404 (Not Found) when the client tries to access the original album.

11.4 When to Use WebDAV Methods

WebDAV (RFC 4918) is an extension of HTTP for the distributed authoring and versioning of resources. This extension extends HTTP and specifies a number of HTTP methods and headers for managing files and documents. This protocol includes the following extension methods:

PROPFIND
    In WebDAV, documents can have properties, and clients can use this method to retrieve those properties.

PROPPATCH
    Clients can use this method to set, add, or remove properties of resources.

MKCOL
    WebDAV lets you group documents into collections, and clients can use this method to create a new collection.

COPY
    Clients can use this method to create a duplicate of a given resource at a destination URI.

MOVE

This is similar to COPY, but the server is expected to delete the source resource as part of this operation.

LOCK

This method lets clients lock a given document. This method enables pessimistic concurrency control.

UNLOCK

Clients can use this method to unlock a previously locked resource.

Problem

You want to know when to use WebDAV specified methods.

Solution

Use WebDAV-specified methods when your web service is a content-authoring application and if your servers can support WebDAV. Avoid using WebDAV for other kinds of applications.

Discussion

It is important to note that WebDAV methods are "file-centric" operations. They assume that resources are like file objects that can be easily copied, overwritten, renamed, etc. However, in most RESTful web services, resources are not files, and such a file-centric view often does not map easily to application resources and business scenarios.

WebDAV is often cited as an example of how to extend HTTP to address the needs of specific application domains. WebDAV extensions are designed to allow clients to edit and manage documents or files on remote servers. Here is an example to copy a resource:

```
# Request to copy a resource
COPY /report/working/2010.pdf HTTP/1.1
Host: www.example.org
Destination:  http://www.example.org/projections/2010.pdf


# Response
HTTP/1.1 201 Created
```

In the request, the client chooses the destination for the copy via a Destination header. The client can apply this method to other WebDAV resources such as properties or collections. The client can also specify whether the server should override any resource that exists at the destination URI by supplying an Overwrite header or can specify a Depth header to indicate the depth while copying a collection.

```
# Request to copy a resource
COPY /report/working/2010.pdf HTTP/1.1
Host: www.example.org
Destination:  http://www.example.org/projections/2010.pdf
```

```
Overwrite: F

# Response
HTTP/1.1 201 Created
```

You can similarly use the MOVE method to move a resource from one location to another location.

```
# Request
MOVE /report/working/2010.pdf HTTP/1.1
Host: www.example.org
Destination:  http://www.example.org/projections/2010.pdf

# Response
HTTP/1.1 201 Created
Location: http://www.example.org/archives/this-resource
```

Both the COPY and MOVE methods are atomic and can even be applied to resources across servers. For instance, the actual move operation may require placing one or more resources from the source server on the destination server and then *removing* the resources on the source server. The server can remove the source only once it has been successfully replicated on the destination server. These methods also require clients to deal with details such as locking, unlocking, or even copying resources across servers.

11.5 How to Support Operations Across Servers

This recipe discusses how to support operations that cross server boundaries. Examples include migrating a user profile from one application to another, importing summaries of pending quotes into a customer relation management application, or publishing a document on the production server that is currently on the drafts server. Such use cases need manipulation of state in multiple servers.

Problem

You want to know how to initiate an operation that involves changes to resources on two or more servers.

Solution

Let servers collaborate with each other to design and implement cross-server operations. This may involve servers agreeing on data formats, backend interfaces, and concurrency control, as well as loading data from one data store, normalizing it to meet the other server's format, and then storing it. Let one of the servers provide a link to clients to trigger the operation.

Discussion

When confronted with operations that cross server boundaries, separation of concerns should be a key concern. Consider two web services: one managing users' contacts running on `http://contacts.example1.org` and the other managing messaging such as email, text messages, voicemail, etc., running on `http://messaging.example2.org`. The use case is to let a user import her contacts into the messaging web service. To support this, assume that the contacts web service includes a link to export contacts into the messaging web service.

Here is the representation of a user's contact list with a link to export the contact list into the messaging web service:

```
# Request
GET /user/smith/contacts HTTP/1.1
Host: contacts.example1.org

# Response
HTTP/1.1 200 OK
Content-Type: application/xml;charset=UTF-8

<contacts xmlns:atom="http://www.w3.org/2005/Atom">
  <atom:link rel="self" href="http://contacts.example2.org/user/smith/contacts"/>
  <atom:link rel="http://contacts.example1.org/rels/export-to-messaging"
    href="http://messaging.example2.org/user/smith/import;
          t=bcb9169866c69410be37f68210a6986c"
    title="Export contacts into to messaging."/> ❶
  <contact>
    ...
  </contact>
  ...
</contact>
```

❶ Link with a URI to export data from one server to another

A client that understands the semantics of the link with relation type `http://con tacts.example2.org/rels/export-to-messaging` can initiate the export operation. Assume that the documentation of this link relation type says that the client needs to submit a POST request to the link's URI to export contacts into the message service. The link's URI contains a security token to prevent the unauthorized use of the link.

```
# Request
POST /user/smith/import;t=bcb9169866c69410be37f68210a6986c HTTP/1.1 ❶
Host: messaging.example2.org

# Response
HTTP/1.1 303 See Other
Location: http://messaging.example2.org/user/smith ❷
Content-Type: application/xml;charset=UTF-8
```

❶ Request to export data

❷ URI that provides the results of the export

When the client submits this request, the messaging service makes a backend request to the contacts web service to get a copy of the contacts. During this process, depending on how security is managed between the servers, the messaging web service may present the token included in the URI to the contacts web service.

In this process, the servers are responsible for making sure to make the contact list data is available on the message server. The client is responsible only for triggering the operation. This keeps the client decoupled from the server's implementation details including concurrency control, atomicity, differences in data formats, etc. This is the result of coordination between the servers.

 When no such coordination is possible because of technical or organizational issues, the client has no choice but to download all contacts from `http://contacts.example2.org/user/smith/contacts` and submit them to the messaging service. See Recipe 2.6 for an example.

11.6 How to Take Snapshots of Resources

This recipe describes how to take a snapshot of the resource before each update. When a client updates a resource via the method PUT, the server updates the current state of the resource, leaving no way for the client to know what existed before the update. However, there are cases when clients expect to be able to go back in time and browse through the history of changes.

For example, imagine that you are designing a web service to provide past and present snapshots of traffic conditions at certain intersections. Most clients would like to see the latest conditions, but some clients may want to browse through past traffic conditions.

Alternatively consider a wiki. For each page on the wiki, the server needs to maintain a revision stack of current and past revisions for each page so that any client can retrieve, compare, and evaluate changes made to any given page.

Problem

You want to know how to keep snapshots of a resource so that clients can browse through previous versions of the resource.

Solution

Every time a client submits a PUT request to update a resource, before updating the resource, implicitly create a snapshot (a copy resource). In the representation of the updated resource, include a link to the snapshot. Also include a link in the snapshot resource to the updated resource.

When a client submits a DELETE request, delete the resource along with all the snapshots.

Discussion

In essence, this recipe lets you build a simple versioning mechanism for resources without requiring clients to learn how to create and manage versions of resources. Clients that do not care about versions can use HTTP's uniform interface as usual without even noticing that the server is maintaining snapshots. Clients that do care about versions can browse through past versions. In the server's storage, each snapshot can be a full copy or a contain just the list of differences from the previous version.

Here is an example that creates a new snapshot:

```
# Request
PUT /trails/ColchuckLake HTTP/1.1
Host: wiki.example.org
If-Unmodified-Since: Sun, 01 Nov 2009 12:34:43 GMT
Content-Type: application/atom+xml;type=entry;charset=UTF-8

<atom:entry xmlns:atom="http://www.w3.org/2005/Atom">
  <atom:author>
    <atom:name>Joe Hiker</atom:name>
  </atom:author>
  <atom:title>Colchuck Lake</atom:title>
  <atom:id>urn:example:wiki:trails:ColcuckLake</atom:id>
  <atom:content xml:lang="en" type="html">
    ... initial draft ...
  </atom:content>
</atom:entry>


# Response
HTTP/1.1 204 No Content
```

In response to a PUT request, the server copies the resource to http://wiki.example.org/trails/ColchukLake/s1.

```
# Request
GET /trails/ColchuckLake HTTP/1.1
Host: wiki.example.org

# Response
HTTP/1.1 200 OK
Last-Modified: Sun, 01 Nov 2009 16:24:56 GMT
Content-Type: application/atom+xml;type=entry;charset=UTF-8

<atom:entry xmlns:atom="http://www.w3.org/2005/Atom">
  <atom:author>
    <atom:name>Joe Hiker</atom:name>
  </atom:author>
  <atom:title>Colchuck Lake</atom:title>
  <atom:id>urn:example:wiki:trails:ColcuckLake</atom:id>
  <atom:link href="http://wiki.example.org/trails/ColchuckLake" rel="self"/> ❶
  <atom:link href="http://wiki.example.org/trails/ColchuckLake/s1" rel="previous"/> ❷
  <atom:content xml:lang="en" atom:type="html">
    ... updated draft ...
  </atom:content>
</atom:entry>
```

❶ Current version of the resource

❷ Snapshot

The link with the **previous** relation is a link to the previous snapshot of the resource. When the client submits another PUT request to modify the resource, the server can repeat the process shown previously to create a new snapshot at http://wiki.exam ple.org/trails/ColchuckLake/s2.

```
# Request to update the resource
PUT /trails/ColchuckLake HTTP/1.1
Host: wiki.example.org
Content-Type: application/atom+xml;type=entry;charset=UTF-8
If-Unmodified-Since: Sun, 01 Nov 2009 16:24:56 GMT

<atom:entry xmlns:atom="http://www.w3.org/2005/Atom">
  <atom:author>
    <atom:name>Joe Hiker</atom:name>
  </atom:author>
  <atom:title>Colchuck Lake</atom:title>
  <atom:id>urn:example:wiki:trails:ColcuckLake</atom:id>
  <atom:content xml:lang="en" type="html">
    ... updated draft ...
  </atom:content>
</atom:entry>


# Response
HTTP/1.1 204 No Content
```

After this step, the resource at URI http://wiki.example.org/trails/ColchuckLake is the latest version. It is preceded by http://wiki.example.org/trails/ColchuckLake/ s2, which further is preceded by http://wiki.example.org/trails/ColchuckLake/s1. Using the link with the **previous** relation type, the client can walk backward to get older snapshots.

After this update, a representation of http://wiki.example.org/trails/ColchuckLake/ s2 includes its own snapshot—http://wiki.example.org/trails/ColchuckLake/s2.

```
# Request
GET /trails/ColchuckLake/s2 HTTP/1.1
Host: wiki.example.org

# Response
HTTP/1.1 200 OK
Content-Type: application/atom+xml;type=entry;charset=UTF-8

<atom:entry xmlns:atom="http://www.w3.org/2005/Atom">
  <atom:author>
    <atom:name>Joe Hiker</atom:name>
  </atom:author>
  <atom:title>Colchuck Lake</atom:title>
  <atom:id>urn:example:wiki:trails:ColcuckLake</atom:id>
  <atom:link href="http://wiki.example.org/trails/ColchuckLake/s2" rel="self"/> ❶
  <atom:link href="http://wiki.example.org/trails/ColchuckLake/s1" rel="previous"/> ❷
  <atom:link href="http://wiki.example.org/trails/ColchuckLake" rel="next"/> ❸
  <atom:content xml:lang="en" atom:type="html">
    ... updated draft ...
```

```
          </atom:content>
      </atom:entry>
```

❶ Current version of the resource

❷ Another snapshot

❸ Later snapshot

The client can use the link with the previous relation type to navigate to previous snapshots and use the link with the next relation to navigate to more recent snapshots.

11.7 How to Undo Resource Updates

On occasion, you may be need to provide an "undo" functionality to clients. For instance, a client may want to undo some recently made changes to a quote. This problem is similar to taking a snapshot with the added capability of making the latest snapshot active again.

Problem

You want to know to how to undo changes made to a resource.

Solution

Every time a client submits a PUT to update a resource, take a snapshot as described in Recipe 11.6.

Provide a controller resource for undo. To undo a change, let the client submit a POST request. Log the current state of the resource in a transaction log for auditing purposes. The server restores the state of the resource from the latest snapshot and redirects the client to the URI of the resource.

Discussion

Consider the document on a wiki at URI http://wiki.example.org/trails/Colcuck Lake introduced in Recipe 11.6. In the representation of the resource, include a link to perform an undo.

```
# Request
GET /trails/ColchuckLake HTTP/1.1
Host: wiki.example.org

# Response
HTTP/1.1 200 OK
Last-Modified: Sun, 01 Nov 2009 16:24:56 GMT
Content-Type: application/atom+xml;type=entry;charset=UTF-8

<atom:entry xmlns:atom="http://www.w3.org/2005/Atom">
  <atom:author>
    <atom:name>Joe Hiker</atom:name>
```

```
    </atom:author>
    <atom:title>Colchuck Lake</atom:title>
    <atom:id>urn:example:wiki:trails:ColcuckLake</atom:id>
    <atom:link href="http://wiki.example.org/trails/ColchuckLake" rel="self"/>
    <atom:link href="http://wiki.example.org/trails/ColchuckLake/s1" rel="previous"/>
    <atom:link href="http://wiki.example.org/trails/ColchuckLake/undo;
                 t=72f2a2342ce7dc806ae7697e138bad71"
           rel="http://wiki.example.org/rels/undo"/> ❶
    <atom:content xml:lang="en" atom:type="html">
      ... updated draft ...
    </atom:content>
  </atom:entry>
```

❶ Link with a URI to undo the current state of the resource

The client can use the link with relation type `http://wiki.example.org/rels/undo` to submit an undo request. The URI in this link is a controller resource capable of undoing a change.

```
# Request
POST /trails/ColchuckLake/undo;t=72f2a2342ce7dc806ae7697e138bad71
Host: wiki.example.org
Content-Length: 0

# Response
HTTP/1.1 303 See Other
Location: http://wiki.example.org/trails/ColcuckLake
```

The controller restores the current state of the resource and logs the undo request for auditing purposes. A subsequent GET request to the resource will have the restored state.

```
# Request
GET /trails/ColchuckLake HTTP/1.1
Host: wiki.example.org

# Response
HTTP/1.1 200 OK
Last-Modified: Sun, 01 Nov 2009 16:24:56 GMT
Content-Type: application/atom+xml;type=entry;charset=UTF-8

<atom:entry xmlns:atom="http://www.w3.org/2005/Atom">
  <atom:author>
    <atom:name>Joe Hiker</atom:name>
  </atom:author>
  <atom:title>Colchuck Lake</atom:title>
  <atom:id>urn:example:wiki:trails:ColcuckLake</atom:id>
  <atom:link href="http://wiki.example.org/trails/ColchuckLake" rel="self"/>
  <atom:content xml:lang="en" atom:type="html">
    ... updated draft ...
  </atom:content>
</atom:entry>
```

You can extend this recipe to support redo.

11.8 How to Refine Resources for Partial Updates

At some point, you are likely to encounter a situation where you need to partially update an existing resource. This may happen if the resource is large and/or the update you want to make is small. In these cases, it may seem wasteful to submit a GET request to get the entire representation, make the small change, and submit a PUT request with the entire representation back to the server to update the resource. When you are confronted with such a situation, one of the first solutions to consider is to refine the resource in question in a way that removes the need for partial updates in the first place. See Recipe 11.9 for an alternative.

Problem

You want to know how to refine resources so that clients can partially update resources.

Solution

Design a new resource that encapsulates the parts of the resource that a client can modify. Let clients use PUT to update that resource, in effect partially updating the original resource.

Discussion

The key advantage of this solution is that it gives clients the ability to update subsets of the original resource by using the HTTP method PUT. It also has the added bonus of making otherwise previously hidden resources accessible via their own URIs to clients.

For example, consider the following representation of a customer resource:

```
# Request
GET /customers/1 HTTP/1.1
Host: www.example.org

# Response
HTTP/1.1 200 OK
Content-Type: application/xml;charset=UTF-8
Last-Modified: Thu, 05 Nov 2009 01:54:19 GMT
ETag: "ca87aa4ff1505934281d91f807b25b3c"

<customer xmlns:atom="http://www.w3.org/2005/Atom">
  <atom:link rel="self" href="http://www.example.org/customers/1"/>
  <name>J. P. Goodright</name>
  <status>active</status>
  <address>
    <street>123 Main</street>
    <city>Byteville</city>
    <state>MD</state>
    <postal-code>12345</postal-code>
  </address>
  <billing-contact>
    <name>P.J. Billingsley</name>
```

```
      <email>pjbill@example.org</email>
      <voice-phone>123-456-7890</voice-phone>
      <fax-line>234-567-8901</fax-line>
    </billing-contact>
    <services>
      <preferred-shipping>two-day</preferred-shipping>
      <billing-method>net-30</billing-method>
      <minimum-order>1000</mininum-order>
      <customer-discount>10%</customer-discount>
    </services>
  </customer>
```

Assume that you want to update the billing contact information for the customer resource. To support this, the server can refine the resource to introduce a new "billing contact" resource that contains the desired elements from the original resource.

```
# Request
GET /customers/1/billing-contact HTTP/1.1
Host: www.example.org

# Response
HTTP/1.1 200 OK
Content-Type: application/xml;charset=UTF-8
Last-Modified: Thu, 05 Nov 2009 01:54:19 GMT
ETag: "d65b17759967753e7eb37b28f1bdb1fa"

<billing-contact xmlns:atom="http://www.w3.org/2005/Atom">
  <atom:link ref="self" href="http://www.example.org/customers/1/billing-contact"/>
  <name>P.J. Billingsley</name>
  <email>pjbill@example.org</email>
  <voice-phone>123-456-7890</voice-phone>
  <fax-line>234-567-8901</fax-line>
</billing-contact>
```

You can then refine the representation of the customer resource to include a link to the billing-contact resource.

```
# Request
GET /customers/1 HTTP/1.1
Host: www.example.org

# Response
HTTP/1.1 200 OK
Content-Type: application/xml;charset=UTF-8
Last-Modified: Thu, 05 Nov 2009 01:54:19 GMT
ETag: "99d37a01bc588d8743f704eaffdb22b0"

<customer xmlns:atom="http://www.w3.org/2005/Atom">
  <atom:link rel="self" href="http://www.example.org/customers/1"/>
  <atom:link rel="related" href="http://www.example.org/customers/1/billing-contact"/>
  <name>J. P. Goodright</name>
  <status>active</status>
  <address>
    <street>123 Main</street>
    <city>Byteville</city>
    <state>MD</state>
```

```
      <postal-code>12345</postal-code>
    </address>
    <services>
      <preferred-shipping>two-day</preferred-shipping>
      <billing-method>net-30</billing-method>
      <minimum-order>1000</mininum-order>
      <customer-discount>10%</customer-discount>
    </services>
  </customer>
```

Clients can now update the billing contact by submitting a PUT request to the resource at URI http://www.example.org/customers/1/billing-contact.

You can extend this approach to other parts of the customer resource. For instance, the following PUT request updates the customer status and preferred shipping method:

```
# Request
PUT /customer/1234/info HTTP/1.1
Content-Type: application/xml;charset=UTF-8
If-Match: "bfcc688bd542e17f27da0f82200c35ea"
If-Unmodified-Since: Thu, 05 Nov 2009 01:54:19 GMT

<customer-info>
  <status>premium</status>
  <preferred-shipping>next-day</preferred-shipping>
</customer-info>
```

Alternatively, consider a case where a client wants to remove the existing email address of the customer but add two new email addresses. In this case, you can represent all email addresses as another resource and let the client update that resource by submitting a PUT request:

```
# Request
PUT /customer/1234/emails HTTP/1.1
Content-Type: application/xml;charset=UTF-8
If-Match: "b5b55c8a7f18dd77b4b2d94eed7f1be5"
If-Unmodified-Since: Thu, 05 Nov 2009 01:54:19 GMT

<emails>
  <email type="work">pjbill1@example.org</status>
  <email type="alt">jane1@example.org</status>
</emails>
```

 Such resources may seem inconsistent, or *polluting*. The resources for "customer info" or "emails" have no reason to exist other than to support certain partial updates of the customer resource. But remember that anything that is appropriate for retrieval and updates is a candidate as a resource.

11.9 How to Use the PATCH Method

The HTTP PUT method is defined for the complete update or replacement of a resource. The PATCH method is designed to support partial updates. See RFC-5789 (*http://tools .ietf.org/html/rfc5789*) to read more about this method.

Problem

You want to know how to use the PATCH method.

Solution

The PATCH method is an unsafe and nonidempotent HTTP method. The body of the request is a representation that describes a set of changes that need to be made to the resource. On receiving this request, the server applies the changes to the resource and returns response code 200 (OK) or 204 (No Content).

Make the implementation of this method conditional by requiring clients to supply If-Unmodified-Since and/or If-Match headers. Return response code 412 (Precondition Failed) if the supplied preconditions do not match.

Advertise support for the PATCH via the Allow header of the OPTIONS response. Also include an Accept-Patch header with the supported media types for the PATCH method.

Discussion

Here is an example of a client submitting a PATCH request to modify the customer's name, add a nickname, and remove the fax number. Except for the representation in the request, this request-response pair is similar to using a conditional PUT request.

```
# Request for a partial update
PATCH /customers/1 HTTP/1.1 ❶
Host: www.example.org
If-Match: "2a7ad61820b6ba89e6c4a119e22f7dfc" ❷
If-Unmodified-Since: Thu, 05 Nov 2009 01:00:01 GMT
Content-Type: application/xml;charset=UTF-8

<diff-customer> ❸
  <replace-name>J. P. Goodright, Jr.</replace-name>
  <add-nickname>Jimmy</add-nickname>
  <remove-fax-line/>
</diff-customer>

# Response
HTTP/1.1 204 No Content
```

❶ Request to partially update a resource

❷ Preconditions for the request

❸ Body of the representation describing changes need to be made

In this example, the server uses an XML format to describe changes for the customer resource as simple commands such as "replace name," "add nickname," and "remove fax line."

 To support the PATCH method, the server needs to define a representation format that can express changes. Solutions to this problem are media-type specific. For example, the way to express patches for an XML document might be very different from the way to express patches to a binary image file. Moreover, there are no IANA registered media types and formats that you can reuse to describe changes.

In the response, the server can include a Content-Location header along with the latest Last-Modified and/or ETag headers. If not, the client must issue an unconditional GET request (see Recipe 10.6) to fetch the updated representation of the resource along with fresh ETag and Last-Modified headers.

 Since the PATCH method is not idempotent, clients must not repeat PATCH requests.

The response codes for the PATCH method are similar to other HTTP methods except for 422 (Unprocessable Entity). Return this when the server cannot honor the request because it might result in a bad state for the resource. Here is an example:

```
# Request for a partial update
PATCH /customers/1 HTTP/1.1
If-Match: "2ce12fc9d303b1eee1ed3efe9713663c"
If-Unmodified-Since: xxx
Host: www.example.org
Content-Type: application/xml;charset=UTF-8

<diff-customer>
  <remove>
    <name/>
    <fax-line/>
  </remove>
</diff-customer>

# Response
422 Unprocessable Entity
Content-Type: application/xml;charset=UTF-8

<error>
  <message xml:lang="en">Name cannot be removed.</message>
</error>
```

You can avoid such failures by making the representation format for the PATCH request include only the valid combinations of changes that, when executed, do not leave the resource in an inconsistent state.

One way to ensure that PATCH requests include only valid combinations of changes is to design a specific format for each resource as in the previous example and avoid general-purpose diff formats. General-purpose diff tools include Unix `diff` or Microsoft's XML Diff and Patch Tool (*http://msdn.microsoft.com/en-us/library/aa302294.aspx*).

Finally, list the media types supported for this method by adding the `Accept-Patch` header to the `OPTIONS` response.

```
# Request
OPTIONS /customers/1
Host: http://www.example.org

# Response
HTTP/1.1 204 No Content
Allow: POST, GET, PATCH
Accept-Patch: application/xml
```

As of writing this book, the specification for the PATCH method is new and may still undergo minor changes before it is finalized. If this is a concern, use Recipe 11.8 or substitute the HTTP method POST for PATCH.

```
# Request for a partial update using POST
POST /customers/1 HTTP/1.1
Host: www.example.org
If-Match: "2a7ad61820b6ba89e6c4a119e22f7dfc"
If-Unmodified-Since: Thu, 05 Nov 2009 01:00:01 GMT
Content-Type: application/xml;charset=UTF-8

<diff-customer>
  <replace-name>J. P. Goodright, Jr.</replace-name>
  <add-nickname>Jimmy</add-nickname>
  <remove-fax-line/>
</diff-customer>

# Response
HTTP/1.1 303 See Other
Location: http://www.example.org/customers/1
Content-Length: 0
```

When using PATCH is not an option, overload POST but not PUT for partial updates. Per HTTP, PUT is meant for fully updating or replacing a resource.

11.10 How to Process Similar Resources in Bulk

When a client needs to submit a number of similar requests for different resources, as long as the operations on each resource are the same and the resources are "similar," you can combine them into a single operation on a collection resource. Recipe 11.11 and Recipe 11.13 present alternatives for solving related "batch processing" problems.

Problem

You want to know how to create, update, or delete several similar resources all at once.

Solution

Use POST and a collection resource to create a number of similar resources at once. Let clients include information about the resources to be created in the request. Assign a URI for all the resources created, and redirect the client to the collection using response code 303 (See Other). A representation of this resource includes links to all the newly created resources.

To update or delete a number of similar resources in bulk, use a single URI that can return a representation containing information about all those resources. Submit a PUT request to that URI with information about the resources to be updated or a DELETE request to delete those resources.

In all these cases, ensure that the processing of the request is atomic.

 Since bulk operations can be long running, restrict the size of requests to prevent overloading the server. If not, clients can accidentally or intentionally cause denial-of-service attacks.

Also, controlling the concurrency and atomicity of bulk operations may involve database locks held for long durations of time, which may reduce performance and scalability.

Discussion

Consider the following use cases:

- Create 10 addresses.
- Delete five books from a user's wish list.
- Update all the favorite movies of a user.

For such use cases, if you can identify the resources involved via a single URI, the client can use an appropriate HTTP method to operate on that collection as a whole. For example, a client can submit a POST request to create 10 addresses.

```
# Request
POST /user/user002/addresses HTTP/1.1 ❶
Host: www.example.org
Content-Type: application/xml;charset=UTF-8

<addresses> ❷
  <address>
    ....
  </address>
  <address>
    ....
```

```
    </address>
      ...
  </addresses>

# Response
HTTP/1.1 303 See Other
Location: http://www.example.org/user/user002/addresses  ❸
```

❶ Collection used as a factory to create resources in bulk

❷ Representation containing data of all the resources to be created

❸ Refer to the collection for results

The client needs to follow the redirect to obtain URIs of all newly created resources.

```
# Request
GET /user/user002/addresses HTTP/1.1
Host: www.example.org

# Response
HTTP/1.1 200 OK
Content-Type: application/xml;charset=UTF-8
Cache-Control: max-age:3600
Last-Modified: Thu, 05 Nov 2009 01:54:19 GMT
ETag: "474263ccac5ad16fbe9f48bf63ef0846"

<addresses xmlns:atom="http://www.w3.org/2005/Atom">
  <address>
    <atom:link rel="self" href="http://www.example.org/user/user002/addr001"/>
    ....
  </address>
  <address>
    <atom:link rel="self" href="http://www.example.org/user/user002/addr002"/>
    ....
  </address>
    ...
</addresses>
```

Operations like the previous reduce the visibility of the uniform interface. In this example, since the server created several resources, it cannot
use response code 201 (Created) and provide a single Location header.
Clients need to read the collection's body to learn the URIs of the resources created.

This is a trade-off between client convenience/network efficiency and
visibility.

You can similarly update several resources at once by submitting a PUT request for that
collection. The following example replaces all the existing favorite movies of a user with
a new set of favorite movies:

```
# Request
PUT /user/user002/favmovies HTTP/1.1
Host: www.example.org
```

```
Content-Type: application/xml;charset=UTF-8
If-Match: "10895276d1cfdabdce24e6e902222198"

<favmovies>
  <favmovie>
    <id>urn:example:movie:2001</id>
    ...
  </favmovie>
  <favmovie>
    <id>urn:example:movie:2002</id>
    ...
  </favmovie>
</favmovies>

# Response
HTTP/1.1 204 No Content
```

You can implement bulk deletion in the same manner.

 The server must implement bulk requests as atomic. If the request is for creating 10 addresses, the server should create all 10 addresses before returning a successful response code. The server should not commit changes partially in the case of failures.

11.11 How to Trigger Bulk Operations

Use cases where a client needs to perform work in bulk are not uncommon. For example, creating summaries for the previous day's sales orders, archiving one or more documents for future reference, approving a selected set of purchase orders, etc., involve tasks that need to be executed in bulk. Use this recipe when the server has most of the data needed to perform the bulk operation. Recipes 11.12 and 11.13 discuss alternatives.

Problem

You want to know how to design an application-specific resource to trigger bulk operations.

Solution

Design a controller resource that, with some client inputs, can start executing a bulk operation. Allow the client to use a POST request to initiate processing. If the processing needs to be tracked by the client or if the client needs to submit a large amount of data for the operation, use Recipe 1.10 to return response code 202 (Accepted). If not, return 200 (OK) or 204 (No Content).

Discussion

This recipe shows how you can use a "fire and forget" strategy to handle bulk operations. For instance, consider the process of applying an address correction process to the addresses of all users in the system created before 2010. The server has a large number of addresses collected from a legacy system and needs to reformat them to the format used by the postal service. One way to approach this problem is to let the client iterate through each address, apply the address correction process, flag each address as being valid or needing manual correction, and then store each address in the following sequence:

```
# Get each address
GET /user/001/address HTTP/1.1
Host: www.example.org

# Apply address correction locally
...

# Store updated address
PUT /user/001/address HTTP/1.1
Host: www.example.org
Content-Type: application/xml;charset=UTF-8

...
```

Since this process involves two requests per address, alternatively the client could fetch all addresses as a single collection, apply address correction to all of them locally, and then use Recipe 11.10 to update all the addresses in a single request.

```
# Get all addresses
GET /addresses?before=2010-01-01 HTTP/1.1
Host: www.example.org

# Apply address correction to all addresses
...

# Store updated addresses
PUT /addresses?before=2010-01-01 HTTP/1.1
Host: www.example.org
Content-Type: application/xml;charset=UTF-8

...
```

As discussed in Recipe 11.10, designing a resource to consume a large volume of data in a single request and process them atomically can be challenging. A simpler alternative is to "ask" the server to apply address correction. The client submits a POST to ask the server to start the address correction. Since there are no other inputs needed, the body of the request is empty.

```
# Request to apply address correction
POST /address-correction?before=2010-01-01 HTTP/1.1  ❶
Host: www.example.org
Content-Length: 0
```

```
# Response
HTTP/1.1 202 Accepted
Content-Type: application/xml;charset=UTF-8
Date: Sun, 13 Sep 2009 01:49:27 GMT

<status xmlns:atom="http://www.w3.org/2005/Atom">
  <state>pending</state>
  <atom:link href="http://www.example.org/address-correction/status/1" rel="self"/>
  <message xml:lang="en">Your request has been accepted for processing.</message>
  <ping-after>2009-09-13T01:59:27Z</ping-after>
</status>
```

❶ Fire and forget a bulk task

If your use cases do not require any client-side tracking of the progress, the server can return 200 (OK) or 204 (No Content).

```
# Request to apply address correction
POST /address-correction?before=2010-01-01 HTTP/1.1
Host: www.example.org

# Response
HTTP/1.1 204 No Content
```

In this example, the client only needs to submit a POST request to a known URI, which initiates the bulk operation. The server applies the address correction process for each address on its own. In essence, the client is "flipping a switch" to start the work.

11.12 When to Tunnel Multiple Requests Using POST

Combining several HTTP requests in a single HTTP request to support batch processing is not an uncommon technique. Here is a commonly used implementation of this technique:

1. The client serializes each HTTP request (including the URI, HTTP method name and HTTP headers) into a JSON object or an XML document or even a single part in a multipart/mixed message.

2. The client creates an envelope format to combine each of those requests into a single message.

3. The client submits that message to the server using POST to a resource that is often termed a *batch end point*.

4. The server, on receiving this message, opens the envelope, reconstructs HTTP requests, and then dispatches them to the respective URIs on the server. Alternatively, the server may bypass HTTP and dispatch these requests directly to the code that can process those requests.

5. The server collects the response for each request and then serializes them into a single message and returns to the client.

6. The client opens the envelope and processes each response message.

Here is an example:

```
# Batch request
POST /batch HTTP/1.1 ❶
Host: www.example.org
Content-Type: application/xml;charset=UTF-8

<batch-request>
  <request method="PUT" uri="http://www.example.org/req/2009/11/1/log"> ❷
    <headers>
      <header name="Content-Type" value="application/xml"/>
    </headers>
    <body>
      ...
    </body>
  </request>
  <request method="POST" uri="http://www.example.org/req/2009/11/2/reject"> ❸
    <headers>
      <header name="Content-Type" value="application/xml"/>
    </headers>
    <body>
      ...
    </body>
  </request>
  ...
</batch-request>

# Batch response
HTTP/1.1 200 OK ❹
Content-Type: application/xml;charset=UTF-8

<batch-response>
  <response status="200" message="OK"> ❺
    <headers>
      <header name="Content-Type" value="application/xml"/>
    </headers>
    <body>
      ...
    </body>
  </response>
  <response status="412" message="Precondition Failed"> ❻
    <headers>
      <header name="Content-Type" value="application/xml"/>
    </headers>
    <body>
      ...
    </body>
  </response>
  ...
</batch-response>
```

❶ An HTTP request to a gateway resource

❷ A serialized version of an HTTP PUT request to update a resource

❸ A serialized version of an HTTP POST request to create a new resource

❹ An HTTP response from the gateway resource containing results

❺ Result of the request to update a resource

❻ Result of the request to create a new resource

This is a process of tunneling several HTTP requests into a single HTTP POST request.

Problem

You want to know if batch processing of several HTTP requests via single POST request is appropriate for your web service.

Solution

Avoid tunneling of multiple HTTP requests within a single POST request. Instead, use Recipe 11.13 to design application-specific resources to process batch requests without tunneling.

Discussion

Here is a design problem that may prompt the previous tunneling technique.

A server manages purchase requisitions. The client provides a user interface for approval and presents open requisitions to the user in lists of 10. The user reviews each and selects a user interface control (e.g., a checkbox) to approve or reject each requisition. In some cases, the user adds a log seeking a clarification. After making these changes, the user presses a "submit" button to process the 10 requisitions shown. The client then repeats the same user interface for the next 10 open requisitions.

The server offers each requisition as a resource and uses HTTP methods as follows:

- PUT to update the log section of each requisition
- POST with a controller resource to reject a requisition
- PUT to accept a requisition

Since the client is processing up to 10 requisitions at a time, it seems natural to bundle up to 10 HTTP requests into a single request and submit them to the server. An argument for doing so is reduced network latency. Instead of opening 10 connections, the client opens a single network connection.

However, such a generalized tunneling approach has several disadvantages:

Concurrency
> HTTP offers Last-Modified and ETag headers as a way to implement optimistic concurrency checks. Batch operations that tunnel multiple HTTP requests in a single request make concurrency checks difficult since the server may need to check for concurrency for each individual task within the batch.

Atomicity

HTTP requests are atomic. Each request performs a single task, and if an error occurs, the server can ensure the atomicity and consistency of data. Batch operations that mix multiple tasks in a single request, especially batches in which the success of some operations is dependent on previous operations in the same batch, can make it much harder for web services to ensure atomicity and recover from failures.

Visibility

Tunneling multiple operations through a single HTTP request makes it impossible for intermediaries to respond to actions described within the batch. Also, typical security measures that inspect requests and guard against abuse attacks are less likely to catch suspect requests carried in a batch. This may lead to denial-of-service attacks.

Error handling

Handling and reporting errors is more complicated for batch operations. The results of a single batch request might be "mixed," with some completed successfully and some not.

Scalability

Typical justifications for batch operations rely on the assumption that batch requests are more scalable than executing each individual request. If most batch operations arrive at a single server, the requests can reduce the responsiveness of that server. An application that makes heavy use of batch client requests sent to a single server for processing may perform poorly when compared to the same application that does not support batch operations.

Whenever an HTTP operation modifies more than one resource, the server should build custom solutions such as the one discussed in Recipe 10.8. However, a generalized solution for processing batch requests makes HTTP requests and responses completely opaque and is not guaranteed to meet the objective of better performance and lower latency. If not designed and implemented well, tunneling HTTP requests via POST can also make the server prone to denial-of-service attacks.

Note that the Internet-Draft "HTTP Multipart Batched Request Format" (see Appendix A) attempts to formalize a multipart/http media type for using HTTP requests or response messages within each part of a multipart message. The use of such media types is prone to all the previously discussed limitations.

11.13 How to Support Batch Requests

Problem

You want to know how to support batch processing of HTTP requests.

Solution

When confronted with a need to tunnel several HTTP requests via a POST request, backtrack to analyze the use case that prompted such an approach. Design an application-specific controller resource that can support the same use case without generalizing the problem into one of tunneling multiple requests via POST.

Discussion

Here is an alternative solution to the purchase requisition example introduced in Recipe 11.12:

```
# Approve 10 requisitions
POST /approvals HTTP/1.1 ❶
Host: www.example.org
Content-Type: application/xml;charset=UTF-8

<approvals> ❷
  <approval>
    <id>001</id>
    <status>approve</status>
  </approval>
  <approval>
    <id>002</id>
    <log>Missing bids</log>
  </approval>
  <approval>
    <id>003</id>
    <status>reject</status>
    <log>Exceeds budget limit</log>
  </approval>
  ...
</approvals>

# Response
HTTP/1.1 303 See Other ❸
Location: http://www.example.org/reqs/2009/11?page=2
```

❶ A request to approve requisitions

❷ A representation containing requisition approval data

❸ A success response

The request message shown previously has the same information as the batch request shown in Recipe 11.12 except that, instead of tunneling HTTP methods inside a POST request, it uses an application-specific resource to submit approvals in bulk. It results in a single response. In the case of success, the server redirects the client to the next page of requisitions. In the case of failure, the server can return an error message.

```
# Approve 10 requisitions
POST /approvals HTTP/1.1
Host: www.example.org
Content-Type: application/xml;charset=UTF-8
```

```
<approvals>
  <approval>
    <id>001</id>
    <status>approve</status>
  </approval>
  <approval>
    <id>002</id>
    <log>Missing bids</log>
  </approval>
  <approval>
    <id>003</id>
    <status>reject</status>
    <log>Exceeds budget limit</log>
  </approval>
  ...
</approvals>

# Batch response
HTTP/1.1 400 Bad Request ❶
Date: Tue, 03 Nov 2009 06:44:39 GMT
Content-Type: application/xml;charset=UTF-8
Content-Language: en
Link: <http://www.example.org/help/approvalcodes.html>;rel="help"

<error>
  <message>Authorization type is missing for requisition ID 001.</message>
</error>
```

❶ An atomic failure response

Such a solution is simpler to implement than a general-purpose HTTP tunneling solution. Since the previous request uses a distinct URI for the resource that is processing the request, the request is visible. Since there is a single status code, the response is visible.

11.14 How to Support Transactions

One of the frequently asked questions about RESTful web services is how to deal with transactions. Usually, one of the following scenarios prompts this question:

- A client goes through a sequence of steps with a server in a flow. The client would like to cancel the flow and undo all the changes done to the data in that flow.

- A client interacts with a number of servers in a sequence to implement an application flow, and the client either wants to revert any resulting state changes or wants to record them permanently.

Transactions are often seen as a missing feature of REST and HTTP. For instance, if HTTP supports transactions, a banking server could let a client deduct some amount from one account and add it to another account within a single transaction, thus guaranteeing atomicity. Such an implementation would also improve the visibility of interactions since each HTTP request could be implemented to not modify any related resource. However, supporting transactions in distributed and decentralized web services reduces the separation of concerns between servers and clients. It also makes the application protocol stateful, thereby reducing scalability.

Problem

You want to know how to support transactions.

Solution

Provide a resource that can make atomic changes to data. Treat uncommitted state as application state, and manage it as per Recipe 1.3. If the server needs to allow clients to undo actions, use PUT, DELETE, or POST as appropriate to make compensating changes.

Discussion

There are a number of types of transaction models. The following are the most notable:

- Short-lived atomic transactions to guarantee properties such as atomicity, consistency, isolation, and durability (i.e., ACID)
- Long-running transactions where changes happen over a period of time and the application has a chance to move forward or apply compensating actions

For instance, creating a user in a data store may happen under an atomic transaction, whereas buying a book or making a travel reservation may need to happen over a long-running transaction.

In the case of HTTP, each request provides a sphere of control for atomic changes. An HTTP request either succeeds or fails. There is no scope for partial failures in HTTP. You can support an atomic operation by submitting changes to a resource and let that resource attempt to commit those changes by using optimistic concurrency control (Chapter 10). The server can provide guarantees such as atomicity, consistency, isolation, and durability as appropriate by delegating the task of committing changes to a transactional backend data store.

For instance, the account transfer example in Recipe 10.8 uses a resource to atomically update two bank account resources within a single request.

```
# Request
POST /transfer;t=e6e3c89d4dfe7f3a818734a6237ccfc5 HTTP/1.1
Host: example.org
Content-Type: application/xml;charset=UTF-8

<transfer>
  <source>urn:example:org:account:1</source>
  <target>urn:example:org:account:2</target>
  <currency>USD</currency>
  <amount>100.00</amount>
  <note>Testing transfer</note>
```

```
    </transfer>

    # Response
    HTTP/1.1 201 Created
    Content-Type: application/xml;charset=UTF-8
    Location: http://www.example.org/transactions/1

    <transfer xmlns:atom="http://www.w3.org/2005/Atom">
      <source>urn:example:org:account:1</source>
      <target>urn:example:org:account:2</target>
      <atom:link href="http://www.example.org/transactions/1" rel="self"/>
      <currency>USD</currency>
      <amount>100.00</amount>
      <note>Testing transfer</note>
    </transfer>
```

As far as the client is concerned, this is an atomic activity. The client is decoupled from the details of how the server implements the atomic activity. The server ensures concurrency control either by checking conditional headers such as `If-Unmodified-Since` or `If-Match` or by encoding preconditions in URIs as shown in the previous example.

 Mimicking transaction protocols such as two-phase commit over HTTP, on the other hand, makes the protocol stateful and may reduce the scalability of web services.

You can use links to introduce compensating actions. For example, the server can provide a link to cancel a travel reservation in the itinerary resource.

```
    # A travel itinerary
    GET /bookings/XAA55Z HTTP/1.1
    Host: www.example.org

    # Response
    HTTP/1.1 200 OK
    Content-Type: application/xml;charset=UTF-8

    <itinerary xmlns:atom="http://www.w3.org/2005/Atom">
      <locator-id>XAA55Z</locator-id>
      <atom:link rel="self" href="http://www.example.org/bookings/XAA55Z"/>
      <atom:link rel="http://www.example.org/rels/cancel"
        href="http://www.example.org/bookings/XAA55Z/cancel"/>

      <!-- details of the itinerary -->
      ...
    </itinerary>
```

The client can use the link with the relation `http://www.example.org/rels/cancel` to cancel the reservation and perform the necessary compensating actions such as canceling each segment of the travel, deducting cancelation fees, and refunding the money.

Using this recipe for managing transactions keeps clients decoupled, keeps interactions stateless, and guarantees atomicity within each HTTP request.

## CHAPTER 12

Security

Security is a term used to describe different things at different layers and parts of a system. For instance, take a web-based application that involves users accessing resources. Securing such a system may require the following:

- Ensure that only authenticated users access resources.
- Ensure the confidentiality and integrity of information right from the moment it is collected until the time it is stored and later presented to authorized entities or users.
- Prevent unauthorized or malicious clients from abusing resources and data.
- Maintain privacy, and follow the laws of the land that govern various security aspects.

There is no one-size-fits-all solution to address all these needs. Each application requires a careful analysis as part of the architecture and design exercise to cover all these aspects of security.

This chapter covers a subset of security-related topics for RESTful web services. It maps common problems such as authentication, authorization, confidentiality, and integrity to established HTTP-based standards and practices.

Recipe 12.1, "How to Use Basic Authentication to Authenticate Clients"
  Use this recipe to learn how to use HTTP basic authentication.

Recipe 12.2, "How to Use Digest Authentication to Authenticate Clients"
  Use this recipe to learn how to use HTTP digest authentication.

Recipe 12.3, "How to Use Three-Legged OAuth"
  Use this recipe to learn how to use the three-legged OAuth protocol to let users authorize clients to access their resources.

Recipe 12.4, "How to Use Two-Legged OAuth"
  Use this recipe to learn how to use the two-legged OAuth protocol to authenticate clients.

Recipe 12.5, "How to Deal with Sensitive Information in URIs"
  Use this recipe to learn how to prevent the tampering of state encoded in URIs and how to keep the state confidential.

Recipe 12.6, "How to Maintain the Confidentiality and Integrity of Representations"
  Use this recipe to find out how to maintain the confidentiality and integrity of representations.

12.1 How to Use Basic Authentication to Authenticate Clients

Basic authentication involves the client exchanging an identifier and a shared secret to authenticate a request with the server.

Problem

You want to know how to implement basic authentication.

Solution

On the server, when a client submits a request to access a protected resource, return response code 401 (`Authorization Required`) along with a `WWW-Authenticate` header.

    WWW-Authenticate: Basic realm="Some name"

On the client, concatenate the client identifier (e.g., the username if the client is making a request on behalf of a user) and the shared secret (such as a password) as `<identifier>:<secret>`, and then compute a Base64 encoding of this text. Include the value of the resulting text in an `Authorization` header in client requests.

    Authorization: Basic <Base64 encoded value>

On the server, decode the text, and verify that the secret is the same.

If the client knows a priori that the server requires basic authentication for a resource, it can include the `Authorization` header with each request and avoid receiving the 401 (Unauthorized) response with the `WWW-Authorization` header. To facilitate this, include authentication requirements in the server's documentation.

Discussion

Authentication protocols like basic and digest authentication (see Recipe 12.2) use a challenge-response protocol. When a client accesses a protected resource, the server uses the `WWW-Authenticate` header to challenge the client to provide an answer. For basic and digest authentication, the question is "Who are you?" The client then responds using the `Authorization` header to provide an answer. For basic and digest authentication, the answer is a function of the password or, more generally, a function of the secret shared between the client and the server.

No secret is truly secret unless it is safely stored in a client implementation.

You can use authentication schemes such as basic and digest authentication for two scenarios: when a client is accessing a protected resource on its own behalf and when a client is accessing a protected resource on behalf of a user.

Basic authentication dates back to HTTP 1.0 and was later specified by RFC 2617. In basic authentication, the client Base64-encodes the shared secret and supplies it via the `Authorization` request header.

Base64 encoding is reversible. Do not use basic authentication when the client is not using TLS to connect to the server.

Here is an initial request from a client attempting to access a resource that requires authentication:

```
# Request
GET /photos HTTP/1.1 ❶
Host: www.example.org

# Response
401 Unauthorized
WWW-Authenticate: Basic realm="Photos App" ❷
Content-Type: application/xml;charset=UTF-8

<error xmlns:atom="http://www.w3.org/2005/Atom">
  <message>Unauthorized.</message>
</error>
```

❶ A request with no credentials

❷ A response with a challenge to supply credentials using basic authentication

Since the resource is protected, the server challenges the client to provide its credentials using an authentication scheme named `Basic`. The `realm` value is an opaque string that identifies a protected space on the server.

Assume that the client/user is identified as `photoapp.001` with the shared secret `basicauth`. The client computes the Base64 encoding of the string `photoapp.001:basi cauth` and sends the following request with the `Authorization` header:

```
# Request
GET /photos HTTP/1.1
Host: www.example.org
Authorization: Basic cGhvdG9hcHAuMDAxOmJhc2ljYXV0aA== ❶

# Response
HTTP/1.1 200 OK
```

```
Content-Type: application/xml;charset-UTF8
```

...

❶ A request with credentials

The server decodes the credentials using Base64 and checks that the shared secret supplied by the client matches the one known to the server and that the client is allowed to access the resource with the supplied credentials. If the server receives a request with no `Authorization` header or if the credentials in the supplied `Authorization` header do not match, the server can return an error with the `WWW-Authentication` response header.

Since authenticated responses may contain sensitive information, make sure that the `Cache-Control` and `Expires` headers are appropriate for the response. For instance, if the response is specific to the client, use `Cache-Control: private` to prevent shared caches from storing or serving the response to other clients.

```
# Request
GET /users/admin HTTP/1.1
Host: www.example.org
Authorization: Basic cGhvdG9hcHAuMDAxOmJhc2ljYXV0aA==

# Response
HTTP/1.1 200 OK
Cache-Control: max-age:3600,private
Vary: Authorization
Content-Type: application/xml;charset-UTF8
```

...

Extending the Authorization Header

The `Authorization` header is extensible. Digest authentication (see Recipe 12.2) and OAuth (see Recipes 12.3 and 12.4) use this header to send credentials to the server. In addition, some proprietary authentication techniques also use this header for supplying credentials. For instance, Amazon's Simple Storage Service (S3) uses this header to let clients authenticate with the server using the following request header:

```
Authorization: AWS AWSAccessKeyId:Signature
```

Here `AWS` is an identifier for the authentication scheme used by Amazon, `AWSAccessKeyId` is an identifier that Amazon assigns to clients, and `Signature` is a digital signature of the request method, certain headers, and the body of the message. Clients compute the signature using a secret generated by Amazon and shared with the client. Amazon verifies the identity of the client by computing the signature of the same data using the shared secret and verifying it against the signature supplied by the client.

12.2 How to Use Digest Authentication to Authenticate Clients

Digest authentication (also specified by RFC 2617) is similar to basic authentication except that the client sends a digest of the credentials to the server. Digest authentication also provides mechanisms to prevent replay attacks.

Problem

You want to know how to implement digest authentication.

Solution

When a client submits a request without including an `Authorization` header to access a protected resource, return response code 401 (`Authorization Required`) along with a `WWW-Authenticate` header, `Digest` authentication scheme, and at least `realm` and `nonce` directives. A *nonce* is a number or a token that can be used once or only a limited number of times.

On the client, include an `Authorization` header that contains a digest of the client or user identifier, the realm, and the shared secret.

Upon verifying that the supplied digest matches a digest of the credentials stored in the server, include an `Authentication-Info` response header. This is a server-side equivalent of the `Authorization` header.

By default, clients use MD5 to compute the digest. Unlike basic authentication, this technique does not exchange an unencrypted shared secret.

Discussion

Here is a sample server response with a nonce and a client request with the `Authorization` header:

```
# Request
GET /photos HTTP/1.1 ❶
Host: www.example.org

# Response
401 Unauthorized
WWW-Authenticate: Digest realm="Sample app", nonce="6cf093043215da528d7b5039ed4694d3",
    qop="auth" ❷
Content-Type: application/xml;charset=UTF-8

<error xmlns:atom="http://www.w3.org/2005/Atom">
  <message>Unauthorized.</message>
</error>

# Request
GET /photos HTTP/1.1
Host: www.example.org
Authorization: Digest username="photoapp.001", realm="Sample app",
```

```
      nonce="6cf093043215da528d7b5039ed4694d3",
      uri="/photos", response="89fba5bf5e5f9dd69865258c21860956",
      cnonce="c019e396409afe784ae9f203b8dfdf7e", nc=00000001, qop="auth" ❸

# Response
HTTP/1.1 200 OK
Content-Type: application/xml;charset-UTF8

...
```

❶ A request without credentials.

❷ Response containing a challenge and a nonce.

❸ Request containing a `response` directive. See the following to learn how to compute this.

Unlike basic authentication, digest authentication requires the client to supply a digest of the credentials. In the second step, the server includes the following directives:

realm

> An opaque string that identifies a protected space on the server.

nonce

> An opaque string uniquely generated with each 401 (Unauthorized) response. Clients are required to use this value while generating a digest. Servers can reject requests containing nonce directives older than some value to prevent replay attacks.

qop

> Digest authentication specifies two values for this directive: auth and auth-int. auth implies that the server uses digest authentication for client authentication only. auth-int implies that the server uses this authentication to also maintain integrity of requests. When qop=auth-int, clients include the body of the request while computing the digest.

In this example, the shared secret is digestauth and the client/user is identified as photoapp.001. The client uses these, the request method, the resource URI, and the nonce to compute the digest as follows:

1. Concatenate the client/user identifier, the realm, and the shared secret as <identifier>:<realm>:<secret>, and compute its MD5 value. Say the value of the result is A1.

2. Concatenate the request method and the request URI as <method>:<URI>, and compute its MD5 value. Say the value of the result is A2.

3. Concatenate A1, nonce, and A2 as <A1>:<nonce>:<A2>, and compute its MD5 value.

The client uses the resulting value as the value of the `response` directive in the Authorization header.

Since the server-supplied nonce is part of the Authorization headers, clients cannot send an Authorization header without first obtaining a nonce value via the WWW-Authenticate header.

Servers can limit the chance of replay attacks by using a one-time or limited-use token as a nonce.

Similar to the one-time tokens used in Recipe 10.9, using one-time or limited-use tokens in requests requires the server to maintain a log of all used tokens.

The WWW-Authenticate header can also include other directives such as domain, opaque, stale, and algorithm directives. Further discussion of these directives and implementation details are beyond the scope of this book. See Chris Shiflett's *HTTP Developer's Handbook* (Sams) for more details of digest authentication.

12.3 How to Use Three-Legged OAuth

OAuth (*http://oauth.net*) is a delegated authorization protocol developed in 2007. Using this protocol, a user can, without revealing her credentials, let a client access her data available on a server. OAuth's authentication protocol is called *three-legged* because there are three parties involved in the protocol: the service provider (i.e., the server), the OAuth consumer (i.e., the client), and a user.

OAuth's three-legged protocol is applicable whenever a client would like to access a given user's resources available on a server. For instance, users of Twitter, Yahoo!, Google, Netflix, etc., use the OAuth protocol to grant access to their data to third-party tools so that those tools can access a user's data without asking users to share their credentials such as username and password. Implementations of this protocol are available in most programming languages.

Problem

You want to know how to implement three-legged OAuth protocol.

Solution

Figure 12-1 shows the role of the OAuth protocol. At the start of the protocol, the server uses a "consumer key" as an identifier for the client and a "consumer secret" as a shared secret. Once a user authorizes the client to access her resources, the server uses an "access token" as an identifier and a "token secret" as a shared secret to access the user's protected resources.

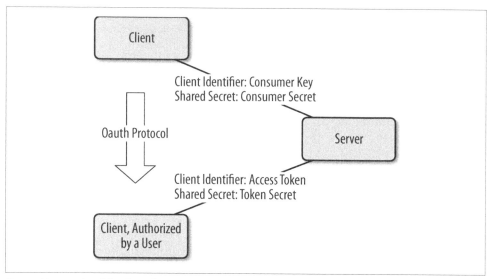

Figure 12-1. Role of the three-legged OAuth flow

OAuth relies on three sets of tokens and secrets issued by the server to the client:

Consumer key and consumer secret
> The consumer key is a unique identifier for the client. The client uses the consumer secret to sign the request to obtain request tokens.

Request token and token secret
> The request token is a temporary one-time identifier issued by the server for the purpose of asking the user to grant permission to the client. The token secret is used to sign the request to obtain an access token.

Access token and token secret
> The access token is an identifier for use by the client to access the user's resources. A client in possession of an access token can access the user's resources as long as the token is valid. The server may revoke it at any time either due to expiry or due to the user revoking the permission. The secret is used to sign requests to access the protected user's resources.

Using three-legged OAuth involves the following steps. The purpose of this flow is to obtain an access token and a secret. The server may grant the access token for a particular period of time and/or to limit access to certain user resources.

1. The client requests the server for a consumer key and a consumer secret out of band.

2. The client uses the consumer key to obtain a request token and a secret.

3. The client directs the user to the server to grant permission to let the client access the user's resources. This process results in an authenticated request token.

4. The client requests the server to provide an access token and secret. These represent an identifier and shared secret that the client can use to access resources on behalf of the user.

5. When making a request to access a protected resource, the client includes an `Authorization` header (or query parameters) containing the consumer key, the access token, the signature method and a signature, the timestamp, a nonce, and optionally the version of the OAuth protocol.

Note that since OAuth is a protocol layered on top of HTTP, servers need to document the following URIs to clients:

- URI to obtain request token
- URI to authorize the server
- URI to obtain an access token

OAuth recommends using `POST` to obtain request and access tokens.

Discussion

Consider the photo album web service introduced in Recipe 11.1. The client needs the user's authorization for it to be able to make a copy of a user's photo album resource. The client approaches the server to obtain an `oauth_consumer_key` and a secret through some out-of-band means. For example, the server may provide a web page for clients to register and obtain the consumer key and consumer secret. Assume that the server assigns `a1191fd420e0164c2f9aeac32ed35d23` as the consumer key and, as the shared secret, `fd9b9d0f769c3bcc548496e4b5077da79c02d7be`.

For the client to initiate the three-legged protocol, the server documents the following URIs:

- A URI to obtain request tokens (e.g., `https://www.example.org/oauth/request_token`)
- A URI to obtain a user's authorization (e.g., `https://www.example.org/oauth/authorize`)
- A URI to obtain an access token (e.g., `https://www.example.org/oauth/access_token`)

 Consider using TLS for these URIs since responses involve shared secrets and user authorization.

These requests involve the following parameters:

`oauth_consumer_key`
    This is the unique identifier issued by the server to each client.

oauth_signature_method

    This is the signing method used when computing a signature. OAuth defines HMAC-SHA1 and RSA-SHA1 as the signing methods. When clients and servers are using TLS, you can avoid signatures and use PLAINTEXT as the value of this parameter.

oauth_timestamp

    This is the number of seconds since January 1, 1970, 00:00:00 GMT.

oauth_nonce

    This is a random string that is unique for all requests sent at a given oauth_timestamp. This parameter helps servers deter replay attacks. Note that, unlike digest authentication, OAuth requires clients to generate nonce values.

oauth_version

    This is the version of OAuth, which is currently 1.0.

Clients can send these parameters as directives of the Authorization headers, or query parameters, or encoded using application/x-www-form-urlencoded in the body of the request. The following examples use the Authorization header for all requests.

The first step for the client is to submit a request to obtain a request token and a secret from the server. The signature in this request is based on the consumer secret that the client obtained along with the consumer key. The signature includes oauth_consumer_key, oauth_signature_method, oauth_timestamp, oauth_nonce, and oauth_version and must be computed as follows:

1. Collect parameters oauth_consumer_key, oauth_signature_method, oauth_timestamp, oauth_nonce, and oauth_version.

2. Percent-encode the parameters, and sort them first by their name and then by their value.

3. Concatenate the parameters into a string just the way you compute an application/x-www-form-urlencoded string. For this example, the value of this string is oauth_con sumer_key=a1191fd420e0164c2f9aeac32ed35d23&oauth_nonce=109843dea839120a&oa uth_signature_method=HMAC-SHA1&oauth_timestamp=1258308730&oauth_ver sion=1.0.

4. Compute a signature using the shared secret. For this example, the signature is d8e19bb988110380a72f6ca33b2ba5903272fe1.

5. Base64-encode the signature, and then percent-encode the resulting text.

Using this signature, the consumer sends a request to obtain a request token.

```
# Request to obtain a request token
POST /request_token HTTP/1.1 ❶
Host: www.example.org
Authorization: OAuth realm="http://www.example.com/photos",
               oauth_consumer_key=a1191fd420e0164c2f9aeac32ed35d23,
```

```
                    oauth_nonce=109843dea839120a,
                    oauth_signature=d8e19bb988110380a72f6ca33b2ba5903272fe1,
                    oauth_signature_method=HMAC-SHA1,
                    oauth_timestamp=1258308730,
                    oauth_version=1.0 ❷
Content-Length: 0

# Response containing a request token and a secret
HTTP/1.1 200 OK
Content-Type: application/x-www-form-urlencoded

oauth_token=0e713d524f290676de8aff4073b1bb52e37f065c
    &oauth_token_secret=394bc633d4c93f79aa0539fd554937760f05987c ❸
```

❶ Request to obtain a request token and secret

❷ Authorization header to authenticate the client

❸ Response containing a request token and a secret

The oauth_token in this response is a request token that the client must use in order to get the user's permission. The client directs the user to visit a resource on the server to grant authorization.

```
# Request to obtain authorization
GET /oauth/authorize?oauth_token=0e713d524f290676de8aff4073b1bb52e37f065c HTTP/1.1
Host: www.example.org
```

The implementation of this resource is up to the server. At this point, the server will need to check whether the user is authenticated with the server. The server may allow the user to select the parts of data that the client can access and the nature of the access. For instance, the user may grant the client permission to edit an album or create a new album but not delete any album or photos. After this step, the server directs the user back to the client. If the client has a web-based user interface, the server may redirect the user to that interface via a callback URI. If not, the server will ask the user to manually enter a verification code in the client's user interface. With either approach, the client obtains a verification code from the server.

The client uses the verification code to obtain an access token. The signature in this request is based on oauth_consumer_key, the request token, the verification code, oauth_signature_method, oauth_timestamp, oauth_nonce, and oauth_version.

```
# Request to obtain an access token
POST /access_token HTTP/1.1 ❶
Host: www.example.org
Authorization: OAuth oauth_consumer_key="a1191fd420e0164c2f9aeac32ed35d23",
                     oauth_token="ad0d1c7a765c9e6e8b14e639c763177312d18e7e",
                     oauth_verifier="988786765423",
                     oauth_signature_method="RSA-SHA1",
                     oauth_signature="698d58fd3316304181e11c6eb8127ffea7e2df46",
                     oauth_timestamp="1258328458",
                     oauth_nonce="109843dea839120a",
                     oauth_version="1.0" ❷
```

```
Content-Length: 0

HTTP/1.1 200 OK
Content-Type: application/x-www-form-urlencoded

oauth_token=8d743f1165c7030177040ec70f16df8bc6f415c7
  &oauth_token_secret=95aec3132c167ec2df818770dfbdbd0a8b2e105e ❸
```

❶ Request to obtain an access token and secret

❷ `Authorization` header to authenticate the client

❸ Response containing an access token and token secret

This response contains an access token and a secret. The server must verify that the request token matches the consumer key before issuing an access token.

The client uses these to construct an `Authorization` header with its requests to access protected resources for that user. The signature in this request is based on the `oauth_consumer_key`, access token, `oauth_signature_method`, `oauth_timestamp`, `oauth_nonce`, and `oauth_version` along with any query parameters in the URI or the body of the request when the request media type is `application/x-www-form-urlencoded`.

```
# Request
POST /albums/2009/08/1011/duplicate;t=a5d0e32ddff373df1b3351e53fc6ffb1 HTTP/1.1 ❶
Host: www.example.org
Authorization: OAuth oauth_consumer_key="a1191fd420e0164c2f9aeac32ed35d23",
                     oauth_token="827fa00c6f15db4063378bb988e1563e0c318dbc",
                     oauth_signature_method="RSA-SHA1",
                     oauth_signature="f863cceebb4f1fe60739b125128e7355dcbf14ea",
                     oauth_timestamp="1258328889",
                     oauth_nonce="3c93e7fdd1101e515997abf84116ef579dccce1a",
                     oauth_version="1.0" ❷
```

❶ Request to access a protected resource

❷ Request containing an `Authorization` header using the access token and token secret

Although the flow appears complex, it is designed to let clients access the user's data without asking for the user's credentials such as a username and password. Moreover, the user can ask the server to revoke the permission to any client.

When considering OAuth, note that the protocol is not associated with any particular resource. For a more in-depth discussion on using this protocol, see the "Beginner's Guide to OAuth" (*http://hueniverse.com/oauth*).

12.4 How to Use Two-Legged OAuth

Two-legged OAuth is similar to a client supplying its credentials to the server via the `Authorization` header using basic or digest authentication with no delegation involved.

Note that the OAuth specification does not specify this style of authentication, but it is widely used as a means of authenticating a client with a server.

Problem

You want to know how to implement two-legged OAuth to authenticate client requests.

Solution

Two-legged OAuth involves the following steps:

1. The client requests the server for a consumer key and a consumer secret out of band. The consumer key is an identifier for the client. The consumer secret is a secret shared between the client and the server.

2. When making a request to access a protected resource, the client includes an `Authorization` header containing the consumer key, the signature method and signature, a timestamp, a nonce, and optionally the version of the OAuth protocol.

The server verifies the signature before granting access to the resource. This approach is called *two-legged* since there are just two parties involved in the authentication flow.

Use two-legged OAuth when the server needs to the authenticate the client to provide access control, logging, metering, rate limiting, metrics, etc.

Discussion

Two-legged OAuth is well suited for cases involving several clients accessing protected resources on a server. The server can issue a consumer key and a secret to each client and require that clients submit an `Authorization` header containing a signature computed as per OAuth. Two-legged OAuth is also convenient to support servers that already support three-legged OAuth.

For instance, consider the hiring process example introduced in Recipe 5.5. In this example, a client interacts with the server to implement an employee hiring process. The client has its own authentication mechanism in place to authenticate its end users. For instance, the client may be a web-based application that uses cookies to authenticate its users. The server requires that the client use two-legged OAuth to authenticate itself to the server with each request. The server issues an `oauth_consumer_key` and a secret to the client through some out-of-band means. Assume that the server assigns `a1191fd420e0164c2f9aeac32ed35d23` as the consumer key and, as the shared secret, assigns `fd9b9d0f769c3bcc548496e4b5077da79c02d7be`.

Assume that the client is submitting the candidate information to create a new resource. To make an authenticated request, the client needs to include an `Authorization` header. See Recipe 12.3 for an outline of how to compute the signature.

The result is the value of the `oauth_signature` parameter. The client then generates the following `Authorization` header and makes a request:

```
# Request to enter candidate info
POST /hires HTTP/1.1 ❶
Host: www.example.org
Authorization: OAuth realm="http://www.example.com/hires",
                     oauth_consumer_key=a1191fd420e0164c2f9aeac32ed35d23,
                     oauth_nonce=85a55859fde262ba,
                     oauth_signature=d8e19bb988110380a72f6dba33b2ba5903272fe1,
                     oauth_signature_method=HMAC-SHA1,
                     oauth_timestamp=1258308689,
                     oauth_version=1.0 ❷
Content-Type: application/json

{
  "name": "Joe Prospect",
  ...
}

# Response
HTTP/1.1 201 Created
Location: http://www.example.org/hires/099
Content-Location: http://www.example.org/hires/099
Content-Type: application/json

{
  "name": "Joe Prospect",
  "id": "urn:example:hr:hiring:099",
  ...
  "link" : {
    "rel" : "http://www.example.org/rels/hiring/post-ref-result",
    "href" : "http://www.example.org/hires/099/refs"
  }
}
```

❶ Request to access a protected resource

❷ `Authorization` header computed using the consumer key and consumer secret

Note that OAuth also allows clients to supply the credentials via query parameters.

```
# Request to enter candidate info
POST /hires?oauth_consumer_key=a1191fd420e0164c2f9aeac32ed35d23&
            oauth_nonce=85a55859fde262ba&
            oauth_signature=d8e19bb988110380a72f6dba33b2ba5903272fe1&
            oauth_signature_method=HMAC-SHA1&
            oauth_timestamp=1258308689&oauth_version=1.0 HTTP/1.1
Host: www.example.org
Content-Type: application/json

{
  "name": "Joe Prospect",
  ...
}
```

However, using the `Authorization` header reduces URI proliferation.

If the client fails to include a valid `Authorization` header, the server should include the `WWW-Authenticate` header and a `401 (Unauthorized)` response header.

```
# Request to enter candidate info
POST /hires HTTP/1.1
Host: www.example.org
Content-Type: application/json

{
  "name": "Joe Prospect",
  ...
}

# Response
401 Unauthorized
WWW-Authenticate: OAuth realm="http://www.example.com/hires"
Content-Type: text/html;charset=UTF-8

<html>
  ...
  <body>
    <p>Unauthorized.</p>
  </body>
</html>
```

This indicates that the server uses OAuth for authentication.

12.5 How to Deal with Sensitive Information in URIs

As discussed in Recipe 1.3, servers can encode application state into URIs. In some cases, such state may be sensitive. Using TLS can help the integrity of such state when URIs are transported over the network, but the server can not control how clients manage URIs. In such cases, servers need to ensure that (a) the URIs have not been tampered with and/or (b) the information in URIs remains confidential.

Problem

You want to know how to maintain the integrity or confidentiality of sensitive information contained in URIs.

Solution

To detect tampering, compute a digital signature of the data in URIs using algorithms such as HMAC-SHA1 and RSA-SHA1. Include the signature as a query parameter in the resource URI.

If the data in URIs is confidential, encrypt the data algorithms such as AES, Blowfish, DES, Triple DES, Serpent, Twofish, etc. Make sure to Base64-encode the result before including it in the URI.

Discussion

Take the insurance quote example introduced in Recipe 1.3. In this example, the server encodes the data used to issued a quote in a link in the representation. The client can use the link to buy insurance based on the quote.

```
# Request
GET /quotegen?fname=...&lname=...&... HTTP/1.1
Host: www.example.org

# Response
HTTP/1.1 200 OK
Content-Type: application/xml;charset=UTF-8

<quote xmlns:atom="http://www.w3.org/2005/Atom">
  <driver>
    ...
  </driver>
  <vehicle>
    ...
  </vehicle>
  <offer>
    ...
    <valid-until>2009-08-02</valid-until>
    <atom:link href="http://www.example.org/quotes/buy?fname=...&lname=...&..."
          rel="http://www.example.org/quotes/buy"/>
  </offer>
</quote>
```

The state encoded in the URI in the link is prone to tampering. To prevent this, the server can include a signature of all the key parameters used to generate the quote.

```
http://www.example.org/quotes/buy?fname=...&lname=...&...
      &sign=f5b244520c2a452a0ee8c8b6ab5b6828317d2f7f
```

The signature in this example is computed using HMAC-SHA1 and a secret known only to the server. When the client makes a request, the server recomputes the signature of the data included in the URI and compare it with the signature included in the URI. Any difference between these values shows that the data has been tampered with.

The server can instead encrypt the state and use the encrypted state.

```
http://www.example.org/quotes/buy?gZwEW9oJIlZhYa1CuJ9IshGyvYJp2Gfo99M5115
      hWRKk497mkAOrnBZhkSb18UBzYftLpnryxUT2YOC8GFDpNT64hypV4kMu
```

When using TLS is not an option, the server can require the client to include the body of the request in the signature. In this case, the server needs to assign an identifier and a shared secret to each client and document the algorithm that clients must use to generate signatures. For instance, OAuth requests to access the resource include a signature of any parameters included in the body of the request. Digest authentication with qop=auth-int also uses the body of the request as part of the digest. Either approach ensures the integrity of the request.

12.6 How to Maintain the Confidentiality and Integrity of Representations

Problem

You want to know how to maintain the confidentiality and integrity of resource representations.

Solution

Use TLS and make resources accessible over a server configured to serve requests only using HTTPS.

Discussion

HTTP is a layered protocol. It relies on a transport protocol such as TCP/IP to provide the reliability of message transport. By layering HTTP over the TLS (RFC 5246) protocol, which is a successor of SSL, you can maintain the confidentiality and integrity of request and response messages without dealing with encryption and digital signatures in client and server code.

> TLS can also be used for mutual authentication where both the server and the client can be assured of the other party's identity. For instance, you can use basic authentication to authenticate users but rely on TLS to authenticate the client and the server.

When you use TLS for confidentiality and integrity, you can avoid building protocols for such security measures directly into request and response messages. Moreover, TLS is message agnostic. It can be used for any media type or request.

Details of setting up TLS are web server and client software specific. These may even change from programming language to language. Consult server- or software-specific material to learn the details of how to set up TLS between clients and servers.

Note that SOAP-based web services rely on WS-Security (*http://www.oasis-open.org/committees/tc_home.php?wg_abbrev=wss*). WS-Security specifies ways to send security tokens as SOAP headers. For instance, to prevent tampering, SOAP-based web services include a signature in the header of SOAP messages as in the following example:

```
# A SOAP message containing a signature
<soapenv:Envelope
xmlns:soapenv="http://schemas.xmlsoap.org/soap/envelope/"
xmlns:xsd="http://www.w3.org/2001/XMLSchema"
xmlns:xsi="http://www.w3.org/2001/XMLSchema-instance">
  <soapenv:Header>
    <wsse:Security
      soapenv:actor="http://www.example.org"
      soapenv:mustUnderstand="1"
      xmlns:wsse="http://schemas.xmlsoap.org/ws/2002/04/secext">
      <Signature xmlns="http://www.w3.org/2000/09/xmldsig#">
        <SignedInfo>
          <CanonicalizationMethod
            Algorithm="http://www.w3.org/2001/10/xml-exc-c14n#"/>
          <SignatureMethod Algorithm="http://www.w3.org/2000/09/xmldsig#rsa-sha1"/>
          <Reference URI="#abcd">
            <Transforms>
              <Transform Algorithm="http://www.w3.org/2001/10/xml-exc-c14n#"/>
            </Transforms>
            <DigestMethod Algorithm="http://www.w3.org/2000/09/xmldsig#sha1"/>
            <DigestValue>... digest value</DigestValue>
          </Reference>
        </SignedInfo>
        <SignatureValue>...</SignatureValue>
        <KeyInfo xmlns="http://www.w3.org/2000/09/xmldsig#">
          ... key info ...
        </KeyInfo>
      </Signature>
    </wsse:Security>
  </soapenv:Header>
  <soapenv:Body>... application data ...</</soapenv:Body>
</soapenv:Envelope>
```

This message contains the application data in the Body element and its signature in the
Header. In contrast, RESTful web services can use HTTPS (i.e., HTTP layered over TLS)
to let TLS deal with digital signatures and encryption independently of the methods
and media types used.

 HTTP's layered architecture thus decouples application-level messages
from transport-level security.

## CHAPTER 13

Extensibility and Versioning

Managing change in any distributed client/server environment can be hard. In these environments, clients count on servers to honor their contracts. RESTful web services are no exception. For these web services, the contract consists of URIs, resources, the structure and content of representations, their formats, and the HTTP methods for each resource.

Any change to a server may seem benign until you consider *backward compatibility*. When a change is backward compatible, you need not upgrade clients at the same time as you modify the server. Clients can ignore the fact that you upgraded the server and continue to use the server as though nothing changed, barring any downtime during server upgrades.

There is another kind of compatibility called *forward compatibility* that may be important when you have several clients and servers upgraded at different points in time. In this case, some newer clients may be interacting with older servers. The purpose of forward compatibility is to ensure that newer clients can continue to use the older servers without disruption albeit with reduced functionality. Whether your application needs to consider backward compatibility alone or both backward and forward compatibility depends on your operating environment. The recipes described in this chapter can help you tackle both.

The characteristic that lets you maintain compatibility is *extensibility*. Extensibility is a design process to account for future changes. As a transfer protocol, HTTP is extensible. You can extend HTTP by adding new methods or headers, with certain caveats (see Recipes 1.12 and 1.13). But that does not mean that applications built over HTTP are automatically extensible. This chapter shows the steps that you can take to maintain the extensibility of web services.

 Managing change takes discipline, careful planning, and defensive coding practices. Most changes have good intentions. Either they fix something broken or they enhance some functionality. However, if not planned well, changes can be disruptive.

Although maintaining compatibility is desirable, making compatible changes is not always possible. For instance, you may have added security measures that require clients to upgrade. In this case, clients have no option. Alternatively, you may have added new functionality to the server that requires clients to make changes to use those features. The challenge is to let existing clients continue to function as usual at least for some period of time, while allowing new clients to take advantage of the newer features in the server. This is a problem of versioning.

 Even if you plan to upgrade all clients to use newer servers, a one-time simultaneous upgrade of all servers and clients is not a realistic task. Your web services may need to operate round the clock, and simultaneous upgrades may require downtime. Therefore, you need to plan for a gradual rollout of upgrades to servers and clients to maintain the availability of the overall system.

Note that both clients and servers need to take the appropriate steps to operate smoothly under change. For the server, the goal is to keep the clients from breaking. For the clients, the objective is to not fail when new unknown data or links appear in representations. This chapter discusses the following recipes:

Recipe 13.1, *"How to Maintain URI Compatibility"*
    Use this recipe to learn how to keep URI changes compatible.

Recipe 13.2, *"How to Maintain Compatibility of XML and JSON Representations"*
    Use this recipe to learn how to extend XML and JSON representations while maintaining compatibility.

Recipe 13.3, *"How to Extend Atom"*
    Use this recipe to learn ways to extend Atom.

Recipe 13.4, *"How to Maintain Compatibility of Links"*
    Use this recipe to learn how to keep links compatible.

Recipe 13.5, *"How to Implement Clients to Support Extensibility"*
    Use this recipe to learn about implementing clients that do not break when the server makes compatible changes.

Recipe 13.6, *"When to Version"*
    Use this recipe to decide when to version the server.

Recipe 13.7, *"How to Version RESTful Web Services"*
    Use this recipe to learn how to version a web service.

13.1 How to Maintain URI Compatibility

Problem

You want to know how to keep changes to URIs compatible with existing clients.

Solution

As described in Recipe 4.4, keep URIs permanent. Treat request URIs containing the same query parameters but in a different order as the same. Clients must be able to get the same behavior irrespective of the order of the query parameters.

When you add new parameters to URIs, continue to honor existing parameters, and treat new parameters as optional. When changing data formats for query parameters, continue to honor existing formats. If that is not viable, introduce format changes via new query parameters or new URIs. By default, treat query parameters in URIs as optional except when such parameters are needed for concurrency or security reasons.

Discussion

Consider the following URIs:

```
http://www.example.org/catalog?q=rest&pub=oreilly&y=2010
http://www.example.org/catalog?pub=oreilly&q=rest&y=2010
```

Since these two URIs are syntactically different, they identify two different resources at the protocol level. However, treating them as equivalent on the server code gives clients flexibility in URI parsing and URI construction.

The following URIs use different formats for a query parameter and hence are compatible:

```
# Original URI format
http://www.example.org/catalog?q=fiction&pubdate=1230796800

# New URI format
http://www.example.org/catalog?q=fiction&pubdate=2009-01-01Z
```

The first URI uses a Unix epoch time for the `pubdate` parameter. The second URI supports an RFC-3339 compliant format for this parameter. The server must continue to support the first format to maintain compatibility with existing clients. If supporting both formats is not viable, say, because of your server-side library not being able to support multiple formats at once, add a new parameter that supports the new format.

```
http://www.example.org/catalog?q=fiction&pubdate=1230796800
http://www.example.org/catalog?q=fiction&published=2009-01-01Z
```

The second URI uses a query parameter with a different name, implying that the first parameter is optional. Designing URIs and server code that can keep query parameters optional gives flexibility to introduce new parameters.

13.2 How to Maintain Compatibility of XML and JSON Representations

This recipe discusses how to make compatible changes to XML and JSON representations. See Recipe 13.3 to learn about extending Atom representations.

Problem

You want to know how to keep changes to XML/JSON representations compatible with existing clients.

Solution

Design an XML format to keep the child elements unordered. When making changes to XML and JSON, preserve the hierarchical structure so that clients can continue to follow the same structure to extract data.

Make new data elements in requests optional to maintain compatibility with existing clients. Clients that do not send new data fields must be able to continue to function.

Do not remove or rename any data fields from representations in response bodies.

Discussion

Although headers are part of a representation, as long as clients and servers use headers correctly as per HTTP, headers should not affect compatibility. Most compatibility problems occur with the body of representations.

Using extensible formats such as XML and JSON is necessary to allow servers to make changes. However, using such extensible formats does not automatically guarantee that the representations are compatible. To keep clients from breaking, you need to preserve the way clients read data from the body of a representation. The following example illustrates a compatible change:

```
# Response before change
HTTP/1.1 200 OK
Content-Type: application/xml;charset=UTF-8

<user>
  <first-name>John</first-name>
  <last-name>Doe</last-name>
  <street>1 Some Street</street>
  <city>Some City</city>
<user>

# Representation body after the change
HTTP/1.1 200 OK
Content-Type: application/xml;charset=UTF-8

<user>
  <first-name>John</first-name>
  <last-name>Doe</last-name>
  <street>1 Some Street</street>
  <city>Some City</city>
  <state>WA</state>
<user>
```

But the following representation introduces an incompatible change:

```
# Representation body after the change
HTTP/1.1 200 OK
Content-Type: application/xml;charset=UTF-8

<user>
  <first-name>John</first-name>
  <last-name>Doe</last-name>
  <address>
    <street>1 Some Street</street>
    <city>Some City</city>
  </address>
<user>
```

The elements that clients need to parse in order to read the name of the city are different in this representation. A client that is written to extract the city name from the city child element of the user element will not find it in the second example. This breaks compatibility.

For any representation format that allows the hierarchical arrangement of data, do not change the hierarchy.

Some applications of XML schema languages for XML representations may limit extensibility. For example, consider the following XML schema for an XML document:

```
<xs:schema xmlns:xs="http://www.w3.org/2001/XMLSchema">
  <xs:element name="address">
    <xs:complexType>
      <xs:sequence>
        <xs:element name="first-name" type="xs:string"/>
        <xs:element name="last-name" type="xs:string"/>
        <xs:element name="street" type="xs:string"/>
        <xs:element name="city" type="xs:string"/>
      </xs:sequence>
    </xs:complexType>
  </xs:element>
</xs:schema>
```

Such a schema prevents you from adding new child elements anywhere except after the city element. Moreover, it requires clients to construct XML as per the document order of child elements. For this particular example, the following schema is a better choice. This schema uses xs:all to keep the child elements unordered.

```
<xs:schema xmlns:xs="http://www.w3.org/2001/XMLSchema">
  <xs:element name="address">
    <xs:complexType>
      <xs:all>
        <xs:element name="first-name" type="xs:string"/>
        <xs:element name="last-name" type="xs:string"/>
        <xs:element name="street" type="xs:string"/>
```

```
            <xs:element name="city" type="xs:string"/>
        </xs:all>
      </xs:complexType>
    </xs:element>
  </xs:schema>
```

You can also use `xs:choice` or substitution groups for unordered child elements. In RelaxNG, you can use the `interleave` pattern to describe unordered elements. See Appendix A for references of books to learn about extensible XML design.

 Use schemas to assist documentation but not to enforce constraints on XML documents at runtime.

In the case of JSON representations, the order of properties for a JSON object does not matter because, by definition, properties are unordered. Hence, the following are equivalent:

```
{
  "first-name" : "John",
  "last-name" : "Doe",
  "street" : "1 Some Street",
  "city" : "Some City"
}

{
  "city" : "Some City"
  "last-name" : "Doe",
  "first-name" : "John",
  "street" : "1 Some Street",
}
```

Note that when a server adds new fields to representations, there is no guarantee that clients submit them back to the server when making PUT or POST requests.

```
# Request
GET /user/001 HTTP/1.1
Host: www.example.org

# Response contains a new email property
HTTP/1.1 200 OK
Content-Type: application/json

{
  "first-name" : "John",
  "last-name" : "Doe",
  "street" : "1 Some Street",
  "city" : "Some City",
  "email" : "john.doe@example.org"
}

# Request to update
```

```
PUT /user/001 HTTP/1.1
Content-Type: application/json

{
  "first-name" : "John A.",
  "last-name" : "Doe",
  "street" : "1012 North 1st Street",
  "city" : "Some City"
}

# Response
HTTP/1.1 204 No Content
```

Clients that do not understand new fields may not store them locally. In this example, the client does not include the `email` property in the `PUT` request. If this causes the server to assume that the user has no email address, introduce a new version of the resource that contains the email. See Recipe 13.7 for an example.

13.3 How to Extend Atom

The Atom format was designed to support future extensions. All elements in the Atom format allow foreign XML elements and attributes. For example, in the following snippet, the `atom:author` element is extended to include the author's telephone number:

```
<atom:author xmlns:atom="http://www.w3.org/2005/Atom">
  <atom:name>John Author</atom:name>
  <atom:uri>http://www.example.org/authors/john-author</atom:uri>
  <atom:email>john.author@mail.example.org</atom:mail>
  <ex:phone xmlns:ex="http://www.example.org/ns">425-123-4567</ex:phone>
</atom:author>
```

This is a valid `atom:author` element. Clients that can understand this extension can interpret the author's phone numbers, and clients that do not understand it can ignore it. You can extend Atom in the following ways:

- Add new link relation types. An example is the "Feed Paging and Archiving" extensions (RFC 5005), which introduce the `first`, `last`, `previous`, and `next` link relation types.

- Add new elements within Atom elements such as `atom:entry`, `atom:feed`, and `atom:link`. Examples include "Atom Threading Extensions" (RFC 4685), which introduces new elements `in-reply-to` and `total`, and "In-Lining Extensions for Atom," which extends the `atom:link` element to include `atom:entry` or `atom:feed` documents of linked resources.

- Use foreign XML or other textual content nested inside `atom:content` elements.

This recipe reviews various ways of extending Atom and presents preferred ways.

Problem

You want to know possible ways to extend Atom.

Solution

Define new link relations as described in Recipe 5.4. Add new child elements or attributes to `atom:feed` and `atom:entry` elements as long as such extensions do not hamper the proper function of clients and other software that does not know about such extensions.

When adding foreign content under the `atom:content` element, provide human-readable text or XHTML under the `atom:summary` element.

Discussion

A key consideration for the introduction of extensions is their effect on interoperability. It is better to avoid extensions that reduce the chances of interoperability. Here is an extension used by OpenSearch (*http://www.opensearch.org*):

```
<!-- Example reproduced from
     http://www.opensearch.org/Specifications/OpenSearch/1.1 -->
<atom:feed xmlns:atom="http://www.w3.org/2005/Atom"
        xmlns:opensearch="http://a9.com/-/spec/opensearch/1.1/">
  <opensearch:Query role="request" searchTerms="General Motors annual report"/> ❶
  <opensearch:Query role="related" searchTerms="GM" title="General Motors stock symbol"/>
  <opensearch:Query role="related" searchTerms="automotive industry revenue"/>
  <opensearch:Query role="subset" searchTerms="General Motors annual report 2005"
  <opensearch:Query role="superset" searchTerms="General Motors"/>
  ...
</atom:feed>
```

❶ Extending by adding optional child elements to `atom:feed`

Clients that do not understand OpenSearch extensions can ignore the extension. Here is another example of an extension that does not reduce interoperability. This is based on the "In-Lining Extensions for Atom" Internet-Draft.

```
<atom:feed xmlns:atom="http://www.w3.org/2005/Atom">
  ...
  <atom:link rel="http://www.example.org/rels/comments" ❶
    href="http://www.example.org/comments"> ❷
    <ae:inline xmlns:ae="http://purl.org/atom/ext/">
      <atom:feed>
        <!-- A complete feed -->
      </atom:feed>
    </ae:inline>
  </atom:link>
  ...
</atom:feed>
```

❶ Extending by introducing a new link relation type

❷ Extending by adding optional child elements to `atom:link`

This example has two extensions. It uses an extended link relation type to introduce a new type of link not defined by Atom. It also extends the `atom:link` element to include the comments feed inside a link used to provide a URI to the comments feed.

The previous examples extend Atom but do not affect interoperability. Here is an example that most Atom-aware tools cannot process. This is variant of the example from Recipe 6.2.

```
<!-- Avoid this -->
<atom:entry xmlns:atom="http://www.w3.org/2005/Atom">
  <atom:title>Johnny Web Sample Production Schedule</atom:title>
  <atom:id>urn:sked:1111</atom:id>
  <atom:updated>2011-11-11T11:11:11Z</atom:updated>
  <atom:author><name>J. W. Smith</name></atom:author>
  <atom:link rel="self" href="http://www.example.org/ps/1111"/>
  <atom:content type="text">
    Johnny Web Sample Production Schedule
  </atom:content>
  <ex:story-development xmlns:ex="http://www.example.org/ns/ps"> ❶
    <ex:days>5</ex:days>
    <ex:planned-start>2012-01-01</ex:planned-start>
  </ex:story-development>
  <ex:pencil-roughs xmlns:ex="http://www.example.org/ns/ps">
    <ex:days>2</ex:days>
    <ex:planned-start>2012-01-10</ex:planned-start>
  </ex:pencil-roughs>
  <ex:layouts-and-ink xmlns:ex="http://www.example.org/ns/ps">
    <ex:days>3</ex:days>
    <ex:planned-start>2012-01-15</ex:planned-start>
  </ex:layouts-and-ink>
</atom:entry>
```

❶ Required elements added to the `atom:entry` or `atom:feed` element reduce interoperability

This representation has several extension elements for the production data. Atom-capable tools that do not know about this extension will see it as follows:

```
<atom:entry xmlns:atom="http://www.w3.org/2005/Atom">
  <atom:title>Johnny Web Sample Production Schedule</atom:title>
  <atom:id>urn:sked:1111</atom:id>
  <atom:updated>2011-11-11T11:11:11Z</atom:updated>
  <atom:author><name>J. W. Smith</name></atom:author>
  <atom:ink rel="self" href="http://www.example.org/ps/1111"/>
  <atom:content type="text">
    Johnny Web Sample Production Schedule
  </atom:content>
</atom:entry>
```

You can make such a representation meaningful to such clients by providing XHTML content or a summary.

```
<atom:entry xmlns:atom="http://www.w3.org/2005/Atom">
  <atom:title>Johnny Web Sample Production Schedule</atom:title>
  <atom:id>urn:sked:1111</atom:id>
```

```
<atom:updated>2011-11-11T11:11:11Z</atom:updated>
<atom:author><name>J. W. Smith</name></atom:author>
<atom:link rel="self" href="http://www.example.org/ps/1111"/>
<atom:content type="xhtml">
  <html>
    <head>
      <title>Johnny Web Sample Production Schedule</title>
    </head>
    <body>
      <!-- HTML formatted production schedule -->
      ...
    </body>
  </html>
</atom:content>
<ex:story-development xmlns:ex="http://www.example.org/ns/ps">
  <ex:days>5</ex:days>
  <ex:planned-start>2012-01-01</ex:planned-start>
</ex:story-development>
<ex:pencil-roughs xmlns:ex="http://www.example.org/ns/ps">
  <ex:days>2</ex:days>
  <ex:planned-start>2012-01-10</ex:planned-start>
</ex:pencil-roughs>
<ex:layouts-and-ink xmlns:ex="http://www.example.org/ns/ps">
  <ex:days>3</ex:days>
  <ex:planned-start>2012-01-15</ex:planned-start>
</ex:layouts-and-ink>
</atom:entry>
```

In general, extensions that can be safely ignored by clients promote interoperability and should be preferred.

13.4 How to Maintain Compatibility of Links

Problem

You want to know how to keep changes to links compatible with existing clients.

Solution

Avoid removing links. Do not change the values of the `rel` and `href` attributes of links. When introducing new resources, use links to provide URIs of those resources to clients.

Discussion

Using links allows clients to treat URIs as opaque resource identifiers. Clients can use link relation types to learn what URI to use. However, clients may store URIs in databases. When a server changes the value of `href`, clients may not update their stored URIs with the new value. For instance, the following change may break clients:

```
<!-- Old link -->
<atom:link rel="edit" href="http://www.example.org/catalog?prodid=32543Y2009"/>

<-- New link -->
<atom:link rel="edit" href="http://www.example.org/catalog/2009/32543Y"/>
```

Clients may have stored the value of this link locally in a data store and may continue to use the old URI. When you need to change URIs, honor old URIs by using server-side URI rewriting rules. See Recipe 4.4 to learn why it is better to keep URIs permanent.

Changing the value of the link relation type will also break client functionality. Instead of changing the name, introduce a new link with the new `rel`.

```
<!-- Link in the old representation -->
<atom:link rel="edit" href="http://www.example.org/catalog?prodid=32543Y2009"/>

<-- Links in the new representation -->
<atom:link rel="edit" href="http://www.example.org/catalog?prodid=32543Y2009"/>
<atom:link rel="http://www.example.org/rels/update"
  href="http://www.example.org/catalog?prodid=32543Y2009"/>
```

Links also play a vital role to keep the web service extensible. For example, if the product catalog now supports user-generated content such as comments, reviews, and photos, the server can introduce this feature by adding new links.

```
# Request
GET /catalog/2009/32543Y HTTP/1.1
Host: www.example.org

# Response contains new links
HTTP/1.1 200 OK
Content-Type: application/xml;charset=UTF-8

<product xmlns:atom="http://www.w3.org/2005/Atom">
  ...
  <atom:link rel="http://www.example.org/rels/ugc-comments"
    href="http://www.example.org/catalog/2009/32543/comments"/>
  <atom:link rel="http://www.example.org/rels/ugc-reviews"
    href="http://www.example.org/catalog/2009/32543/reviews"/>
  <atom:link rel="http://www.example.org/rels/ugc-photos"
    href="http://www.example.org/catalog/2009/32543/photos"/>
</product>
```

The new links in this representation provide URIs of collections for user-generated content, thus extending the representation. Clients that support the new link relations can take advantage of the new functionality.

13.5 How to Implement Clients to Support Extensibility

Problem

You want to know how to implement a client such that it does not fail when the server makes compatible changes.

Solution

When parsing bodies of representations, look for known data. In the case of XML, look for known elements and attributes by name and not by position. Implement the client to not fail when it finds unrecognized data. If the client is capable of storing the complete representation locally, store everything.

Do not assume that the representation received from the server is of a fixed media type, character encoding, content language, or content encoding. As described in Recipe 3.2, read these values from the corresponding `Content-*` headers, and process them accordingly.

Discussion

A key rule to remember when writing client applications is to not falter on any data that is not relevant for the client functionality. For instance, in the case of an XML representation, a server may enhance user profile representations to include the user's blog address and an email.

```
# Response before the change
HTTP/1.1 200 OK
Content-Type: application/xml;charset=UTF-8

<person>
  <first-name>John</first-name>
  <last-name>Doe</last-name>
  <street>1 Some Street</street>
  <city>Some City</city>
<person>

# Response after the change
HTTP/1.1 200 OK
Content-Type: application/xml;charset=UTF-8

<person xmlns:atom="http://www.w3.org/2005/Atom">
  <first-name>John</first-name>
  <last-name>Doe</last-name>
  <atom:link href="http://blog.example.org/johndoe" rel="related"/>
  <email>...</email>
  <street>1 Some Street</street>
  <city>Some City</city>
<person>
```

Implement the client such that it does not fail when it finds a link after the second child of the person element.

13.6 When to Version

Problem

You want to know when to introduce a new version of a web service.

Solution

Consider versioning when the server is unable to maintain compatibility. Also consider versioning if some clients require behavior or functionality different from other clients.

Discussion

Versioning is sometimes seen as a simpler task in comparison to maintaining compatibility. To maintain compatibility, you have to constantly assess whether a given change breaks clients and then proceed with caution. Sometimes simple changes to the server code break clients. In reality, versioning may introduce new problems.

- Data stored by a client for one version of a web service may not automatically work with the data from a different version of the same web service. Clients may have to port resource data stored locally before migrating to the new version. You can avoid this by making compatible changes.

- Version changes may involve new business rules and new application flow. These require code changes in clients.

- Maintaining multiple versions of resources at the same time is not trivial. You may need to partition your servers or code or data stores for each version.

- When you use links to convey URIs to clients, clients may store them locally. When you assign new URIs, clients will have to upgrade those URIs along with other stored data of resources.

However, there are exceptions. For instance, you may have consolidated all customer data stores in your organization, and for some servers that serve the customer data to clients, the fields used are completely different. Similarly, a photo-sharing site now wants to support videos for microblogging, and the resource definitions for videos cannot be shoehorned into the resource definitions used for photos.

Another exception is when servers are required to maintain a different set of features customized for each client. This is common in the case of multitenant or "software as a service" platforms. For example, a server that provides health insurance management for employers may need to maintain separate versions of the server software for each employer. Each version may include special customizations.

See Recipe 13.7 to learn how to introduce a new version.

13.7 How to Version RESTful Web Services

When making compatible changes is no longer an option, version some or all resources to isolate changes from existing clients.

Problem

You want to know how to introduce a new version of a web service.

Solution

Add new resources with new URIs when there is a change in the behavior of resources or a change in the information contained in representations. Use easily detectable patterns such as v1 or v2 in subdomain names, path segments, or query parameters to distinguish URIs by their version.

Avoid treating each version as a new representation with a new media type of the same resource.

Discussion

Versioning a RESTful web service involves versioning resources with new URIs. This is because HTTP dictates everything except URIs of resources and their representations. Although you can add custom HTTP methods and headers, as discussed in Recipe 1.12 and Recipe 1.13, such additions may impair interoperability with other clients and servers. This leaves you with resources for versioning.

Here are some URIs using version identifiers:

```
http://www.example.org/v1/customer/1234
http://www.example.org/v2/customer/1234
http://www.example.org/customer/1234?version=v3
http://v4.example.org/customer/1234
```

Of these, what works best may depend on your software stack and server deployment. When the same server manages multiple versions, then using path segments or query parameters may be convenient.

Consider the email example from Recipe 13.2. Since the email field is new and editable by clients, the server introduces a new version of the person resource with a new URI.

```
# Request
GET /v2/person/001 HTTP/1.1
Host: www.example.org

# Response contains a new email property
HTTP/1.1 200 OK
Content-Type: application/json
```

```
{
  "first-name" : "John",
  "last-name" : "Doe",
  "street" : "1 Some Street",
  "city" : "Some City",
  "email" : "john.doe@example.org"
}

# Request to update
PUT /v2/person/001 HTTP/1.1
Content-Type: application/json

{
  "first-name" : "John A.",
  "last-name" : "Doe",
  "street" : "1012 North 1st Street",
  "city" : "Some City",
  "email" : "john.doe@example.com
}

# Response
HTTP/1.1 204 No Content
```

Clients that use the new version will see or be able to update the email. Clients that use the old version do not.

When a server uses this approach to introduce new versions of existing resources, clients need to upgrade their data stores to support new fields of new versions of resources. For instance, in the data store, the client may have the following data stored for user resources:

```
# Use ID, First name, Last name, URI, ...
user001    "John"    "Doe"    "http://www.example.org/user/001"    ...
user002    "Jane"    "Doe"    "http://www.example.org/user/002"    ...
user003    "Bob"     "Coder"  "http://www.example.org/user/003"    ...
...
```

 Clients storing URIs in databases is like bookmarking. However, since clients may use one set of servers for development and another set for production, you may need to store just the path portion of the URIs, leaving the domain name configurable.

When the server introduces a new version of these resources, the client needs to update its database to point to the new URIs.

```
# Use ID, First name, Last name, email, URI, ...
user001  "John"  "Doe"    -  "http://www.example.org/v2/user/001"
user002  "Jane"  "Doe"    -  "http://www.example.org/v2/user/002"
user003  "Bob"   "Coder"  -  "http://www.example.org/v2/user/003"
...
```

Well-recognizable version identifier URIs can help with the migration of URIs on the client side. For instance, the client may write code to replace all occurrences of http://www.example.org/user/ with http://www.example.org/v2/user/ in the database as part of its upgrade process to support the new version. After upgrading the URIs, the client can fetch new fields to update the stored data.

```
# Use ID, First name, Last name, email, URI, ...
user001  "John"  "Doe"    "john.doe@emample.org"   "http://www.example.org/v2/user/001"
user002  "Jane"  "Doe"    "jane.doe@example.org"   "http://www.example.org/v2/user/002"
user003  "Bob"   "Coder"  "bob.Coder@example.org"  "http://www.example.org/v2/user/003"
...
```

Note that some server applications prefer extending media types with version identifiers instead of using version identifiers in URIs, as shown in the following example:

```
application/xml;version=1
application/vnd.user+xml;version=1
application/vns.user+xml;version=2
```

The idea of this approach is to treat each version of the resource as a different representation so that clients can negotiate for a given version by submitting an Accept header with a media type for that version. If the server supports that version, it will return a representation of that version. When the client is upgraded to support the new version, it can change the media type used in the Accept header to switch to the new version.

 Avoid introducing new media types for each version since it leads to media type proliferation, which may reduce interoperability with other servers/clients as well as existing HTTP-level tools.

## CHAPTER 14

Enabling Discovery

When building RESTful web services, you need to address two kinds of discoverability. These are design-time discoverability and runtime discoverability. Design-time discoverability helps others design and build clients. It describes all the essentials that client developer teams and administrators need to know in order to build and launch clients. Runtime discoverability, on the other hand, helps maintain loose coupling between clients and servers and enables plug-and-play-style automation. Runtime discovery involves HTTP's uniform interface, media types, links, and link relations. This chapter is about design-time discoverability.

Design-time discoverability simply means describing your web service in prose, whether such prose is generated by some tools or created manually by the designers or developers of the web service. Client developers can consult this prose to understand the "semantics" of the resources, media types, link relations, and so on, and implement clients.

This chapter discusses the following recipes:

Recipe 14.1, "How to Document RESTful Web Services"
    This recipe illustrates what to document to help client developers learn about your web service.

Recipe 14.2, "How to Use OPTIONS"
    Use this recipe to learn when and how to use the OPTIONS method.

14.1 How to Document RESTful Web Services

The best way to promote design- and development-time discoverability is to unambiguously document the information needed to implement clients.

Problem

You want to know how to document your web service.

Solution

Fully describe the following in human-readable documentation:

- All resources and methods supported for each resource
- Media types and representation formats for resources in requests and responses
- Each link relation used, its business significance, HTTP method to be used, and resource that the link identifies
- All fixed URIs that are not supplied via links
- Query parameters used for all fixed URIs
- URI templates and token substitution rules
- Authentication and security credentials for accessing resources

For XML representations, if your clients and servers are capable of supporting XML schemas, use a schema language as a "convention" to describe the structure of XML documents used for representations in requests and responses. For other formats, use conventions to describe representations in prose.

Discussion

No machine-readable description can replace human-readable documentation. Documenting your web service in human-readable format such as HTML is the most useful way to enable design-time discovery. When documenting your service, include all the information necessary to implement a client.

> Lack of a standard description language is often cited as a limitation of REST. In reality, machine-readable description languages do not communicate the semantics necessary for client developers to write code. See, for examples, the documentation of web services by Yahoo! (*http://developer.yahoo.com*), Flickr (*http://www.flickr.com/services/api/*), Twitter (*http://apiwiki.twitter.com/*), and Google Data Protocol (*http://code.google.com/apis/gdata/*). All these services provide extensive human-readable documentation with examples.

Here is an example of what to include when documenting a RESTful web service. Consider the album example from Recipe 11.2 to support finding, creating, editing, duplicating, and merging albums. Tables 14-1, 14-2, and 14-3 illustrate how to document such a web service.

Table 14-1. Resources

Resource	Methods	Description
Photo	GET, PUT	This resource contains photo metadata and a link to a related binary photo media resource (such as a JPEG file).
		Media types: application/xml
Photo media	GET, PUT	This resource represents the uploaded photo. Submit a POST request with media type `multipart/form-data` to the album resource to create a photo and a photo media resource.
		Media types: image/jpeg, image/gif, image/png
Album	GET, DELETE, and POST	This resource contains zero or more photos. Use POST to add photos to an album.
		Media types: application/xml, multipart/form-data
Album collection	GET, DELETE, and POST	This resource contains zero or more albums. Use POST to add a new album to the collection.
		Media types: application/xml
Duplicate album controller	POST	This resource lets a client duplicate an album.
		Media types: application/xml
Merge album controller	GET and POST	This resource lets a client merge albums.
		Media types: application/xml

Table 14-2. URIs

Resource	URI	Description
Album collection	`http://www.example.org/albums`	Use this URI to get the 10 latest albums using GET or to create a new album using POST.
		Use links with the relation types `next` and `previous` to browse through all the albums.
Album search	`http://www.example.org/albums?q={keyword}&ym={year-month}`	Use this URI template to search for albums.
		The token `{keyword}` takes a keyword, and the token `{year-month}` takes either a year or a year and month. Here are some example URIs after token substitution:
		`http://www.example.org/albums?q=paris&ym=` `http://www.example.org/albums?q=hiking&ym=2009-08` `http://www.example.org/albums?q=&ym=2000`
Album merge	`http://www.example.org/albums/merge?src={srcid1}&src={srcid2}`	Use this template to get a link to merge two albums into a new album. The server will delete the original albums after this operation. This operation cannot undone.
		In this template, the tokens `{srcid1}` and `srcid2` are identifiers of the albums to be merged.

Table 14-3. Link relation types

Name	Description
http://www.example.org/rels/duplicate	Use a link with this relation type to submit a POST request to duplicate an existing album.
http://www.example.org/rels/merge	Use a link with this relation type to refer to a controller resource to merge albums.

For the sake of brevity, the previous documentation excludes details of the XML documents and form parameters used.

14.2 How to Use OPTIONS

By implementing the HTTP OPTIONS method, you can help tools learn about resources in your web service.

Problem

You want to know how to provide information about a resource or the server to clients using the OPTIONS method.

Solution

On the server side, implement OPTIONS to return the list of supported methods via the Allow response header.

When a resource supports the PATCH method (Recipe 11.9), add an Accept-Patch header listing the media types supported for PATCH requests.

Optionally add a Link header with a link containing a human-readable document that describes the resource.

Discussion

Consider the photo album example again. For each of the resources in that example, you can provide a link to human-readable documentation along with the list of supported methods to help tools learn more about your resources. Here is an example:

```
# Request
OPTIONS /photos HTTP/1.1
Host: http://www.example.org

# Response
HTTP/1.1 204 No Content
Allow: POST, GET
Link: <http://www.example.org/docs/photos>; type=text/html; rel=help
```

In this example, in addition to advertising to clients that this resource supports the HTTP methods POST and GET, the server provides a link to documentation about the resource that client developers may browse. You might develop a plug-in for your favorite browser to automatically show the documentation about the resource when you type the resource URI in the browser.

Although you can use this method at runtime to discover the methods supported by any given resource at runtime, doing so is expensive. In HTTP, the OPTIONS method is not cacheable. For instance, the following sequence of requests introduces extra latency into the client application:

```
# Request
OPTIONS /photos HTTP/1.1
Host: http://www.example.org

# Response
HTTP/1.1 204 No Content
Allow: POST, GET
Link: <http://www.example.org/docs/photos>; type=text/html; rel=help

# Submit a POST request to create a photo
POST /photos HTTP/1.1
Host: http://www.example.org
Content-Type: application/xml;charset=UTF-8

<photo>
  ...
</photo>

# Response
HTTP/1.1 201 Created
Location: http://www.example.org/photo/4312
Content-Type: application/xml;charset=UTF-8

<photo>
  ...
</photo>
```

Instead of using OPTIONS at runtime, use development-time knowledge of the server and links to discover URIs and make requests.

Additional Reading

Books

Anderson, Ross J. *Security Engineering: A Guide to Building Dependable Distributed Systems, 2nd Edition.* Indianapolis, IN: Wiley, 2008.

Bowen, Rich, and Ken Coar. *Apache Cookbook.* Sebastopol, CA: O'Reilly, 2007.

Burke, Bill. *RESTful Java with JAX-RS.* Sebastopol, CA: O'Reilly, 2009.

Flanders, Jon. *.NET.* Sebastopol, CA: O'Reilly, 2008.

Gourley, David, and Brian Totty. *HTTP: The Definitive Guide.* Sebastopol, CA: O'Reilly, 2002.

Lewis, Emily P. *Microformats Made Simple.* Berkeley, CA: New Riders, 2009.

Richardson, Leonard, and Sam Ruby. *RESTful Web Services.* Sebastopol, CA: O'Reilly, 2007.

Ristic, Ivan. *Apache Security.* Sebastopol, CA: O'Reilly, 2005.

Ruby, Sam, Dave Thomas, and David Hansson. *Agile Web Development with Rails.* Raleigh, NC: Pragmatic Bookshelf, 2009.

Shiflett, Chris. *HTTP Developer's Handbook.* Indianapolis, IN: Sams, 2003.

van der Vlist, Eric. *RELAX NG.* Sebastopol, CA: O'Reilly, 2003.

——. *XML Schema.* Sebastopol, CA: O'Reilly, 2002.

Wessels, Duane. *Squid: The Definitive Guide.* Sebastopol, CA: O'Reilly, 2004.

——. *Web Caching.* Sebastopol, CA: O'Reilly, 2001.

References

Foundation

"Architectural Styles and the Design of Network-Based Software Architectures," Doctoral dissertation of Roy Fielding, *http://www.ics.uci.edu/~fielding/pubs/dissertation/top.htm*

HTTP Authentication: Basic and Digest Access Authentication, *http://tools.ietf.org/html/rfc2617*

HTTP Extensions for Web Distributed Authoring and Versioning (WebDAV), *http://tools.ietf.org/html/rfc4918*

HTTP Multipart Batched Request Format, *http://tools.ietf.org/html/draft-snell-http-batch*

Hypertext Transfer Protocol: HTTP 1.0, *http://tools.ietf.org/html/rfc1945*

Hypertext Transfer Protocol: HTTP 1.1, *http://tools.ietf.org/html/rfc2616*

PATCH Method for HTTP, *http://tools.ietf.org/html/draft-dusseault-http-patch*

Uniform Resource Identifier (URI): Generic Syntax, *http://www.ietf.org/rfc/rfc3986.txt*

URI Template, *http://tools.ietf.org/html/draft-gregorio-uritemplate-03*

URN Syntax, *http://tools.ietf.org/html/rfc2141*

Web Linking Internet-Draft, *http://tools.ietf.org/html/draft-nottingham-http-link-header*

Atom and AtomPub

The Atom Publishing Protocol, *http://tools.ietf.org/html/rfc5023*

The Atom Syndication Format, *http://tools.ietf.org/html/rfc4287*

Atom Threading Extensions, *http://tools.ietf.org/html/rfc4685*

Feed Paging and Archiving, *http://tools.ietf.org/html/rfc5005*

In-Lining Extensions for Atom, *http://tools.ietf.org/html/draft-mehta-atom-inline*

Caching

Caching Tutorial, *http://www.mnot.net/cache_docs/*

HTTP Cache Channels, *http://ietfreport.isoc.org/idref/draft-nottingham-http-cache-channels*

The stale-if-error HTTP Cache-Control Extension, *http://tools.ietf.org/html/draft-nottingham-http-stale-if-error*

The stale-while-revalidate HTTP Cache-Control Extension, *http://tools.ietf.org/html/draft-nottingham-http-stale-while-revalidate-01*

Formats and Media Types

The application/json Media Type for JavaScript Object Notation (JSON), *http://tools.ietf.org/html/rfc4627*

BCP 47: Matching of Language Tags, *http://tools.ietf.org/html/bcp47*

Date and Time on the Internet: Timestamps, *http://tools.ietf.org/html/rfc3339*

English country names and code elements, *http://www.iso.org/iso/english_country_names_and_code_elements*

Extensible Markup Language (XML) 1.0 (Fifth Edition), *http://www.w3.org/TR/REC-xml/*

HTML 4.01 Specification, *http://www.w3.org/TR/html401/*

Internet Assigned Numbers Authority (IANA) MIME Media Types, *http://www.iana.org/assignments/media-types/*

ISO 4217 currency names and code elements, *http://www.iso.org/iso/support/currency_codes_list-1.htm*

Olson Time Zone Database: Sources for Time Zone and Daylight Saving Time Data, *http://www.twinsun.com/tz/tz-link.htm*

RDFa in XHTML: Syntax and Processing, *http://www.w3.org/TR/rdfa-syntax/*

Tags for Identifying Languages, *http://tools.ietf.org/html/rfc5646*

XML Base (Second Edition), *http://www.w3.org/TR/xmlbase/*

XML Media Types, *http://tools.ietf.org/html/rfc3023*

XML Schema Part 2: Datatypes Second Edition, *http://www.w3.org/TR/xmlschema-2*

Security

Beginner's Guide to OAuth, *http://hueniverse.com/oauth/*

HTTP Authentication: Basic and Digest Access Authentication, *http://tools.ietf.org/html/rfc2617*

OAuth Core 1.0, *http://oauth.net/core/1.0a*

Overview of REST

REST stands for Representational State Transfer. To understand what it means, consider a simple web-based social application.

1. A user visits the home page of the application by typing the address in the browser.
2. The browser submits an HTTP request to the server.
3. The server responds with an HTML document containing some links and forms.
4. The user types her status in a form and submits the form.
5. The browser submits another HTTP request to the server.
6. The server processes the request and responds with another page.

This cycle continues until the user stops browsing. Except for a few exceptions, most websites and web-based applications follow the same pattern. Let's see how this application is related to REST.

Uniform Resource Identifiers

What the user types into the browser at the start of the previous interaction is a Uniform Resource Identifier (URI). Another commonly used name for this is a Uniform Resource Locator (URL). URI is a more generalized term that you can use to refer to either a location (URL) or a name.

A URI is an identifier of a resource. In most cases, URIs are opaque for clients.

Resources

A *resource* is anything that can be identified by a URI. In the first step of the previous flow, the URI typed by the user is the address of a resource that corresponds to a web page. In a typical static website, every web page is a resource.

In the fourth step, the part of the server that updates the user's status is another re-source. The HTML form that is used to submit the form has the address (URI) of this resource encoded as the value of the `action` attribute of the `form` element.

Representations

The HTML document that the server returns to the client is a *representation* of the resource. A representation is an encapsulation of the information (state, data, or mark-up) of the resource, encoded using a format such as XML, JSON, or HTML.

A resource may have one or more representations. Clients and servers use *media types* to denote the type of the representation to the receiving party (the client or the server). Most websites and applications typically use HTML format with `text/html` as the media type. Similarly, when a user submits the form, the browser submits a repre-sentation using the URI-encoded format using the `application/x-www-form-urlenco ded` media type.

Uniform Interface

Clients use the Hypertext Transfer Protocol (HTTP) to submit requests to resources and get responses. In the first step, the client submits a `GET` request to fetch an HTML document. In the fourth step, the client submits a `POST` request to update the user status.

These two methods are part of HTTP's *uniform interface*. Use of a uniform interface makes the request and responses self-describing and visible. In addition to these two methods, this interface consists of other methods such as `OPTIONS`, `HEAD`, `PUT`, `DELETE`, `TRACE`, and `CONNECT`. Of these methods, except for the `CONNECT` method, which HTTP 1.1 reserves for tunneling TCP-based protocols such as TLS, HTTP defines the seman-tics of each method.

HTTP is a protocol between clients and resources. In this protocol, except when you define new methods to extend HTTP, the list of methods and their semantics is fixed. Those semantics are independent of the resources. That is why HTTP is called a uni-form interface. This is unlike remote procedure calls (RPC) or SOAP-based web services where the semantics of each request are application specific.

Hypermedia and Application State

Finally, each representation that the client receives from the server represents the state of the user's interaction within the application. For instance, when the user submits the form to receive another page, the user changes the state of the application from her point of view. When a user, just browsing a website, the user changes the state of the application with each click on a link to load another page.

In this example, to change the state of the application, the user relies on forms and links found in the HTML. HTML is an hypermedia format, allowing link and form controls to let you flow through the application and thereby change the state of the application.

This way of using hypermedia of the representation (such as HTML) to denote and manage the state of the application is called *hypermedia as the engine of application state*, or in short form the *hypertext constraint*.

HTTP Methods

HTTP's uniform interface consists of the OPTIONS, GET, HEAD, POST, PUT, DELETE, and TRACE methods. This appendix provides a short primer on using these HTTP methods, listed in the order used by RFC 2616.

OPTIONS

Use this method to find the list of HTTP methods supported by any resource or to ping the server.

Request: Headers but no body.

Response: Headers but no body by default. The server may provide a description of the resource in the body.

Examples:

```
# 1. Request to find methods supported by a resource
OPTIONS /movie/gone_with_the_wind HTTP/1.1
Host: www.example.org

# Response with the methods supported by the resource
HTTP/1.1 204 No Content
Allow: HEAD, GET, OPTIONS, PUT, DELETE

# 2. Request to ping the server or find the version of HTTP supported
OPTIONS * HTTP/1.1
Host: www.example.org

# Response
HTTP/1.1 204 No Content
```

GET

Use this method to retrieve a representation of a resource.

Request: Headers but no body specified by HTTP 1.1.

Response: A representation of the resource at the request URI usually with a body. Response headers such as `Content-Type`, `Content-Length`, `Content-Language`, `Last-Modified`, and `ETag` correspond to the representation in the response.

Examples:

```
# A request to get a representation of a resource
GET /tx/1234 HTTP/1.1
Host: www.example.org

# Response
HTTP/1.1 200 OK
Content-Type: application/xml;charset=UTF-8
Content-Length: xxx

<status>
...
</status>
```

HEAD

Use this method to retrieve the same headers as that of a GET response but without any body in the response. In other words, this method returns the same response as GET except that the server returns an empty body. Clients can use this method to check whether a resource exists or to learn its metadata (see Recipe 3.1).

Request: Headers, with no body specified by HTTP 1.1.

Response: Headers but no body. Servers must not include a body.

Examples:

```
# Request to get a representation of a resource
HEAD /movie/gone_with_the_wind HTTP/1.1
Host: www.example.org

# Response
HTTP/1.1 200 OK
Content-Type: application/xml;charset=UTF-8
Content-Length: xxx
```

POST

Use this method to let the resource perform a variety of actions on the server side such as creating new resources, updating existing resources, or making a mixture of changes to one or more resources.

Request: A representation of a resource.

Response: A representation of the resource or instructions for a redirect. If there is a representation in the body that corresponds to a URI of a resource other than the request URI, include a `Content-Location` header with the URI of that resource.

Examples:

```
# 1. Perform some resource specific action
POST /admin/purge HTTP/1.1
Host: www.example.org

HTTP/1.1 204 No Content

# 2. Request to create a resource
POST /user/smith HTTP/1.1
Host: www.example.org
Content-Type: application/xml;charset=UTF-8

<address>
  <street>1, Main Street</street>
  <city>Some City</city>
</address>

# Response
HTTP/1.1 201 Created
Location: http://www.example.org/user/smith/address/1
Content-Location: http://www.example.org/user/smith/address/1
Content-Type: application/xml;charset=UTF-8

<address>
  <id>urn:example:user:smith:address:1</id>
  <atom:link rel="self" href="http://www.example.org/user/smith/address/1"/>
  <street>1, Main Street</street>
  <city>Some City</city>
</address>

# 3. Request to modify a resource
POST /user/smith/address_merge HTTP/1.1
Host: www.example.org
Content-Type: text/csv;charset=UTF-8

John Doe, 1 Main Street, Seattle, WA
Jane Doe, 100 North Street, Los Angeles, CA
...

# Response
HTTP/1.1 303 See Other
Location: http://www.example.org/user/smith/address_book
Content-Type: text/html;charset=UTF-8

<html>
  <head> ... </head>
  <body>
    <p>See <a href="http://www.example.org/user/smith/address_book">address
```

```
    book</a> for the merged address book.</p>
  </body>
</html>
```

PUT

Use this method to completely update or replace an existing resource or to create a new resource with a URI specified by the client.

Request: A representation of a resource. The body of the request may or may not be same as a client would receive for a subsequent GET request. In some cases, the server may require clients to include only the mutable portions of the resource.

Response: The response can be a status of the update. You can include a complete representation of the updated resource in the response, but clients cannot assume that the response contains a complete representation unless the response includes a Content-Location header. If the server does not include this header, clients must submit an unconditional GET request to get the updated representation along with Last-Modified and/or ETag headers.

Examples:

```
# 1. Request to update a resource
PUT /movie/gone_with_the_wind HTTP/1.1
Host: www.example.org

# Response
HTTP/1.1 204 No Content

# 2. Request to create a new resource
PUT /movie/gone_with_the_wind HTTP/1.1
Host: www.example.org

# Response
HTTP/1.1 201 Created
Location: http://www.example.org/movie/gone_with_the_wind
Content-Length: 0
```

DELETE

Use this method to let a client delete a resource.

Request: Headers but no body. If you must submit data to delete a resource, use POST with a controller resource as in Recipe 2.6.

Response: Success or failure. The body may include the status of the operation.

Examples:

```
# Request to delete a resource
DELETE /movie/gone_with_the_wind HTTP/1.1
Host: www.example.org
```

```
# Response
HTTP/1.1 204 No Content
```

As far as the client is concerned, the resource is gone after a successful response.

TRACE

Use this method to let the server echo back the headers that it received. Servers supporting this method may be prone to the cross-site tracing (XST) security vulnerability.

Request: Headers and body.

Response: The body contains the entire request message.

Example:

```
# Request
TRACE /movie/gone_with_the_wind HTTP/1.1
Host: www.example.org
Accept: text/html

# Response
HTTP/1.1 200 OK
Content-Type: message/http

TRACE /movie/gone_with_the_wind HTTP/1.1
Host: www.example.org
Accept: text/html
```

Atom Syndication Format

This appendix provides a quick overview of how to use Atom entry and feed documents for resources. Figures D-1 and D-2 show a high-level view of the structure of Atom entry and feed elements. For a complete description of these elements, see RFC 4287.

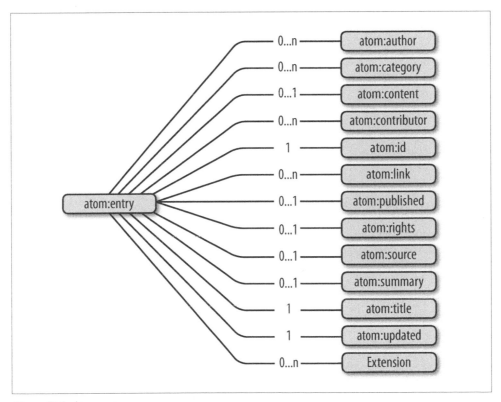

Figure D-1. Atom entry

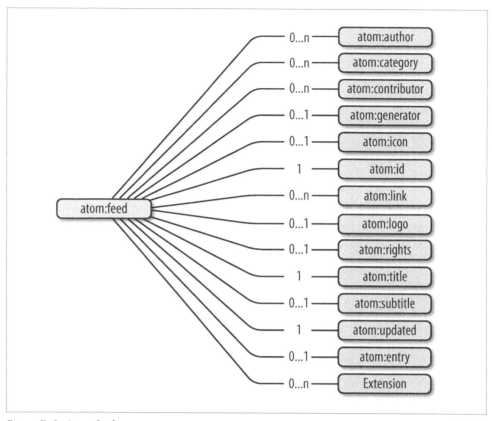

Figure D-2. Atom feed

Key Elements of Feeds and Entries

Here is a list of the key elements within the Atom entry and feed elements. Note that both feeds and entries are extensible, and you can introduce new attributes and elements.

atom:author

Contained in: atom:feed and atom:entry

The atom:author element represents the person or entity that created the entry or feed. It can contain several child elements including atom:name, atom:uri, and atom:email. A single Atom entry or feed can contain more than one atom:author element. Each atom:author element should have at least an atom:name element. The atom:uri and atom:email elements are optional.

Here is an example of the `atom:author` element:

```
<atom:author xmlns:atom="http://www.w3.org/2005/Atom">
  <atom:name>J. P. Williams</atom:name>
  <atom:uri>http://www.example.org/jpwill</atom:uri>
  <atom:email>jpwill@example.org</atom:email>
</atom:author>
```

If the Atom feed has an `atom:author` element, each Atom entry need not have an `atom:author` element. Also, if each Atom entry has an `atom:author`, the Atom feed need not have an `atom:author` element. However, always including an `atom:author` element for each entry and for the feed itself simplifies coding to process feeds and entries.

atom:content and atom:summary

Contained in: atom:entry

Each Atom entry should have an `atom:content` or `atom:summary` element.

The purpose of the `atom:summary` element is to provide a short summary or description of the entry. Similar to the `atom:title` element, this element supports a `type` attribute.

You can use the `atom:content` element in the following ways:

- To include the content of the entry as plain text or HTML or XHTML
- To include any other content with a media type
- To link to an arbitrary resource using the `src` and `type` attributes

Here are examples of valid `atom:content` elements:

```
<!-- Inline plain text -->
<atom:content xmlns:atom="http://www.w3.org/2005/Atom" type="text">
  This is some plain text
</atom:content>

<!-- Inline HTML -->
<atom:content xmlns:atom="http://www.w3.org/2005/Atom" type="html">
  &lt;p&gt;This is some HTML.&lt;/p&gt;
</atom:content>

<!-- Inline XHTML -->
<atom:content xmlns:atom="http://www.w3.org/2005/Atom" type="xhtml">
  <div>
    <p>This is some XHTML.</p>
  </div>
</atom:content>

<!-- Inline other content -->
<atom:content xmlns:atom="http://www.w3.org/2005/Atom" type="text/csv">
name,email
"John Doe","john@example.org"
"Jane Doe",jane@example.org"
</atom:content>
```

```
<!-- External content -->
<atom:content src="http://www.example.org/reports/2009.pdf" type="application/pdf"/>
```

atom:id

Contained in: atom:entry

The `atom:id` element contains the globally unique identifier of the entry. The value is in the form of a URN (for example, `urn:guid:550e8400-e29b-41d4-a716-446655440000`). The value of `atom:id` must never change even when the entry or feed is updated or moved. Clients should be able to compare these identifiers to check whether two entries or feeds are the same. See Recipe 3.10 for other use cases for such identifiers in representations.

atom:link

Contained in: atom:feed and atom:entry

Each Atom entry or feed can contain several `atom:link` elements. See Recipe 5.1 for the structure of this element. The rules for when to include `atom:link` elements are detailed in RFC 4287 and are summarized here:

- Each feed and entry must contain a single `atom:link` element with a `rel` value of `self`.
- You can include additional `atom:link` elements with a `rel` value of `alternate` as long as the combination of `type` and `hreflang` attribute values are unique. See Recipe 7.8 for an application.
- You can also include additional `atom:link` elements to link to related resources.

atom:title

Contained in: atom:feed, atom:entry, and atom:source

This element contains a string representation of the title of the entry or feed (e.g., `<atom:title type="text">My Title</atom:title>`). The `title` element supports a `type` attribute with a value of `text`, `html`, or `xhtml`. `type="text"` is the default. When the type is `html` or `xhtml`, you must entity-escape the value of the element, as in `<atom:title type="html">&lt;em&gt;My Title&lt;/em&gt;</atom:title>`.

atom:updated

Contained in: atom:feed and atom:entry

This element contains the date-time at which the entry or feed was last updated. See Recipe 3.9 for the format.

Other Atom Elements to Consider

atom:category

Contained in: atom:feed and atom:entry

The purpose of this element is to categorize feeds and entries. Each Atom entry can contain one or more `atom:category` elements.

```
<atom:category term="animal"
  scheme="http://example.org/categories/animal"
  label="Animal">Animal</atom:category>
```

atom:contributor

Each Atom entry can contain one or more `atom:contributor` elements.

```
<atom:contributor>
  <atom:name>E. Pound</atom:name>
  <atom:email>epound@example.org</atom:email>
  <atom:uri>http://epound.example.org</atom:uri>
</atom:contributor>
```

atom:generator

Contained in: atom:feed and atom:source

You can use this element to indicate the software that generated the feed or source of an entry. Each Atom entry can contain one `atom:generator` element.

```
<atom:generator uri="http://www.example.org/generator/"
      version="1.0">Atom Generator 1.0</atom:generator>
```

atom:icon

Contained in: atom:feed

Each feed can contain an `atom:icon` element.

```
<atom:icon>http://example.org/image/icon.png</atom:icon>
```

atom:logo

Contained in: atom:feed

Each feed can contain an `atom:logo` element.

```
<atom:logo>http://example.org/image/logo.png</atom:logo>
```

atom:published

Contained in: atom:entry

Each Atom entry can contain one `atom:published` element. This is usually the date-time value the entry was first published.

```
<atom:published>2010-06-24T12:15:30Z</atom:published>
```

atom:rights

Contained in: atom:entry

Each Atom entry can contain one `atom:rights` element to describe rights, such as copyright.

```
<atom:rights type="text">©2010 All rights
        reserved.</atom:rights>
```

atom:subtitle

Contained in: atom:feed and atom:source

Each Atom entry or source can contain one `atom:subtitle` element.

```
<atom:subtitle type="text">How I learned to
        love the Atom format</atom:subtitle>
```

Link Relation Registry

This appendix lists all the registered link relation types documented at *http://www.iana .org/assignments/link-relations/link-relations.xhtml* and when to use them. The Web Linking Internet-Draft will consolidate this list when it is finalized.

alternate

Use this type when providing a URI to an alternative version of the same resource. You can use links with this type whenever a resource has alternate representations with distinct URIs.

```
<!-- Link to an alternate representation in the PDF format -->
<atom:link rel="alternate"
      href="http://www.example.org/report.pdf" type="application/pdf"/>

<!-- Link to an alternate representation in French -->
<atom:link rel="alternate"
      href="http://www.example.org/report.fr.pdf" hreflang="fr"
      type="application/pdf"/>
```

appendix

Use this type when linking to a resource that serves as an appendix for a collection of resources. Links with this relation type may be useful in content-centric applications.

```
<atom:link rel="appendix"
      href="http://www.example.org/books/restful-webservices-cookbook/appendix"/>
```

bookmark

This link relation type is used by blogging platforms such as WordPress to create permanent links to resources from their summaries.

```
<div id="p1">
  <h2>My First Post</h2>
```

```
    <p>Hello world. This is my first post.</p>

    <p><a href="/2009/10/1.html" rel="bookmark">Read more</a>.</p>
</div>
```

chapter, section, subsection

These relation types can be used to link to chapters, sections, and subsections in a collection of resources.

```
<book xmlns:atom="http://www.w3.org/2005/Atom">
  <title>RESTful Web Services Cookbook</title>
  <atom:link rel="chapter" title="Introduction"
        href="http://www.example.org/contents/ch01.xml"/>
  <atom:link rel="chapter" title="Using the Protocol"
        href="http://www.example.org/contents/ch02.xml"/>
  ...
</book>
```

contents

This relation type can be used to link to a table of contents for a collection of resources.

```
<book xmlns:atom="http://www.w3.org/2005/Atom">
  <title>RESTful Web Services Cookbook</title>
  <atom:link rel="contents" title="Table of Contents"
        href="http://www.example.org/contents/toc.xml"/>
  ...
</book>
```

copyright

This relation type can be used to link to a copyright statement for a resource.

```
<book xmlns:atom="http://www.w3.org/2005/Atom">
  <title>RESTful Web Services Cookbook</title>
  <atom:link rel="copyright" title="Copyright"
        href="http://www.example.org/contents/copyright.xml"/>
  ...
</book>
```

current

This relation type refers to a resource containing the most recent item or items in a collection. Here is an example providing a link to the latest articles:

```
<atom:feed xmlns:atom="http://www.w3.org/2005/Atom">
  <atom:title>Archives - 2008</atom:title>
  <atom:link rel="current" href="http://www.example.org/latest"/>
  <atom:link rel="self" href="http://www.example.org/2008/archive"/>
```

describedby

This link relation type refers to a resource that describes the link's context. For instance, you can use this relation type to link to a document that describes a user's hometown.

```
<user xmlns:atom="http://www.w3.org/2005/Atom">
  <name>John Doe</name>
  <location>
    <latitude>47.45</latitude>
    <lingitude>122.30</logitude>
    <atom:link rel="describedby" href="http://www.example.org/places/Seattle"/>
  </location>
</user>
```

edit

Use this relation to link to a URI that clients can use to retrieve, update, or delete the resource.

```
<user xmlns="http://www.w3.org/2005/Atom">
  <atom:link rel="edit"
       href="http://www.example.org/users/john.doe/profile"/>
  <name>John Doe</name>
  ...
</user>
```

When you include a link with this relation in a resource that is not a collection, it usually means that the client can use the link's URI to retrieve (via GET), update (via PUT), or delete (via DELETE) the resource. Although it is common to have the value of the link the same as the request URI used to fetch the representation of the resource, in some cases the server may choose to offer a separate URI for editing purposes.

The presence of a link with this relation does not automatically mean that such editing is possible. The client must check the HTTP OPTIONS response and server's documentation before attempting to edit the resource.

edit-media

This relation type is used by Atom entry documents that have an associated media resource. An example is an article with a video resource attached. Clients can use a link with this relation type to edit such associated media.

```
<atom:entry xmlns:atom="http://www.w3.org/2005/Atom">
  <atom:title>Balloon Boy</atom:title>
  <atom:content type="text/html"
    src="http://news.example.org/balloon_boy.html"/>
  <atom:link rel="edit-media"
```

```
      href="http://media.example.org/balloon_boy.mov"
      type="video/quicktime"/>
  ...
</atom:entry>
```

enclosure

Use this relation type to refer to a related resource that is potentially large. Here is an example of a preview of a video podcast linking to a full podcast:

```
Content-Type: video/quicktime
Link: <http://www.example.org/podcasts/what-is-rest.mov>;
      type="video/quicktime;length="124143";rel="enclosure"

...
```

first, last, next, next-archive, prev, previous, prev-archive, start

Use these relation types to provide links to scroll through a collection of resources. Here is an example of a collection:

```
<result xmlns="http://www.w3.org/2005/Atom">
  <atom:link rel="first" href="http://www.example.org/item/12321"/>
  <atom:link rel="last" href="http://www.example.org/item/6721"/>
  <atom:link rel="next" href="http://www.example.org/item/54674"/>
  ...
</result>
```

glossary

Use this relation type to link to a resource that provides a glossary of terms.

```
<book xmlns="http://www.w3.org/2005/Atom">
  <title>RESTful Web Services Cookbook</title>
  <atom:link rel="glossary" title="Glossary"
        href="http://www.example.org/contents/glossary.xml"/>
  ...
</book>
```

help

Use this type to link to a resource offering information or help about the current resource.

```
<div class="approval">
  <a href="/help.html" rel="help"/>
  <form ...>
```

```
    </form>
  </div>
```

index

Use this relation type to link to a resource that provides an index.

```
<book xmlns="http://www.w3.org/2005/Atom">
  <title>RESTful Web Services Cookbook</title>
  <atom:link rel="glossary" title="Index"
        href="http://www.example.org/contents/index.xml"/>
  ...
</book>
```

license

You can use a link with this relation type to link to license of a resource such as an article, graphic, etc.

```
Content-Type: video/quicktime
Link: <http://creativecommons.org/licenses/by-nd/3.0/us/>;rel="license"

...
```

payment

Use this relation type to link to a resource that provides a link to purchase or conduct some payment. Here is an example of a link to buy a book:

```
<book xmlns="http://www.w3.org/2005/Atom">
  <title>RESTful Web Services Cookbook</title>
  <atom:link rel="payment" title="Buy this book"
        href="http://my.safaribooksonline.com/9780596809140"/>
  <atom:link rel="chapter" title="Using the Protocol"
        href="http://www.example.org/contents/ch02.xml"/>
  ...
</book>
```

related

Use this to link to a related resource.

```
<book xmlns="http://www.w3.org/2005/Atom">
  <title>RESTful Web Services Cookbook</title>
  <atom:link rel="related" title="RESTful Web Services"
        href="http://my.safaribooksonline.com/9780596529260"/>
  ...
</book>
```

This relation is generic and simply says that the resource at the link's URI is related to the containing resource. If you prefer to be more specific, use extended link relations such as `http://www.example.org/rels/photos/owner` for a photo resource to link to a owner resource, and such as `http://www.example.org/rels/friend` for a user resource to link to a friend resource.

replies

Use this link relation type to link to a resource that is a reply to the context of the link. Links of this relation type may be relevant in content-centric systems or on servers managing user-generated content.

```
<article xmlns="http://www.w3.org/2005/Atom">
  <title>State of the State</title>
  <atom:link rel="replies" title="Comments"
        href="http://www.example.org/ch01/comments"/>
  ...
</article>
```

self

Use this type to link to the preferred URI of the resource. Here is an example:

```
<user xmlns:atom="http://www.w3.org/2005/Atom">
  <name>John Doe</name>
  <atom:link rel="self" href="http://www.example.org/users/0012"/>
</user>
```

service

A link with this relation type refers to a service document of Atom feeds.

```
<atom:feed xmlns:atom="http://www.w3.org/2005/Atom">
  <atom:title>Sci-Fi Books</atom:title>
  <atom:link href="http://www.example.org/books" rel="self"
    hreflang="en" type="application/atom+xml"/>
  <atom:link href="http://www.example.org/service" rel="service"
    hreflang="en" type="application/atomsvc+xml"/>
  <atom:updated>2013-12-13T18:30:02Z</atom:updated>
  ...
</atom:feed>
```

stylesheet

This well-known link relation is used by documents to link to stylesheets.

```
<html>
  <head>
```

```
      <title>Hello World</title>
      <link rel="stylesheet" type="text/css" href="/style.css" />
   <head>
   <body>
     ...
   </body>
</html>
```

up

Clients can use links with this relation type to navigate up a hierarchy of resources. Here is an example:

```
<place xmlns:atom="http://www.w3.org/2005/Atom">
  <name>Seattle </name>
  <atom:link rel="self" href="http://www.example.org/us/wa/seattle"/>
  <atom:link rel="up" href="http://www.example.org/us/wa"/>
</user>
```

via

Use this type to identify a resource that is the source of the information. In this example, an Atom entry attributes the source to another resource:

```
<atom:entry xmlns:atom="http://www.w3.org/2005/Atom">
  <atom:title>...</atom:title>
  <atom:link rel="alternate" type="text/html"
     href="http://www.subbu.org/archives/2009/10/15/announce.html"/>
  <atom:id>urn:example:10001</atom:id>
  <atom:link rel="via" type="text/html"
     href="http://www.example.org/blog/213"
     title="Jeffrey Veen"/>
</atom:entry>
```

Index

We'd like to hear your suggestions for improving our indexes. Send email to *index@oreilly.com*.

auto insurance application example, 7

B

backward compatibility, 235
bank transfer application example, 176
Base64 encoding, security, 219
batch HTTP requests, 211
binary data, representations, 66
bookmark link relation type, 277
bookstore example, 41
bulk operations, resources, 203–208

C

Cache-Control headers, 148–151
caching, 147–158
    composite resources, 154
    content negotiation, 136
    expiration caching headers, 148–154
    keeping caches up-to-date and nonempty,
        156
    POST method, 143, 144
    proxy HTTP caches, 31
    queries, 144
caching proxy servers, 163
capital letters, URIs, 79
category documents, AtomPub, 116
chapter link relation type, 278
character encoding negotiation, 129
characters, encoding mismatch, 50
charset parameter, 51
clients
    agent-driven negotiation, 134
    application state, 7
    authentication, 218–223
    client preferences and content negotiation,
        124
    conditional GET and HEAD requests, 165
    conditional PUT and DELETE requests
        from clients, 174
    convenience versus visibility, 6
    decoupling from application state, 95
    expiration caching headers, 153
    extensions and interoperability, 244
    HTTP error codes, 71
    links in, 103
    media types and HTTP clients, 132
    safety and idempotency, 12
    supporting extensibility, 246

unconditional GET requests, 172
    URIs as opaque identifiers, 81
collections
    representations of, 59–62
    resources, 32
comma (,), URIs, 76
compatibility
    forward and backward, 235
    links, 244
    URIs, 236
composite resources
    caching, 154
    combining into, 34–37
compression, content negotiation, 130
concurrency control
    DELETE requests, 174
    PUT requests, 167, 174
    types of, 159
concurrency, tunneling, 210
conditional requests, 159–181
    conditional DELETE requests in servers,
        171
    conditional GET and HEAD requests from
        clients, 165
    conditional POST requests, 176
    conditional PUT and DELETE requests
        from clients, 174
    conditional PUT requests in servers, 167–
        170
    GET requests in servers, 162–165
    Last-Modified and ETag Headers, 161
    one-time URLs for POST requests, 179
    unconditional GET requests from clients,
        172
conneg (see content negotiation)
content encoding, 130
content model, Atom, 111–116
content negotiation, 123–136
    agent-driven content negotiation, 133
    character encoding negotiation, 129
    client preferences, 124
    compression, 130
    expensiveness of implementing, 135
    language negotiation, 127
    media type negotiation, 126
    negotiation failures, 132
    server-driven negotiation, 135
    Vary headers, 131
Content-Encoding headers, 49

F

failures, negotiation failures, 132
feed documents, Atom, 108
feed elements (Atom), 272
feed resources, AtomPub, 118
Fielding, Roy, REST, ix
filesystems, storing application state, 8
first link relation type, 93, 280
formats
    JSON, 58
    for media types, 55
    portable data formats in representations,
        62–64
    representation formats, 52–56
forward compatibility, 235
forward proxy caches, 154
forward-slash separator (/), URIs, 76
freshness lifetime, defined, 148
full stop (.), URIs, 78
functions, supporting processing functions, 37
    (see also methods)

G

GET method, 13, 142, 266
GET requests
    combining resources into composites, 35
    conditional, 160
    conditional GET requests from clients, 165
    conditional GET requests in servers, 162–
        165
    unconditional GET requests from clients,
        172
glossary link relation type, 280
granularity, resources, 31

H

hcard microformat, 69
HEAD method, 266
HEAD requests
    conditional HEAD requests from clients,
        165
    limitations of, 175
headers
    Accept-* headers, 124
    Accept-Charset headers, 129
    Accept-Language headers, 128
    Age headers, 150
    Authorization headers, 220, 226

    Cache-Control header, 148–151
    custom HTTP headers, 25–27
    entity headers annotating representations,
        46–49
    ETag headers, 161, 169
    expiration caching headers, 148–154
    Expires headers, 148
    interpreting entity headers, 49
    keeping interactions visible, 2
    Last-Modified headers, 161, 169
    link headers, 91
    representations, 47
    Slug headers, 119
    Vary headers and content negotiation, 131
help link relation type, 280
hiring process example, 229
homogeneous collections, 61
HTML representations, serving, 67
HTTP, 1–27, 23
    (see also methods)
    application state, 7
    batch HTTP requests, 211
    caching headers, 151
    custom HTTP headers, 25–27
    custom methods, 23
    DELETE, 22
    GET, 13
    media types and HTTP clients, 132
    optimistic concurrency control, 160
    POST, 14, 16, 19–22
    PUT, 18
    safety and idempotency, 9–13
    security, 233
    visibility of interactions, 2–6
hypermedia, defined, 262
hyphen (-), URIs, 76

I

IANA (Internet Assigned Numbers Authority),
    52
idempotency
    and safety in clients, 12
    and safety on servers, 9–12
identifiers, entity identifiers in representations,
    65
    (see also URIs)
identifying resources from domain nouns, 30
image-processing web service example, 20
index link relation type, 281

interface (see HTTP)
Internet Assigned Numbers Authority (IANA), 52
interoperability
  Atom, 108
  extensions, 244
interpreting entity headers, 49

J

JSON representations
  compatibility of XML and, 237–241
  designing, 58
  links, 90

L

language formats, 64
language negotiation
  content versus server driven negotiation, 136
  implementing, 127
last link relation type, 93, 280
Last-Modified headers
  about, 49
  generating, 161
  sending on requests, 169
latency
  network cost, 36
  network latency, 6
  query requests with large inputs, 143
  unconditional GET requests, 174
  web caching, 147
length, URIs, 142
license link relation type, 281
link elements
  about, 87
  JSON, 90
  XML, 88
link relation types, 277–283
links, 87–105
  application flow, 95–99
  in clients, 103
  compatibility, 244
  contextual links, 97
  ephemeral URIs, 99
  headers, 91
  links in JSON representations, 90
  relation types, 93
  self links, 56

storing application state, 9
URI templates, 101
XML representations, 88
localization, language negotiation, 127
LOCK WebDAV method, 190

M

mapping
  database tables or object models, 32
  operations to methods, 42
max-age Cache-Control directive, 149
media resources, AtomPub, 119–122
media type negotiation, 126
media types
  Atom and AtomPub, 109
  HTTP clients, 132
  list of, 53
  multipart media types, 66
  representation formats, 52–56
  versioning, 250
memcached, 147
merging resources, 186
metadata, representation metadata, 46
methods, 265–269
  (see also conditional requests; GET
    requests; HEAD requests; POST method;
    POST requests; requests)
  custom methods in HTTP, 23
  DELETE method, 11, 22, 268
  GET method, 13, 142, 266
  HEAD method, 266
  mapping operations to, 42
  OPTIONS method, 254, 265
  PATCH method, 201
  PUT method, 18, 193, 268
  safety and idempotency, 10
  TRACE method, 269
  WebDAV methods, 189
microformats, 68
mimicking transaction protocols, 215
MKCOL WebDAV method, 189
modeling
  Atom content model, 111–116
  mapping object models, 32
modeling resources using Atom, 108–111
MOVE WebDAV method, 190
moving resources, 188
multipart media types, 66
must-revalidate Cache-Control directive, 149

About the Author

Subbu Allamaraju is an architect at Yahoo!, where he developed standards and practices for designing RESTful web services, and now provides architectural oversight for certain developer-facing platforms. Prior to that, Subbu developed web services/Java-based software and contributed to the JCP and OASIS standards at BEA Systems, Inc. Subbu has contributed to four books on J2EE, all published by Wrox. See *http://www.subbu.org* to learn more about him.

Colophon

The animal on the cover of *RESTful Web Services Cookbook* is a great fringed lizard or *Hatteria punctata*. *Hatteria*, more commonly known as *tuatara*, are endemic to New Zealand; "tuatara" is a native Maori word meaning "peaks on back" (referring to their spiky, or fringed, spines). The name "great fringed lizard" is a misnomer; though they resemble common lizards, tuatara are quite different anatomically, and, unlike lizards, they're nocturnal and enjoy cool weather. Misclassified as lizards by the British Museum in 1831, tuatara were reclassified by zoologist Albert Günther in 1867 as *Rhynchocephala*, an order from which many Mesozoic fossil species are known. In fact, some scientists refer to these reptiles, the only living representative of *Rhynchocephala*, as "living fossils."

Tuatara grow very slowly—they don't reach maturity until they are 13–20 years old and don't stop growing until they are about 30. It is believed that tuatara in the wild can reach the impressive age of 80 or older. Their average length is 20–31 inches and they weigh 1–3 pounds. They can be gray, olive, or brick red, and their coloring can change over their lifetime. As adults, they shed their skin at least once per year. Other physical characteristics include a diapsid skull (two openings on either side), a lack of external ears, acrodont tooth structure (meaning the teeth are fused to the jawbone—another fact that distinguishes tauatara from lizards), and a third eye. This third eye grows on top of the head—under the skin in adults—and has a retina, lens, and nerve endings, although it is not used for seeing. It is, however, sensitive to light and is thought by some to help the tuatara detect the time of day or season.

Despite an endangered status, the tuatara maintains high visibility in and around New Zealand. Until October 2006, it was featured on one side of New Zealand's 5-cent piece, but the coin has since been phased out. The reptiles also figure prominently in Maori culture; they are esteemed as *ariki* (god forms). According to indigenous legends, they're messengers of Whiro, the god of death and disaster, and Maori women are forbidden to eat them. They also represent *tapu*, the line marking all things sacred and beyond which lie potentially serious consequences (*manu*). Maori women have been known to tattoo lizards or tuatara near their genitals to symbolize the concept of *tapu*. Today, tuataras are regarded as a *taonga* (treasure), and as the *kaitiaki* (guardian) of the trails to the mental and spiritual realms that give humans life.

The cover image is from Wood's *Animate Creation*. The cover font is Adobe ITC Garamond. The text font is Linotype Birka; the heading font is Adobe Myriad Condensed; and the code font is LucasFont's TheSansMonoCondensed.

Get even more for your money.

Join the O'Reilly Community, and register the O'Reilly books you own. It's free, and you'll get:

- $4.99 ebook upgrade offer
- 40% upgrade offer on O'Reilly print books
- Membership discounts on books and events
- Free lifetime updates to ebooks and videos
- Multiple ebook formats, DRM FREE
- Participation in the O'Reilly community
- Newsletters
- Account management
- 100% Satisfaction Guarantee

Signing up is easy:

1. **Go to: oreilly.com/go/register**
2. **Create an O'Reilly login.**
3. **Provide your address.**
4. **Register your books.**

Note: English-language books only

To order books online:
oreilly.com/store

For questions about products or an order:
orders@oreilly.com

To sign up to get topic-specific email announcements and/or news about upcoming books, conferences, special offers, and new technologies:
elists@oreilly.com

For technical questions about book content:
booktech@oreilly.com

To submit new book proposals to our editors:
proposals@oreilly.com

O'Reilly books are available in multiple DRM-free ebook formats. For more information:
oreilly.com/ebooks

Spreading the knowledge of innovators oreilly.com

©2010 O'Reilly Media, Inc. O'Reilly logo is a registered trademark of O'Reilly Media, Inc. 00000

Have it your way.

O'Reilly eBooks

- Lifetime access to the book when you buy through oreilly.com
- Provided in up to four DRM-free file formats, for use on the devices of your choice: PDF, .epub, Kindle-compatible .mobi, and Android .apk
- Fully searchable, with copy-and-paste and print functionality
- Alerts when files are updated with corrections and additions

oreilly.com/ebooks/

Safari Books Online

- Access the contents and quickly search over 7000 books on technology, business, and certification guides
- Learn from expert video tutorials, and explore thousands of hours of video on technology and design topics
- Download whole books or chapters in PDF format, at no extra cost, to print or read on the go
- Get early access to books as they're being written
- Interact directly with authors of upcoming books
- Save up to 35% on O'Reilly print books

See the complete Safari Library at safari.oreilly.com

O'REILLY®

Spreading the knowledge of innovators.   oreilly.com

©2011 O'Reilly Media, Inc. O'Reilly logo is a registered trademark of O'Reilly Media, Inc. 00000